growing up
PSYCHIC

About the Author

Michael Bodine is a professional psychic whose clients include many celebrities. It wasn't always that way. Michael grew up in a typical American family, in a typical midwestern suburb, until ghosts started appearing at his house. Before long, his mother and sister were hosting psychics and ghostbusters in the family kitchen, and Michael had acquired his own guardian angel. NBC TV's *Paranomal Borderline* show called them "the world's most psychic family."

Michael has been interviewed on dozens of radio and television shows, including appearances on the Biography network series, *Celebity Ghost Stories*. His life story is being optioned for a feature film, and a television series featuring Michael and his sister, Echo, was filmed last summer for a network TV broadcast next year.

Foreword by **Echo Bodine**—Best-selling Author and Ghost Hunter

growing up
PSYCHIC

From Skeptic To Believer

Michael Bodine

Llewellyn Publications
Woodbury, Minnesota

First Edition
Second Printing, 2010

Cover art © Bike image by Comstock Images, House image iStockphoto.com/
 by Jill Battglia
Cover design by Kevin R. Brown
Editing by Connie Hill
Interior photos provided by the author
Llewellyn is a registered trademark of Llewellyn Worldwide Ltd.

Library of Congress Cataloging-in-Publication Data
Bodine, Michael, 1957–
 Growing up psychic : from skeptic to believer / Michael Bodine ; foreword by Echo
Bodine. — 1st ed.
  p. cm.
 ISBN 978-0-7387-1961-0
 1. Bodine, Michael, 1957– 2. Psychics—United States—Biography. I. Title.
 BF1027.B56A3 2010
 133.8092—dc22
 [B]   2009048390

Llewellyn Worldwide does not participate in, endorse, or have any authority or responsibility concerning private business transactions between our authors and the public.

All mail addressed to the author is forwarded but the publisher cannot, unless specifically instructed by the author, give out an address or phone number.

Any Internet references contained in this work are current at publication time, but the publisher cannot guarantee that a specific location will continue to be maintained. Please refer to the publisher's website for links to authors' websites and other sources.

Llewellyn Publications
A Division of Llewellyn Worldwide Ltd.
2143 Wooddale Drive
Woodbury, Minnesota 55125-2989
www.llewellyn.com

Printed in the United States of America

Dedication

To my mom, thank you for staying, even after all of your friends have left. To Katie, Bianca, and Blake, thank you for giving my life meaning.

Acknowledgments

Scott S., thank you for pushing me. Melody B., thank you for directing and believing in me. Echo, thank you for helping me. Lewis, thank you for your kind words. Therese W., thank you for resurrecting my belief in getting it done. Buddy, thank you for inspiring me.

Contents

Foreword by Lewis Black

What is Lewis Black doing writing a foreword for a book like this?

There must be some mistake.

This is the New Age Spiritual Hoodoo Voodoo section of the bookstore.

Well, yes, but that begs the question. For those of you who don't know me, this is the last place even Michael, the gifted psychic who wrote this book, would have expected to find me because, as good a psychic as he is, he wasn't sure I would be willing to do something like this. I have a reputation to uphold, and appearing in this section of the bookstore would ruin it.

If, twenty years ago, someone had told me I would be writing the introduction to a book about someone who spends his days hanging out with dead people, I would have said they were stark raving mad. And I wouldn't have written this if I hadn't met Michael.

In 1997, I got a call from my friend Tamara Nerby, a comic from Minneapolis. She told me she'd been talking to her good friend Michael Bodine, a psychic, and that he had talked about me. He told her that she had to stop worrying about her friend, Lewis Black, because he was going to be very successful. Tammy never mentioned me in her conversation. She had never talked to Michael about me. There is no way he could know me, because I was barely known outside the community of comics. She was stunned, as was I. Up to this point I had always felt that psychics were like a magic act without props. I told Tammy the next time I was in Minneapolis I wanted to meet this guy. And could she have him call my agents and get them up to speed.

Several months later, I met Michael for the first time in Minneapolis. He looked like a surfer dude, or what I imagined one to look like. He was not what I was expecting at all. I guess I figured he'd be more of a nerd type with sunken eyes, his shoulders stooped by the weight of the nether world. This guy was all bright eyed and eager and sincerely happy, bouncy even.

He asked if I had any questions for him. Did I want to know about my future? Not really, I replied, as I was freaked out enough by a guy knowing about my future, my successful future, and I'd never even met the guy. I just wanted to know how he knew of me. I wanted to find out how someone learns to see the unseen—certainly a world I had never had access to. And so Michael, quite calmly and without any fanfare, much the way he matter-of-factly expresses his gifts in this book, explained to me how he had become a psychic. I was astonished. I had never met anyone like him. I had heard stories from friends who had experiences with psychics, but this was different. Michael was either a man with a real gift, or he certainly knew how to sling the bull. Michael spoke to dead people or spirits or call them whatever you want, and they told him about me. It was no big deal to him. He didn't try to impress me. He saw dead people and they communicated. It was that simple. Michael is a professional psychic and he spoke about his work in the same fashion one might if one worked in an insurance agency. (Even now when I call him, I say, "How are you doing?" and he says, "I spend my day talking to dead people. How do you think I'm doing?")

I was impressed, but when Michael started talking to me about my brother (who I had not mentioned, nor had my friend Tammy) and the fact that he had cancer, my mind was officially blown. There is absolutely no way he could have known about my brother's condition. He said it was going to be an extremely difficult battle for him and it was certainly one that he could easily lose. Up until this point, all the news my brother Ron had given me had been positive. That even though he had cancer, he had no doubts that he would be cured. It certainly helped open my eyes. I cannot express how vital this information was to me as it deepened my awareness of how precious the time I had with him was. (Sadly, we need those reminders, even if our family is healthy.)

What made this all truly impressive and worthy of noting was that Michael had no interest in me as some sort of client. He came to meet me because he was a friend of a friend and I guess the dead people said I was interesting.

He reiterated the fact that I was going to do very well. That my career was going to take off. And, sure enough, it did. Not immediately, as a psychic's timeline may be off. But Michael has since told me things that have happened in my career that no one who I work with professionally had expressed as possible.

We have been friends now for years and I am not writing this because he is my friend. It is because he opened up a world whose existence I never would have ever truly believed even remotely possible. I could list instance after instance where Michael has been aware of things happening in my world that one could only know by standing next to me while they were happening. I don't know how else to describe it to you. I do know that I wouldn't have written this if I hadn't been overwhelmed by the experience.

I had told Michael, on more than one occasion, that he should tell his life story. If only for me, I am glad he has written this book. I had a glimpse of his upbringing during our talks, but this book has been an eye-opener.

I am sure there are many who will read it and not believe a word of it. Why should they? In a world like ours, this all sounds like a bunch of nonsensical magic and hocus-pocus.

As Shakespeare so aptly put it, "There are more things in heaven and earth, Horatio, than are dreamt of in your philosophy."

I know Michael. I know this is a true story.

And for many, in a world that grows madder by the day, this book will bring some comfort. And if not comfort, it may make you question the nature of the real world, and where that might lead you can be better than all the answers you think you have.

Foreword by Echo Bodine

My dear, sweet brother Michael should come with a warning label: **Handsome, extremely gifted, funnier than all the comedians combined (sorry Lewis), incredibly blunt, and you will fall in love with him.**

I have had the pleasure of knowing him his whole life, and for the most part, it's been an honor to be his sister, his ghost-busting partner, and his friend. I say for the most part because when he was a little guy, I've never met a more hyper, wound up tighter than a top, ADD, sensitive, psychic, skinny kid in my life. And since we didn't know then what we know now, we'd feed him sugar when he got hyper, hoping to calm him down—and, well, you know the rest.

Looking back on his life, I would have to say Michael has been psychic since the day he was born. He's always been uniquely *knowing*. He's *known* things about people and situations that we could never understand. And as a little guy, he'd talk about the colors around people's heads, further convincing us that our dear baby brother had lost it even before he found it.

I think you are going to thoroughly enjoy reading about Michael's journey as the youngest child growing up in a family of psychics. His life has not been easy. Far from it. He has suffered from numerous phobias and gone through many of life's tough lessons, including alcoholism and drug addiction, and losing his first-born son, but with his incredible sense of humor, he's always found a way to cope with whatever life handed him.

As I read through his book, the one thing I was struck with was how little he actually talks about the excellent work that he's done over the years. Michael is, by far, the best psychic I've ever met. He has read for thousands of people, including many of Hollywood's finest. He's been sought after for television shows and movies. He really truly is a very gifted human being and I know you're going to fall in love with him as you read through his journey.

Just remember the warning: **Handsome, extremely gifted, funnier than all the comedians combined (sorry Lewis), and incredibly blunt.**

Enjoy,
Echo Bodine,
Michael's big sister.

Introduction

On a warm, muggy night in the late summer of 1971, I found myself driving with my mother, my cousin, and my cousin's friend to a house long-since abandoned and reportedly very haunted. I was thirteen. The city lights of Minneapolis behind us, we drove deeper and deeper into the winding hills and lush forest. Our reasons for being there were as varied as our emotional states. My mother was excited. She saw this as an adventure and yet another chance to learn about ghosts and how to deal with them. My cousin and his friend were curious, curious to see if this place was as bad and scary as it had been rumored to be. And I was there because I had to be. According to *my teachers* it was my time to confront my fears and come to terms with whatever issues I might have towards ghosts and demons. My issues were that *they scared the crap out of me.* As the houses disappeared and the car slowed and the scariest looking mansion anyone could imagine appeared out of the pitch-black night, I knew my life was over.

It wasn't. It was the beginning of my career as a ghost buster.

My name is Michael B. and I'm a psychic. I say this with as much resolve as an addict would at their first AA meeting. And like an addict, being a psychic was never something I aspired to become. In fact, I've done everything I could not to be psychic. I threw this *gift* in the corner and tried to ignore it. I misused it in the hopes it would be taken away. And when it wasn't, I begged God to take it from me. To

1

many people, being psychic appears to be a wonderful thing. Who wouldn't want to know what your boss or lover is thinking or doing, to be able to predict events, or talk to dead people to comfort the living? But for me, the realities of this so-called *gift* are not all Kumbaya and bonbons. For all the reasons a person can think of to be psychic, I can think of more why not to be. If you don't prove yourself every time you work, you don't work. If you do predict something that comes true, you're a novelty. If you're wrong, you're a fraud.

If I tell someone what I do, whether it's when I'm playing golf or going to my kids' school conferences, most people think I'm kidding. They crack a joke or look astonished. But when I assure them I'm not kidding, they get a *where's my Bible* look on their faces and start heading for the exits. It gets uncomfortable when they get quiet or, worse, snicker to themselves and look at their friends like I'm one of those. But it can be equally uncomfortable when the person reacts in the opposite extreme. For every skeptic floating around, there are fifty people who have had some sort of supernatural experience. And if you're a psychic, you get to hear their story. Something about us and what we do gives people the impression that we'd understand anything, no matter how weird. I can't tell you how many times somebody has come up to me and confessed how Uncle Harry hears the theme to *Star Wars* every time he goes to the bathroom and then asks if that's ever happened to me.

What I want to tell these people, but don't, is that I'm not the keeper of odd information. Yes, I talk to dead people, and yes, I've had some strange things happen to me because I'm psychic, but I don't have the answers to all life's odd little happenings. Granted, in my business you have to stay open-minded about things, but that doesn't mean we walk around wearing pyramids on our heads. I don't say this to people because in many ways psychics are at the bottom of the food chain when it comes to professions, and we always have to be cognizant of people's attitudes toward us.

My solution to these problems is to tell most people I meet in casual situations that I'm a waiter. Waiters threaten few people. The conversations stay light, I don't get the judgment vibe, and nobody asks me to contact a dead relative when I'm on the golf course.

My gift is pretty basic. I get pictures and images of things and words but not balls of death hitting the earth. I see things like where a person has been, where they're going, and what they're doing now. I can see short-term future opportunities like relationships, jobs, health, and sometimes stocks and bonds. I made some choices a while back to keep it simple. Because I didn't want to walk around being a psychic victim, I put certain restrictions on my abilities, which I'll explain later.

Even when I'm not working and I'm not opened up psychically, there are times when I still feel people's vibes. For example, when I go to a party and people are drinking, I feel like I have the hangover the next day. If I'm around someone who's depressed, I feel depressed. If I go to a stadium to watch a football game with fifty thousand people huddled together screaming for the hometown boys, I sit and vibrate from all the energy.

This book is about coming to terms with my gift and psychic phenomena as a whole—something I've had trouble with my whole life. I wrote it for a few reasons. One, being a psychic is an odd job.

Also, I know there are other people who have had similar experiences and might be able to relate. Because some psychics have made themselves bigger than life, they appear more powerful than the average person. There's nothing worse than psychics who take themselves too seriously. We don't all have to spin and levitate to get our point across. Being a psychic can be a normal, natural thing and hopefully some day it will be treated as such.

Finally, the main catalyst for this book wasn't something I learned as a result of heavy therapy or a near-death experience. It was sparked by a simple ghost busting job I went to in 1995.

Sitting in that car driving to my certain death at my first ghost busting job in 1971, I never dreamt that twenty-four years later I would still be doing the same thing. But here I was driving to another haunted house, this time with my sister Echo, also a professional ghost buster and psychic. Only now I wasn't afraid or nervous or even excited. I was just going. Haunted houses and dealing with ghosts had become routine.

I still liked the idea of helping people. I wouldn't do these jobs if I didn't. But by this time, Echo was writing books, traveling, and speaking about her psychic experiences and I was raising my two kids and doing readings for corporations and Hollywood actors.

The reality was, I was sick of it all—the ghost busting, the exorcisms, and the way the psychic world was becoming so prevalent. You couldn't get away from it. It was there, even when you turned on the television. *Call now and receive a free reading.* Driving down the street, you saw a psychic shop every four blocks. There are classes on past lives and future lives. If you want to be a psychic, take a one-day class. If you take a two-day class, you can teach the stuff. There are psychic doctors, psychic dentists, psychic salesmen, and psychic dog therapists.

And you don't talk to a *psychic.* You talk to a *clairvoyant* or a *clairaudient* or a *medium* or an *intuitive counselor.* If the person you go to has a flare for the dramatic, then you're talking to a *channeler.*

It doesn't matter if you don't know what you're doing. You could be washing the dishes one day, get possessed by an ancient spirit, and the next day charge a fortune to let people watch you perform. It's hip, it's happening, get a reading, get a crystal.

A few years back, more and more of the religious folks decided to sell their wares on TV. Lying, cheating, and greed were all fruits of that decision. Many years ago when psychic phenomena were still underground, one of the first things our family was taught was that psychics would do the same. They would become popular, in demand, and because of that popularity would be taken more seriously and thrown into the spotlight.

But, just like with the religious folks, psychics would start to take themselves too seriously. They'd start to believe they had the power and forget it comes from a higher source. As a result ego, greed, and cheating would become common, and psychics would again be forced to go underground with their work and beliefs.

With the first part of this prediction unfolding, the next part had to be close behind. Being a psychic has never been the most stable of career choices, but it felt like it was about to get worse.

I had been doing this for so long that I had gone beyond being bored. I had started to become indifferent. The thought of being in a room with an insurance salesman scared me more than being in a room with floating heads. Even Echo wasn't afraid of going on ghost busting jobs anymore and she used to get nervous watching *Bewitched*.

I found myself asking how I got in this place. More importantly, how did I end up doing the one thing I least wanted to do? The logical place to find that answer seemed to be in the beginning, and that's where my story begins.

One
Guess Who's Coming to Dinner?

"Okay, this one time, I'm in the kitchen, it was the middle of the day and I hear someone coming up behind me. I'm thinking it's my daughter, but when I turn around, nobody's there. Then this other time, somebody tapped me on the shoulder and whispered my name. The scariest time was when my friend Ellen was over and she ran out of the house because her coffee cup started moving by itself. I told my husband about it, but he just thinks I'm crazy. What do you think—do you think I saw a ghost?" "Either that," I replied, *"or you're crazy."*

Back when all this started, what now seems like three hundred years ago, our family didn't believe in ghosts. We were too busy being normal. I grew up in a white house with purple trim in an upper-middle-class neighborhood. A trimmed three-foot hedge surrounded the house. If you wanted to shoot a commercial for Wonder Bread, this was the place. Every house on our cul-de-sac had kids. Nobody locked their doors, and to me, everything seemed right with the world—until that autumn of 1964.

I remember it as a cool evening and even though I was only seven, I was slightly depressed because at six PM, it was already dark outside. I knew this meant that within a month it would be dark at four PM. There'd be the usual fourteen feet of snow on the ground and any skin exposed to the elements for more than three seconds would freeze and turn black. This, they say, makes Minnesotans hardier and gives us a longer life expectancy. *Obviously, because we're frozen for nine months out of the year.*

We were all sitting around eating dinner except for my teenage cousin, who was way too cool to wait for everyone else to finish. More importantly, if he was going to be the future Ringo Starr, he had to practice on his new drum set.

My mother was busy running around, dishing up plates, and pouring the milk. She was up and down so much it was like a Catholic service. But then, that was her job. If you offered to help, she'd consider it an insult. She was a beautiful black-haired, brown-eyed woman in her mid-thirties. A Jackie O. prototype, she was elegant and mysterious, yet nothing was more important to her than her kids, and nobody was more important to me than my mom.

My father was a tall, strong man, both physically and mentally. Because he had very little when he was young, it was important for him to have it all as an adult—and at thirty-five, he was well on his way. He started his own business helping kids stop wetting the bed several years earlier, and his drive for success kept him on the road two hundred days of the year.

My oldest sister Echo was an attractive seventeen-year-old girl, even with her horned-rimmed glasses and beehive hairstyle. She was at an age where she was becoming more aware of her independence. A slight competition was developing between her and my mother.

My cousin Lance lived with us. He had blonde hair and blue eyes, and more girlfriends than Hugh Hefner. There's a five-year difference between us and for the most part, we stayed away from each other. He struck me as too serious to be thought of as human and he thought of me as a ferret with lips.

My youngest sister Nikki was a beautiful, blonde-haired, blue-eyed girl of ten. Quiet and shy, she was my father's favorite. To everybody else, she was sweet and innocent. To me, she was sent to earth to torment me. In our teenage years, we would become close but back then, the only time we didn't fight was when we were sleeping.

As for me, I was a hyper, blonde-haired, crew-cut-wearing seven-year-old who was so skinny, I looked like a Bangladesh poster child. My mind was constantly going—usually off in some imagery adventure. This left little time to spend in reality, which meant my concentration level was low. I usually started dinner by spilling my milk. I always felt bad for doing that, but since I never meant to do it in the first place, I couldn't see how I could stop myself from doing it again. My siblings were convinced that my father was going to kill me by age ten.

For our family, this night was a typical one. It was warm, safe, and comfortable. Echo and Nikki were talking to my mom about makeup and I was trying to stretch eating time as far as I could so I wouldn't have to do my homework. In the background was the banging of Lance's hack drumming, along with the clanking noise of dishes being put away.

The drumming started out sounding normal, if you consider the sound of loud, irrational banging normal. But as time went on, it sounded better and tighter. At one point even my father commented on how good Lance sounded. Not wanting to give Lance any credit, Echo insisted it was a record, one of those *how to play the drums by numbers* type of deals. But it wasn't. It was Lance. Just about the time I started to like the drumming, it stopped.

We heard the door downstairs burst open, slam shut, and then we heard Lance racing urgently upstairs. By the time he got to the kitchen, we were waiting in silence for an explanation. When he came through the door, he looked scared, really scared. He was pale, glassy-eyed, and out of breath. I'd never seen him like that before. None of us had. He was, after all, the golden boy—the star athlete, the brilliant artist who rarely showed his feeling, except anger, and never showed fear, especially around my father who saw fear as a weakness.

We waited a second or two, half-expecting Lance to snap out of it and make a joke. When he didn't, my mother approached him. She tried to put her arms around him and asked him what was wrong. When she did, it broke whatever trance he was in. Remembering he was a teenager, he shrugged his shoulders and told my mother he was all right. My father, slightly relieved that his nephew hadn't totally lost his mind, decided to take control.

"What's the matter, Lance?" he said. "You look like you just saw a damn ghost."

All eyes were on Lance as he looked down at his feet and pondered his next words. "I did," he said quietly.

My father instantly went from being concerned to being annoyed. He had that look on his face that he gets when he puts his hands in a sink full of wet bread. "Lance, really. Come on. What happened?"

Lance paused for a second, his eyes scanning the floor like he was looking for an answer. "I saw … something. I don't know. A figure." He put his hands over his face, struggling with what had just happened.

My father was now becoming officially pissed off. His tone became more serious. "Come on. What the hell are ya talking about? YOU saw a figure! WHAT figure?"

This line of questioning made it harder for Lance. I, however, liked seeing Lance on the hot seat for a change.

Sensing Lance's frustration, my mother stepped in. "Honey, come over here," she said. She pointed to a chair and had him sit. She gave my father one of those *I'll take care of it* looks. She then walked over to Lance, bent over, and looked in his eyes.

"Tell me what happened," she said calmly.

Lance studied her for a moment, then finally felt comfortable enough to talk. He said he was playing the drums as usual. Frustrated because he wasn't playing as fast as he wanted to, he decided to concentrate and put his head down as he played. Then he sensed something to his left. He looked up and saw a man, a black man, coming through the wall toward him as he was playing. He quickly put his head back down and kept playing. Then he felt the figure right in front of him. The adrenaline from the fear made him play faster and faster. He was too afraid to get up and too afraid to stop. A tear came out of his eye. "Would you please leave?" he said, talking more to the air or himself than the ghost, because he still could not believe what he was seeing. The *man,* apparently sensing Lance's anxiety, left through the other wall. That's when Lance threw down his drumsticks and bolted upstairs.

We all just sat there. I for one was still waiting for the punch line, but there was none. That warm, safe feeling that was so strong just a minute ago was gone. A strange, scared, awful feeling—like there was something else in the house—replaced it. It could have been my imagination (I was right up there with Walt Disney as far as imagination was concerned) but it did feel like *someone* was there.

This *feeling* would later become routine as more things happened in our house, but because this was the first time I felt it, it had more of an impact on me. People talk about how fun it would be to see a ghost, not understanding that there's more to it than just *seeing* a ghost. There's the *feeling* that goes with it.

I wanted my mom and dad to handle the problem and make this feeling go away, but they seemed just as much in the dark as us kids. Finally my dad stood up and said he was going downstairs to check it out. I remember feeling relieved that my father was taking charge and being brave. But his plan to go downstairs and check things out differed from my plan, which was to start packing. My mother, still calm, started asking Lance more questions. *Was he okay? What did this man look like? Was he hurt in any way?* She also tried to reassure Lance that he wasn't crazy and that there was probably some explanation for what happened. Lance didn't want to talk about it.

Well, I wanted to talk about it. There's nothing worse than being afraid and not being able to talk about it. And I was afraid. I was there and heard the drumming get better. I saw the look on Lance's face when he came flying through the kitchen door. I could feel that weird feeling in the air. The way I saw it, something had just happened. Either Lance was playing a huge joke on all of us, in which case somebody needed to hit him hard, or something really did happen and we needed to deal with it and make it go away. You don't just have a ghost go through your den and then go watch *Laugh-In*.

I asked my mom if Lance really did see a ghost, truly expecting her to tell me everything was all right, even though I knew it wasn't—like when I cut myself or got really sick. I wanted her to look at me with that look of disgust and say *no* with authority. Instead she quietly said, "I don't know honey. We don't know what your cousin saw. But I'm sure it will all be fine."

She wasn't very convincing. I don't think she believed herself. But you couldn't blame her for trying. Saying *yes* would have raised a lot of unanswerable questions. Plus she knew I would never sleep again. Still, I was hoping to be more convinced. At age seven, your parents are God and if they don't have the answers, you're screwed.

I looked to my sisters for help, but they had already booked passage on the River Denial. This was obvious by the blank, vacant stare in their eyes. They each had different reasons for their emotional departures. Echo was coming from a place of practicality. It wasn't practical to believe in ghosts unless they did the dishes or took out the trash. Even if Echo did think there might be something to Lance's story, she wasn't going to let him think she did. Lance had been known to play practical jokes, and Echo usually bore the brunt of his jokes. So now if Lance felt a little crazy, Echo wasn't going to lose any sleep over it. If anything, the wheels were turning in her head as to how she could use Lance's turmoil to her advantage.

As for Nikki, I don't know what the hell she was thinking. When I looked at her, she had that *look* on her face. I got the feeling that if I did say anything to her, it might damage her, like when you wake up a sleepwalker and they go off on you. Besides, given the climate of the night so far, I knew that a verbal exchange would get me in trouble. I decided instead to hit her on the head with one of my peas. At the time I thought it would be a nice icebreaker but as I loaded my spoon, I could hear my father shutting the door to the downstairs den and all my attention turned back to what had gone on earlier.

As my father came back up the stairs, visions of the movie *Invasion of the Body Snatchers* danced in my head. I calculated the distance between the front door and me just in case he was possessed and I had to make a break for it. But when he came in, he looked normal. I looked at him as he looked at my mom, and he looked disgusted.

"Well, I didn't see anything odd down there, except," and he looked at Lance, "you managed to leave *every* goddamn light on."

He was pissed off because he actually went downstairs to look for something he knew wasn't there to begin with, and in doing so, his dinner got cold. He hated his dinner getting cold. A possible poltergeist was a drag, but having his dinner get cold, that was a *real* problem.

However uneducated his reaction might have been, my father did calm everybody down. As far as he was concerned, he took care of the problem. We all went back to our routines and kept whatever opinion we had to ourselves. Denial's a funny thing. If everybody in the room acts as if it's okay, you can convince yourself it's okay. And who was I to question it? Maybe everything was okay. Maybe Lance had been playing so hard he hit himself accidentally with a drumstick and hallucinated all of this. Who knew? All I know was that I was starting to feel better.

Lance had by now composed himself. He asked my mother to be excused, another sign of how weird things were that night. Lance hadn't asked to be excused since the Kennedy administration. My mother knew that nobody wanted to talk about it anymore so she said yes and everybody went their own way.

A week passed and again we were all sitting around eating dinner, this time with Lance. Even though he said he wasn't afraid, he said he wouldn't go downstairs alone without an armed guard and a priest or at least without one of the family. We were almost done with dinner and Lance was getting anxious to go down and play the drums. Echo had volunteered to go downstairs with Lance this particular night and just to emphasize her control over him, she decided to take her time by eating her peas one at a time—with chopsticks.

Suddenly, as we were talking, a salt and pepper shaker in the middle of the table levitated. It moved up, across the table, and then fell to the floor.

This time, we all saw it. When it first moved we just kept talking but as it got higher and higher, everybody stopped talking and focused on the floating objects. When they hit the floor, we just sat and stared at each other for what felt like a week.

"Did you all see that?" Echo finally said.

Nobody said a word. Then Nikki said, "Mom, what was that?"

Still, nobody had an answer.

My father jumped in. "Mary O (my mother's nickname—her name was really Mae, but Dad liked to compare her to Jackie O), what just happened?" Then he looked at Lance, who had that look on his face again, and asked him if he had anything to do with this, implying that he rigged up some sort of string or contraption to make the salt shaker move.

Lance blew up. All week long he had felt crazy because of seeing this *ghost*, and because this *ghost* chose to appear to him as opposed to Echo or Nikki or myself, he felt somehow responsible for the whole thing. Because we had given him so much crap all week for supposedly seeing this *ghost,* he wasn't going to take the responsibility for whatever was happening to us anymore.

He turned to my dad. "You saw it. We all saw it," he said in a high, loud, cracking fourteen-year-old voice. "I didn't do a thing and I'm not crazy. There is something in this house."

My father didn't buy it. "Well, if you didn't do it, who did? Somebody did this," he said. "Things don't just float around like that for no reason!" My dad looked at my mother for support, but she was in shock.

Then my cousin said what we'd all been thinking but didn't want to say, "It was a ghost, Dad. A GHOST moved that thing. A GHOST was downstairs with me last week and a GHOST just moved that salt shaker. There's no other explanation for it, Dad. WE HAVE A GHOST!"

The room was still. We were afraid to breathe. We were all trying to come to terms with this but we didn't have a clue what those terms would be. We were actually having a loud argument about ghosts, except for Lance, who seemed at peace with himself for accepting it.

For a second my father looked like he was giving credence to what my cousin said. But then he looked at my mom (like he always did when he was in over his head) and said, "Mary O, talk some sense to your nephew, will ya?"

My mother was more concerned with Lance. She looked at Lance. "Honey, we'll find out what's going on. Don't worry," she said.

The conviction in her voice made me feel a little better. She seemed as anxious to find out what was going on as my father was to dismiss the situation as swamp gas. Her attitude also helped my cousin. He appeared calmer. When he looked at my mother and said "*Okay, Mary,*" he said it with belief. This made us all feel better.

Even my dad was impressed. He looked at my mom, surprised that she broke protocol by not totally backing him, but relieved that calm was once again restored to the house. "See there? Your mom's got it under control."

Dad went into the living room while the rest of us stayed in the kitchen. By the look he gave my mother when he got up, you could tell they were going to have one of those closed-door conversations when they went to bed.

With my mother's assertion, I felt better, but I couldn't escape the feeling of being doomed. I didn't know what was going to happen next or to whom it was going to happen. I had no idea why this was happening to our family or when it was going to stop. But I did know one thing. That night I was going to put so many lights on in my room, small planes would be able to land on our roof.

Two

Who Ya Gonna Call?

"Look, I didn't come here looking for life's little answers, I don't even believe in this crap. I just want to know if I'm going to win the lottery." She took out a cigarette, leaned back and lit it up. I made sure we had eye contact and then spoke. *"No, you're not going to win the lottery, but if you don't stop drinking you are going to die. You hate your job, you hate your life ... the only thing you don't hate is the 25-year-old mechanic you're having the affair with, but even that will get old."* I stopped. She looked at the floor, took a deep drag on her cigarette and with a blank stare looked back up at me. *"Hmm,"* she said, as she exhaled with an almost last breath feel. *"You really don't think I'm going to win the lottery?"*

The next day, my mother decided to find some help. She sat down and made a list of people she could talk to about this problem. The list was short. There were only three possible choices: our minister, Reverend Crowler, the Catholic Church, or Mrs. Rupe.

Reverend Crowler was a young, handsome, ambitious minister who led a large Baptist congregation. He was also a thoughtful, kind man. Every Sunday when we went to church, my dad insisted we sit in the very front row. Whether we were late or on time, we had to sit in the front. On the days we were running late, my dad would parade us down the middle of this huge church with everybody looking at us, waiting for our butts to sit so they could start the service. We'd all be purple by the time we reached the pew, except my dad. We'd look up at the Reverend Crowler. He'd look down at us, smile a genuine smile, say good morning, and start the service.

He never made us feel bad, never said anything judgmental, and I liked him for that. The only problem with Reverend Crowler as I could see it was that he was spiritually handcuffed. He may have wanted to help us. Maybe he could have helped us. But he was an ambitious man and my mom felt he would jeopardize his place in the church by helping us. Besides, we had some clout in the church. My dad gave a lot of money for additional wings and children's camps (that's probably why the Reverend was always smiling at us) and my mom felt it would put Reverend Crowler in a bad position if he couldn't help us.

Either way—by helping or not helping us—Rev. Crowler would lose. He was out.

The Catholic Church was the religion in which my mother was raised—not the best place for the alternative thinker. That meant she was raised with the prehistoric notion that anything to do with ghosts and psychics was evil. If you even thought of those things, you were considered Satan's little helper. At a young age, I got the impression some Catholics thought their religion was far better than any other. I felt bad for them, even as a youngster, because that attitude seemed so self-righteous and fearful—two emotions that are the opposite of what a religion is supposed to give you. (I later learned that the shortcoming of instilling those emotions in people was just as strong in the psychic community as anywhere else.)

Either my mother couldn't find her rosary or she just plain had too many bad memories from that place, but she couldn't bring herself to go to the Catholic Church and ask for help. It wasn't a safe environment in which to discuss that sort of thing.

That left Mrs. Rupe.

Mrs. Rupe was my mother's counselor, someone my mother would go to from time to time when things got too difficult at home. She was a soft-spoken little woman who turned out to be a major influence in my mom's life. She had been through a lot in her life—she knew her own gifts and where to apply them. I liked Mrs. Rupe because she had the greatest back yard for a kid, full of little plastic trolls and deer. She'd always have something for me to eat and the place always smelled like a cookie. Everybody knew Mrs. Rupe and most people liked her. For my mother, she was the only option.

When my mother went to see Mrs. Rupe, she told her about the things that were happening at the house and also her concerns if other people were to find out. My mom laid it all out and was surprised by how calm Mrs. Rupe was. She didn't throw crosses at her and demand that she leave. Instead she was more concerned about how all this weird stuff was affecting my mother and her family. After their session, Mrs. Rupe said that she knew someone who might be able to help us with our problem. She said a friend of hers had gone to see this woman named Mrs. Olsen, a medium who lived just across the river in St. Paul.

She said Mrs. Olsen had helped her friend and if my mom wanted, she would give her the number, too. This was a suggestion my mother probably wouldn't have taken if Mrs. Rupe hadn't been so understanding.

The thought of going to a medium scared my mother. It was opening a door that she wasn't sure she wanted to go through. And she knew it might lead to a place she wasn't prepared to go. She did, however, trust Mrs. Rupe, and she didn't want to appear ungrateful for her solution. So she thanked Mrs. Rupe for the number, put it into her purse, and hugged her goodbye.

On the way home, my mother started feeling better about the situation. Talking with Mrs. Rupe seemed to help and just knowing she wasn't crazy also seemed to take some of the edge off. She also knew that if things got worse around the house, if something started floating or the walls started bleeding, she could call this Mrs. Olsen. But for now she was going to go home, try to put this stuff out of her head, and take a nap. She had been up all night the night before discussing things with my dad and she was tired. We kids weren't going to be back from school for a couple more hours and my dad wasn't coming home until late, so this would be a perfect time.

When my mother got home, she entered the house, hung up her coat, and went upstairs to lie down. The house was quiet and, according to her, felt normal. As she was taking off her earrings, she looked in the mirror and in the reflection she saw all the Bibles in the house—even the ones that were supposed to be packed away—lying on the bed in a big circle. She dismissed this as nothing out of the ordinary. Her first thoughts were that one of us kids had done it or maybe she had stacked the Bibles on her bed when she was looking for a psychic reference. Either way, she wasn't going to make a mountain out of a Bible hill. She went about putting them away without giving it much thought.

She was nearly done when the phone rang. It was her best friend, Rosie. Rosie and my mother had known each other for years. They had been through the mill together and both had come out okay. But even with their bond as strong as it was, my mother didn't feel comfortable talking to her about what was happening around the house. She kept the conversation light and they talked for about ten minutes. Finally my mom said she wanted to take a nap before all the kids got home. She hung up the phone, walked back in the bedroom, and there were all the Bibles back in a circle in the middle of the bed.

My mother turned around, went back to the hall, picked up the phone, and called Mrs. Olsen.

"Hello, dear. I've been expecting your call," Mrs. Olsen said, in her slight English accent, as soon as my mother identified herself.

As unsettled as my mother was about the Bibles moving around, Mrs. Olsen's reaction to my mother's call was even more disturbing. Assuming Mrs. Rupe had talked to Mrs. Olsen, my mother let it go. But when Mrs. Olsen continued by saying the reason the Bibles were in a circle was to get my mother's attention, my mother was dumbfounded.

How did Mrs. Olsen know all of that, especially since it just happened? (While she was trying to figure it out, she almost forgot she was on the phone.)

"Hello? Are you still there, dear?" Mrs. Olsen said.

"Uh, yes. I'm sorry," my mother said, coming back to reality. She tried to explain her shock by telling Mrs. Olsen how new all of this was and how normal our family was, and well, just how amazing it was that she knew about the Bibles.

Again Mrs. Olsen interrupted, not interested in my mother's ramblings. "Don't worry about that spirit your nephew saw in the basement, dear," Mrs. Olsen said. "He's there to help the boy. His name is Dr. Fitzgerald. He was a drummer when he was alive—quite a good one from what he says—but he expired a few years ago."

Mrs. Olsen paused for a moment, probably realizing she was scaring my mother. "He's harmless," she said, referring to the dead guy floating in our basement. "He really is. He's just attracted to your nephew's life force," she said, trying to reassure her (as if that would somehow calm my mother down). She then asked my mother if she would like to come to see her.

"Yes, I would," my mother said (as soon as she pulled her jaw off of the floor). "Very much."

Mrs. Olsen jumped in again. "I'd like you to bring your eldest daughter with you. Would that be all right? Spirit has some things to discuss with her," Mrs. Olsen said, before my mother had a chance to ask why.

Believing, by this time, that Mrs. Olsen knew what she was talking about, my mother agreed. They made arrangements and my mother hung up the phone.

Still in shock over what had just happened, my mother went to the edge of the bed and sat down. She looked at the Bibles that were still in a circle on top of the bed, rolled her eyes, and pushed them off the bed. Half-seriously, she told them to put themselves back. She lay on her back, stared at the ceiling, and reviewed the day's events.

On one hand, it felt good, like she was making some progress. This woman, this medium person—whatever she was—seemed to have answers, and my mother liked her.

On the other hand, what was she getting herself and her family into? Was this the gateway to Hell? It didn't feel that way but in the Bible it says the Devil can be tricky. Was Mrs. Olsen the Devil in a blue dress? What were the religious ramifications?

As time went on and my mother got to know Mrs. Olsen better, she would hear her constantly talking about God and Jesus Christ. If Mrs. Olsen was the Devil—as some religious people might suggest— why would she talk so much about God and Jesus?

Eventually my mother would resolve this conflict, but for now there were too many things to figure out, all at once. If she were to go forward with this process she knew that, unlike the religion she was raised in, she needed to have an open mind about things she might learn and not be judgmental. Ironically, it was that same closed-minded thinking and sharp criticism of other people's beliefs that made my mother want to be more open-minded about this new area. And in her heart, it felt right to do so. Having had that realization, her most immediate problem was how she was going to get Echo to go to the reading.

Echo was not into this at all. She liked her world neat and organized, so organized that she would iron her socks. Not that she was closed off or stuffy. Echo was friendly and everybody liked her, including me. She was thoughtful and sincere, and probably more maternal at times than my mother. But to envision her getting a reading was like hearing Mary Tyler Moore talk about going to the bathroom. It just didn't seem right. In many ways, Echo reminded me of Mary Tyler Moore, and Echo's life plans did not include dealing with floating candles, dead people, or *mediums* named Mrs. Olsen. Echo was going to marry at age nineteen, have fourteen kids, and live happily ever after.

The only way I could see my mother convincing Echo to go on this psychic rendezvous would be to tell her they were going to a class on how to fold towels. Or better yet, a *friends of Elvis* meeting. But as it turns out, not only did my mother tell her the truth, Echo surprisingly agreed to go.

I remember coming home from school that day and having that same feeling come over me that I had when my cousin saw that ghost. It felt like walking into a thick cloud—heavy and stifling. It was eerie. I knew something was up, but when I went upstairs and asked my mom, she denied it. She looked a little stupid saying nothing was wrong as she fumbled with all those Bibles, but a part of me really didn't want to know.

I had decided earlier that denial was the best way to go. It seemed to work for thousands of people for thousands of years. The only requirement to join this group was I had to stop trusting my eyes and ears. And seeing how easy it was for my dad, I figured it could probably work for me. So when my mother later told me that she and Echo were going to see Mrs. Olsen, I was unaffected. As far as I was concerned, it was for a knitting class.

My mother said when they arrived at Mrs. Olsen's house, it looked like a place where a *medium* might live. It was old, painted dark brown, and the yard was overgrown with thick, uncut grass and shrubbery. An older gentleman met them at the door—presumably Mr. Olsen—but he didn't say much. He led them upstairs to a waiting area. All the furniture was dark, as were the draperies and carpet.

Later, when my mother dragged me there the first time, the place gave me the Willies. It was clean, but it smelled old and I was afraid to touch anything in case Lurch jumped out at me. I could feel there were other people around me, even though I was sitting there by myself waiting for my mother. Being the hyper little nipper that I was, I kept looking over my shoulder and around the room.

As spooky as the place was, Mrs. Olsen was not. She was short with black hair, and she was gentle, loving, and genuine. She was the first person, other than my family, that I met who displayed unconditional love. You could feel it when you talked to her. Right away she took a shine to my mother and sister. She greeted them both with a big smile and insisted they call her Eve.

My mother went in for her session first. When I was there, I got the feeling anything could happen to me. I imagine my mother felt the same way. Being the parent, she probably thought if someone were to get possessed, it should be her. If this did happen, Echo would have to find a different way home, but it was a risk my mother was willing to take. Eve led my mother into this little dark room and had her sit down. Then she lit some candles and sat down.

There was a glass of water on the light stand by her chair. She didn't drink it. It just sat there. We found out later it was for a spirit, apparently a dehydrated one who was, as she put it, her spirit guide. She started with a prayer. She was always saying prayers and not just generic ones. These prayers were personal and from the heart. I was surprised at how spiritual she was. Now it makes sense, but back then, I was expecting chants instead of prayers. I really thought that *those people* didn't believe in God, at least not a normal god—a god with the tail of a goat maybe, but certainly not J. C.

Eve talked more about God than anybody I knew, including Rev. Crowler. At times, it seemed more like a church service than a reading.

There were pictures of Jesus all over the place, plus a Bible was always in view, either on the table or close by. She didn't go overboard, but she made it clear that whatever gift she had came from Jesus and that the readings were secondary to the influence of God. Today, in my life, that thinking is mandatory. If you start thinking you're better than your gifts, you tend to lose those gifts.

At that time, however, it bugged me that there was so much emphasis on God. I didn't want to talk about Jesus. I wanted to know whether or not I was going to pass my spelling test. Important stuff like that. Still, it was reassuring to me that she had such a strong faith.

When my mother went in, Eve started to do her prayer thing. She asked Jesus to come down and help her with the questions my mother might have. (Normally when you went in to a reading with Eve, you had some prepared questions to ask.) She asked that the reading be blessed, and because of that, I think my mother started feeling a little safer and more relaxed.

Suddenly, Eve got quiet. She closed her eyes and started talking to herself. She nodded her head, like she was saying yes and no. This was unnerving for my mother because when Eve was saying yes or no, she mentioned my mother's name from time to time. Then she started thanking someone (supposedly the Big Guy), slowly opened her eyes, and started telling my mother all about what *they* had to say. She explained that these words were not her words, but words from my mother's *spirit guides*. She said these spirit guides were with us all the time. They helped us when they could, but they also learned from us, as well.

She went on to say that my mother's spirit guides were anxious to talk to my mom. They had told her that my mother had natural psychic abilities and it was time for her to develop and use them. This was something my mother didn't know she had, or if she did have a slight notion she had a gift, she had suppressed it a long time ago. (Just another joy of being raised Catholic.) She told my mother that these *gifts* were passed down from generation to generation. My mother's mother had the gift and she gave it to my mother, and she in turn gave the gift to us kids. She said that out of the four kids, three would end up using these gifts. The fourth would have the gift, but not use it.

She continued by saying that the psychic activity at the house would increase. As a family, we were about to experience many unusual things, but we should not be frightened by them. These experiences were all part of the learning process. We needed to keep an open mind and take in as much as we could, and most importantly, trust the process. She said that this was a spiritual journey. Being on a spiritual journey, we would find that there was a light side and a dark side. The light side was when you used your gift to help other people to bring out the good in them—to show people their gifts and path. The dark side was when you used your gift to manipulate or control someone through fear or the illusion that you have more power than they do. She said we needed to be careful, to always ask for protection from Jesus, and she explained that asking for protection meant seeing a white light from God surround you like a flashlight. This, she said, would help protect us when we became afraid or felt we were in danger.

She said there were many spirits around us and they would help, but ultimately the choice about what side we wanted to be on was ours, and that there was no middle ground. With that, Eve stopped talking.

There was now an awkward silence in the room. My mother didn't know if the session was over or if Mrs. Olsen had suddenly broken down. She was thinking maybe she should ask if they were finished when she noticed Mrs. Olsen, with her eyes still shut, bowing her head as if she was listening to someone give her instructions. "Thank you," Eve said. Then Eve lifted her head and said to my mother, "Dear, so you know I'm talking to spirit, I will give you three truths, things only you would know. Do you understand, dear?"

My mother, not sure what to say, said, "Uh, sure. That's fine."

Again, Eve put her head down and went back to talking to herself.

After a minute or so, she lifted her head and started by saying there was someone who wanted to talk to my mother, that it was her mother. She told her that her mother's name was Laura and that Laura had passed away about ten years earlier. Then she described Laura to my mother. Eve's voice was now more endearing than factual. "Your mother has black hair, like you, except it's quite thick. She stood about five-foot-seven, and had a hard time breathing when she was alive here on earth."

She stopped for a second, then with a sheepish smile said, "Oh, I'm sorry, dear. That's how your mother says she died. Her lungs were bad." She paused again, then said, "Your mother had a hard time this last time on earth. She had a hard life. She says she feels good about how you two reconciled near the end, but that your relationship was strained ever since you married *that man*."

"She doesn't care much for your husband," Eve whispered to my mom. "Anyway your mother says you must not be ashamed of your gypsy blood. She wished that she would have been more comfortable with it herself while she was on earth, but she could never get past the stigma of being a gypsy.

"She said that she would sneak down to the river at night from time to time, whenever she knew the gypsies were in town. She would go to visit and catch up on all the latest gossip and news. She said some were relatives and some were friends, but they all felt like family. She said it was the only time she felt truly happy. The only thing that stopped her from just going with the gypsies when they moved on was one, she knew it would be no life for you, and two, she didn't want to disappoint her Irish Catholic husband. He hated the gypsies and made her promise she would stay away from them forever.

"He was the one who took her away from that lifestyle. He offered stability and a home, two things Laura didn't have growing up with the gypsies. Life had been hard for her growing up. Food and money were hard to come by. Staying in one place for more than nine months was unheard of. When Boyd (my grandfather) came along, he was kind, responsible, and truly cared about Laura. She decided to settle down and live life in a different way. And for a few years she was content."

(They got married, bought a house in St. Paul, had my mother and settled down to what Laura thought was the normal way to live. Boyd worked as a printer and preferred a more quiet life. Laura stayed home and raised my mom and read romance novels. As time passed and my mother grew, Laura started to miss her friends and family. It started to become important to her to get in touch with her roots, but knowing it was impossible to bring her gypsy family into her home, she chose to go to theirs. She would sneak down to the river when she thought they might be in town and visit with them. She kept the visits a secret because she didn't want to mix worlds.)

"She tried to tell you about the gypsies and her roots," Mrs. Olsen continued, "but at the time you were a teenager and there was a war on. You seemed busy with your friends and life. She wanted to tell you how wonderful those people were to her and how much they loved you. She said she'd bring you down to the river when you were a baby, and you always seemed so happy and giggly.

"Do you remember any of that?" Mrs. Olsen asked my mother. But my mother was in a different world. She was way back at the point in the reading where Mrs. Olsen said, "Your mother's name is Laura."

Mom was amazed that Mrs. Olsen was actually talking to her mother and, even though that thought frightened her, it also excited her to think that maybe her mother wasn't really dead, and if that was true, maybe there wasn't any such thing as death—at least the kind of death my mother was used to. But then what?

My mother was full of questions. She wanted to learn more about *how* her mother was doing. She wanted to know *what* she was doing. She wanted to know what heaven was like, what it looked like. Her mind started going a mile a minute—all these questions—and yet when Mrs. Olsen asked her if she understood everything, the only thing my mother could say was *yes*.

With that, Mrs. Olsen continued, only this time her tone was more serious. "Your mother wanted to tell you it was *those people*, the gypsies, who helped her understand her gift. But she said it scared her too much to use it all the time. She only used it for little things like feeling out whom she could trust or whom she couldn't, or how to react when her husband came home upset or troubled. Your family (the Bodine family) has a chance to get beyond the fear and make a difference. You can help educate people, show them the gifts that they have—not in a grandiose way, but in a subtle way. Your mother said she would help you as much as she could."

Again Eve became quiet. She took a deep breath, exhaled, and finished by telling my mother that it was time for her mother to leave.

Eve asked my mother if there was anything she wanted to say to her mother before she left. My mother quickly asked how she could stay in contact with her.

"Now that you have made contact with her, she won't be afraid to contact you."

With that Mrs. Olsen said thank you to the spirit, then said another prayer as she slowly opened her eyes. She looked at my mother. "Did that help, dear?" she asked.

"Yes it did," said my mother, still in shock. "Thank you."

Mrs. Olsen asked to have five minutes alone and then to please send Echo in. My mother thanked Mrs. Olsen again and went to the other room to get my sister.

My mother was blown away. In that short forty-five-minute period, her eyes had opened and her life felt different. The things that Eve had said were too accurate for my mother to dismiss as a fluke or a lucky guess. She realized that there was so much to learn and it was time for her to start school—not just because she was curious, but because, as she found out, it was a part of who she was. Maybe she knew that all along, deep down, but Eve's session gave her permission to explore that side of her. What had just happened up there in that room excited her. She was also more comfortable sending in Echo, although Echo's anxiety level peaked when she saw my mother coming at her with her eyes glazed over and a blank smile on her face, saying *"you're next, honey. Go ahead. I think you'll like it."*

Echo must have felt like the turkey on Thanksgiving when the farmer says, *"Hey let's go for a walk."*

When Echo walked in to see Eve, her anxiety caused her to go from being a middle-aged teenager to a six-year-old in a minute. She felt afraid and alone. Since my mother was already possessed, Echo had no choice but to go through with it.

Eve was still tired from her session with my mother, but when she saw Echo, she perked up. She greeted Echo with a big smile and took her hand to show her where to sit. This put Echo at ease. Echo could sense Eve's gentle nature, and she knew she wasn't going to be harmed.

As Echo settled in, Eve took the glass of water that was on the light stand, went in the other room, poured out the water, filled it up again, and brought it back to the light stand. Echo, assuming that it was for her said, "No thanks. I'm fine."

Eve chuckled. "Oh no, dear," she said. "This is for spirit." Eve put the glass down and started going through the same routine that she did with my mother. She closed her eyes. She said the prayers. She talked to herself.

While Echo was watching all this, a couple of things came to mind. One, maybe Mrs. Olsen was off her rocker. And two, if something started to drink that glass of water, she was out of there. The best thing to do was to watch Eve closely in case she went off. When Echo first met Eve, she didn't look at her closely because Echo was nervous. But now, it was in her best interests to study her.

She noticed a small lump in the middle of Eve's forehead, right where you would put a third eye, if you had one, like a Cyclops. At first, Echo just thought it was interesting, but as happens when your imagination goes wild, you start seeing things. The more Echo looked at it, the more it looked like it was growing bigger and bigger. After a while, Echo couldn't take her eyes off it.

Now, she was getting uncomfortable. What if Eve saw her staring at her giant bump? Maybe she already knew she was thinking about it. After all, she was a medium. Echo couldn't just ignore it. It was now as big as a zeppelin. What could Echo do? She was in this tiny, dark room with an old lady who talked to herself and had a house growing out of her forehead.

Echo started thinking maybe she should just leave. She didn't want to embarrass Eve by thinking about her forehead anymore and she was sure Eve knew what she was thinking. She started to fidget in her chair as though she was about to leave when Eve came out of her trance, looked up at Echo, and said, "My dear, you are a very gifted human being."

Echo decided to stay.

"You were born with many talents, but your biggest gift is your gift of healing. You will be a famous healer someday."

Suddenly, the bump on Eve's face didn't look so big. Echo's concerns shifted from physical deformities to mental abnormalities. Echo wasn't going to be a healer. She didn't even like being a candy striper. She was going to be a mother and housewife and all she wanted to know was when was she going to get married.

But Eve continued. "You also have the gifts of clairvoyance and clairaudience, which means the gifts of being able to see and hear spirits. Again, people will know who you are because of these gifts."

Eve once again became quiet, apparently to get more information. Echo saw this as her opportunity to orally refresh Eve as to why she was really there. "Excuse me, Mrs. Ol…Eve, is there anything about, um, marriage? I'm just curious because …" Echo's voice trailed off. She could see she was talking to herself because Eve wasn't listening. Eve was deep in thought with her *spirit friends*. Echo decided to wait for the question-and-answer portion of the show to finish her question.

Eve finished talking to her buddies and continued with the reading. "Your father's at home in pain. Go to him and put your hands where the pain is coming from; you will see your healing abilities for yourself. Don't be frightened by these gifts, as they'll serve you well."

Eve got quiet again. Then in a softer voice, she said, "I do have some disappointing news for you dear. You won't marry until your mid-thirties. You will have one child, but you will be young when you have him and you will not raise him. I believe you give him up for adoption. But don't worry, you will become close when the two of you meet in his early twenties. He will also have the gift of healing. Your main purpose here on earth is to teach and help people."

To Echo, this new information wasn't music to her ears. To say she was disappointed would be like saying Jeffrey Dahmer was a little quirky. She was downright bummed out. She couldn't, wouldn't, and didn't believe what Eve was telling her. There was no way that she was going to be a *healer*. Dogs heel, not people. And a clairvoyant, or a clairaudient—whatever they call it—well, Eve obviously had the wrong person.

But when Eve started telling Echo information only Echo knew— like about her boyfriend, the job she had, and things that she hid in her car—Echo knew she was talking about her. Everything Eve said was right on, and Echo just kept getting more and more depressed.

Eve, on the other hand, was getting downright giddy. She was truly excited about Echo's future and she knew that eventually Echo would be too. She also knew that later on in their lives, she and Echo would become friends and see each other often. Eve found it best to leave that part out of the reading for now.

They finished their talk and met my mother in the sitting room. My mother asked Echo how the reading went, but the only thing Echo would tell her was *we'll talk later*. My mother thanked Mrs. Olsen, as did Echo, and we headed home.

Three
Psychic 101

"I said you would see life differently when we started psychic development classes, and you might experience some psychic phenomena, but I wasn't talking within the first twenty minutes," I told the class. But that light just went off by itself for no reason. Kay said, "I saw it, you saw it. They must be trying to contact us. But why would they be trying to contact us now? It must mean something." The group got quiet, and all attention was on me. "Yes, it does mean something," I said. "It means I have a timer." Everyone, including Kay, became noticeably depressed. I continued. "If we stop to observe every brick in the road, it's going to be a long trip." I let them think about it while I grabbed my notebook and scribbled three simple words: "return the clapper."

The ride home was a particularly long one for Echo. If she could get rid of that gnawing feeling in the pit of her stomach that said *Eve was right*, she could hop back on the River Denial with me and everything would be fine. But she couldn't. That gnawing feeling wasn't only telling Echo that Eve was right, it was also telling her she might like being a healer, and that was something she couldn't deal with.

My mother's attitude wasn't helping Echo block out her fears. As much dread as Echo felt, my mother felt equal amounts of excitement. She wouldn't stop talking about all the things that Mrs. Olsen had said and with every word she seemed energized. This was truly what my mother needed in her life, and the timing couldn't be better. Her life was passing her by.

With my father's business going full guns, the money was flowing in. Mom was becoming a rich Edina housewife. (Edina is an affluent upper-middle-class town with expensive property and lots of attitude. The nickname for people from Edina was *cake-eater*.) This was a role my mother never felt comfortable in.

My mother was a product of the depression and World War II. Money was hard to come by. Her dream wasn't living in a big house with fancy clothes. She was comfortable with what she had and who she was. She wanted kids and maybe some stability, but she would have been just as happy in a middle-class house with middle-class neighbors and a middle-class dog.

Middle-class was not in my father's plans. He was out to conquer the world and nothing was going to stop him. He went from foster home to foster home until he was twelve, and then the Bodines adopted him and put him to work. He enlisted in the Navy as soon as he looked old enough to do so and he got both knees shot to hell in Normandy. You might say the man had a few issues. But to his credit, he didn't become a victim. The anger and frustration that had festered inside of him for years fueled a bombastic desire to show the world he was better than the people who had called him a bastard all his life.

He once told me a story about when he was nine and living in the orphanage. Every Christmas, this *rich prick* (as he put it) would drive up in his shining black Cadillac and hand out apples. And every year, he said, he would get his butt kicked because he wouldn't thank the guy for his apples. He resented the fact that the guy could afford a Cadillac but not a turkey or a decent present. He said he made up his mind at that time that he was going to buy his own Cadillac, go back to the orphanage, and give the kids some real presents.

So the first chance he got, he went out and bought a new Cadillac and took some toys to the orphanage. Since that day, every car he bought had to be a Cadillac or whatever was the most prestigious. He loved cars—the more expensive the better—and everything the man bought had to be the best, or somehow it wasn't worth buying. We didn't just have housekeepers, we had housekeepers from Germany living with us. We didn't just have dogs and cats, we had monkeys and alligators. We had toys galore and every new gadget that came out. Every weekend, the whole family would go to the Mississippi River where our yacht was parked and take trips up and down the river with other rich people who would talk about how wonderful life was. We were living the American dream, and as comfortable as I was in that role, my mother was not.

My mother got lost in all the baubles, and for the last few years had resigned herself to being a trophy wife. She had no reason to believe her life would change until her visit with Eve. Their meeting woke her up. She knew there was more to life than material belongings and money, but it had been awhile since she cared. Suddenly she did and now Echo was on her own as far as pooh-poohing this psychic stuff.

Echo's only hope to calm the fires of enthusiasm burning in my mother was what happened when she got home. If my father wasn't in pain, she could dismiss all of this as the ramblings of an old woman. But if my dad did have a headache, the chances of being any help to him were ridiculous.

She wasn't sure how she was going to approach him. He was already bugged that they went to a psychic in the first place. Now to announce that she had *healing powers* and would he mind if she conducted a little experiment might send him over the top. Still, if his headache were bad enough, maybe he'd be willing to try anything.

My father was a good man. He was just a product of the forties and fifties—a hunter-gatherer type. In his mind, his job was to take care of us. He worked hard, set up the moral code for the rest of the family, and didn't have much time for things like the occult or psychics.

He wasn't what you'd call a *light* guy. For fun he would read law books or play chess. It was important for him to always have the upper hand and his philosophy was *he who had the most toys when he died, won.* He was funny and at times could be sensitive. I never saw my father cry, but he'd be there if you needed him and because of his size, nobody messed with our family (at least anybody living). I loved my father, although there were times I didn't understand him.

When my mother and Echo arrived home, the house was quiet. On the way home, Echo had told my mother everything Eve said, so they were both curious about my father's condition. As soon as my mother put down her purse to go upstairs, she heard my father yell down, "Mae, is that you?"

"Yes honey. We're back," my mother replied.

My father asked her to come upstairs to the bedroom. He had a headache and would she please bring some aspirin.

My mother and Echo looked at each other.

"Go upstairs and put your hands on your father's head," my mother said. "Tell him I'll be upstairs shortly with the aspirin. You don't have to tell him what Eve said."

Echo went upstairs and saw my father lying on his back in bed. His arms covered his eyes so when Echo walked in, he thought it was my mother.

"Well, you're finally back. Could you get some aspirin?"

"No, Dad, it's me," Echo said.

He moved his arms to look up at her. "Oh hi, honey," he said wearily. "My head is killing me. Would you get me some aspirin?"

"Mom's getting it," Echo said.

She stepped closer. "Dad, Eve told me you had a headache and she told me I could heal you, if I put my hands on your head," Echo said. "Do you mind if I try?"

He paused for a second. "Eve told you that I had a headache? Really?"

Echo walked closer to him. "Yeah, Dad. She did. Weird, huh?"

As she started toward him, her hands started to get warm, then hot. "Do you mind?" she asked.

Apparently, his headache was bad. "Yeah, what the hell. I'll try anything," he said.

She put her hands on my father's head and he noticed how hot they were. He told her that her hands felt soothing and then asked her about their night. She talked a little about what went on, but the subject changed and he started talking about his job, and how that must be the reason for the headache.

My mother walked in the room with the aspirin. "Here's your pills," she said. "Are you okay?"

He said *yes*, he was feeling better. He started to get up and looked around, puzzled. "I'll be damned. The headache's gone."

My mother asked if he was okay. Again he said, "That's weird. It's really gone."

My mother and sister looked at each other. Suddenly, my father wanted to know everything that went on that night. My mother told Echo she'd explain everything to my dad and that she could leave.

Echo could hear my mother and father talking to each other as she walked out the door. She just kept walking, staring at her hands, amazed at what she had just done, and not too sure what she was going to do next.

Like Mrs. Olsen had predicted, it didn't take long for things to start happening around the house. You could hear people walking up and down the stairs. Lights were going on and off for no reason. When you opened the cupboard, objects like the vanilla would slide out and drop in your hands. There was a constant thumping at night, and a general feeling of someone being there who wasn't.

With so many things happening around the house, I'd try to convince myself it was all a dream, but I'd get so sick of slapping myself trying to wake up, it wasn't worth it. Denial was becoming less effective. On the plus side, when things happened, they didn't always come with that weird feeling of that first night, so in some ways it was easier to deal with. When I went to the cupboard and something slid out into my hands, it seemed almost natural. I found myself wanting to thank whoever slid it to me. It wasn't all light and fluffy. We had a Ouija board.

I remember the first time I saw a Ouija board. It didn't look like any board game I'd ever seen before. It had mystical signs, dark scary looking ghosts, and it just felt weird. For a seven-year-old, it was a little intimidating and not just because it looked spooky. The whole idea was something I wanted to stay away from. You'd put your fingers on this little floating saucer with a window and a ghost or spirit would move it to spell out answers to questions. According to the company that made the game, it was all supposed to be in fun, but how do you figure having your hands manipulated by a dead person is fun?

For our family to have a Ouija board was like asking Michael Jackson to babysit—you're asking for trouble. We didn't play it as a family. We all did our own thing with it. At first, I treated it like it was just a game. I'd get together with my friends and goof around with it. We'd say something like *Oh, great Ouija, tell me, is J.J. a dipstick?* Then we'd beat each other up trying to point to the *no/yes* symbol. We'd laugh and kid each other about the whole idea of having a spirit communicate to us, but I think it gave my friends the creeps just as much as it did me.

Being boys, you couldn't say it scared you. You had to go along with it so that your friends wouldn't think you were a pussy. But nothing really happened in those early days, and if it did, it was probably our imagination.

It was when my we started learning about all this psychic stuff that the Ouija board took on its own personality. We were becoming attractive to dead people and they used the Ouija board to get through. Pretty soon, every time one of us used the stupid thing, something weird would happen.

One night, Echo and her friends were having a slumber party and they decided to play with the Ouija board. They dragged it out and started asking the usual questions. They asked for a sign. The Ouija board pointed to *S* and then *L*. They asked what that meant and the board pointed to *13 ghosts* and then to *three AM*.

None of this made sense but they didn't care. They wanted to get down to some real questions, like what hairspray worked best under certain wind conditions and would that slut, Mary Jo Anderson, ever get hers for stealing Molly Limpet's boyfriend? They got so involved with their serious questions, they completely forgot about what the Ouija board had said when they started.

A little before three in the morning, their party was winding down. A couple of them had already nodded off and the few remaining were sitting on the bed talking. Suddenly, all the lights started going on and off, like someone was at the switch doing it by hand. At first, the girls who were awake were silent, then they woke up the ones sleeping so they could witness what was going on. Then everybody was awake, and more than just a tad freaked out.

The lights stopped going on and off and stayed on. The tension was relieved for a bit when the girls started talking to each other about what just happened. Their conversations were interrupted when they noticed a stuffed snake hanging from the top off the canopy bed move back and forth. Nobody said a word as it started to go faster and faster until it gained enough momentum to fly off the bed and onto the floor.

The next thing I knew, I was woken up by a herd of screaming girls as they ran out of the bedroom. I struggled to the hall, half-asleep, wondering what was going on. As I passed Echo's room, I could feel that weird feeling. I knew something had just happened. I didn't know the specifics, but I knew *somebody* had been there.

I went back to my room, shut the door, turned on the radio—and all the lights. I could hear the girls crying and my parents trying to calm them down. I knew it wasn't a good time to ask them what had just happened; they probably wouldn't have told me, and besides they had their hands full with hysterical teenagers.

As I was sitting with my blanket over my head, breathing in my own air, it started to hit me that maybe denial wasn't the best way to go. Maybe I should at least try to accept some of what was happening, so when stuff like this did occur, I could deal with it a little easier. Since we were now knee-deep in this, I needed to change some of my thinking. Sleep was becoming harder to come by.

The next day, my mother called Mrs. Olsen to ask her what to do about the Ouija board. Before she could even start to explain, Mrs. Olsen interrupted her. She told my mother to burn the Ouija board immediately. There was urgency in her voice. My mother asked why. Mrs. Olsen paused for a minute and then, like a mother would talk to her daughter, calmly explained why she was concerned.

She told her that spirits were the souls of people who died. She said when most people die, they go to the light—some people call it heaven. But she said that some people don't go to the light for a variety of reasons. They might be afraid. They may feel guilty if they've committed suicide or died from a drug overdose. Some just don't know that they're dead. All of these spirits are considered *earthbound spirits*.

Earthbound spirits sometimes feel alone and afraid—and always bored. Ouija boards are like antennas for bored spirits. The Ouija board picks up and gives these spirits a chance to mess around with the living. Some of these spirits, just like some people, are negative and actually use these Ouija boards to manipulate vulnerable people. Mrs. Olsen again said we must burn the Ouija board and told my mother to do so as soon as she got off the phone.

My mother was taken aback by the urgency, but she thought burning it was a little dramatic. She agreed to get rid of the Ouija board and told Mrs. Olsen if she had any more problems, she would call her back. When she hung up the phone, she got the Ouija board from the bedroom closet and threw it in the garbage. As far as my mother was concerned, that would be enough. She went back to her housework, and after a while, forgot about the whole thing.

When my mother worked her way back upstairs and into her bedroom, there it was, sitting on the bed. This freaked my mother out. She grabbed the board and hurried down to the fireplace to burn it. She was no longer thinking that Mrs. Olsen was being too dramatic. My mom was scared, really scared.

She threw the wooden board in the fireplace. She grabbed newspaper and kindling, and stuffed it underneath the Ouija board. She lit a match. She said it felt like the Ouija board was alive, like an evil male spirit. She was half-expecting the board to start talking to her, begging for its life.

Mrs. Olsen was right. She had to burn it NOW. She watched as the newspaper and kindling caught fire. But the Ouija board wouldn't burn. My mother started to get nervous. She grabbed more newspapers and threw them in. The board still wouldn't burn. She ran to get some charcoal fluid and poured it all over the board. Finally, it caught fire. Finally, my mother felt relieved.

Later on, my mother would tell me that when it finally did start to burn, it made weird noises, like it was alive. My mother watched as the board slowly burned. She wasn't going to feel comfortable until the whole thing was gone.

When I got home from school that day, I went upstairs to get the Ouija board. Since I'd half-decided to go with the program the night before, I thought I'd take it out for a spin. Besides, I wanted to see if all the activity from the night before had caused it to change shape or grow hair. And now that it was so willing to talk, maybe I could ask the Devil's version of Concentration some important questions, like if Tammy Roberts really liked me. But when I went upstairs, I couldn't find it. I asked my mother where it was.

She looked at me with a harried look on her face, said *"It's gone,"* and walked away.

Unaffected, I pressed on. "Mom, really, where is it? It's important."
I was more than just a little impressed with how assertive I sounded.

My mother, on the other hand, wasn't. She turned around and
walked toward me. She was serious. "What did you want to know?
If Tammy Roberts likes you? Yes, she does like you." (Apparently, my
mother's psychic powers were kicking in.)

"Now, I want you to listen to me," she continued. "Forget about
the Ouija board. It's gone. I burned it." She softened a bit. "I know
you looked at it as a toy, but it wasn't a toy. Honey, it started to control
our lives, so I got rid of it."

I interrupted her. "Mom, could we go back to that part about
Tammy liking me?"

If this were my father, his veins would have started popping out
if I asked a question like that under those circumstances, but for my
mother, it had the opposite effect. She could tell she wasn't getting
anywhere talking at me, so she decided to talk with me. She smiled.
"Yes, I'll tell you later about that," she said. "But it's important you
listen to me."

I agreed, and we sat down and talked.

She told me what Mrs. Olsen said about the Ouija board and why
she had to burn it. She told me what happened when she tried to burn
it and how it seemed alive. She reminded me how it felt the night before when the girls were playing with the Ouija board. There was a
seriousness to her story, like it was important for me to get it. She told
me what Mrs. Olsen said about what was happening to our family. She
told me we had to be careful, that because of the learning process we
were going through, negative—as well as positive—forces were going
to be attracted to our family.

Pretty heavy conversation for an eight-year-old. Still, I was getting
it. I was also starting to feel better. She was letting me in on what was
going on and that gave me a sense of power. She said that when I was
feeling afraid, like when *they* were around, to ask for protection—to
visualize a white light from God surrounding me, like a flashlight. She

told me that would protect me from negative spirits. She told me positive spirits wouldn't scare me, because they didn't want to. They were generally more evolved spiritually. And they had unconditional love for people and would only show themselves to you when they knew you were ready.

These *positive* spirits were old souls. They had been around for a while. She told me to concentrate on them and not be taken in by the negative ones. The negative ones might be more interesting, especially with my nose for trouble, but they manipulated, lied, and were not to be trusted. She also said that I needed to be able to recognize that in people, as well as in spirits.

I was surprised at how much my mother knew. Don't get me wrong. I didn't think my mom was stupid, but we're talking 1965 here. Moms were moms. They cooked and cleaned and went to the store and drove us around to places, but they didn't think. At least my mom wasn't a thinker.

I asked her where she had learned all that stuff, and, as excited as I have heard her in a long time, she said she'd been reading anything she could get her hands on—Edgar Cayce, Jane Roberts, Ruth Montgomery—anything that had to do with the paranormal. She said it was difficult to find, but that made it even more of a challenge. She also said talking to Mrs. Olsen helped. I was surprised at how my mother was changing. She was on a mission, and because of that, seemed stronger. For eight years, she had just been my mom. Now she was becoming my teacher and I had to be impressed.

What she told me that day was the foundation—the cornerstone—of everything I was to learn about the paranormal. My mother continued to learn everything she could, and maybe it was just a coincidence, but more psychic activity was happening in the house. There would be a couple of months where there wasn't anything going on, but then it would start up again. Besides the usual stuff, things were now disappearing and then reappearing—like keys or clothes. Shadows were starting to take the shape of people, and then there was the sound of someone typing under the stairs.

Individually, the activity was also picking up. Echo's hands would get hot anytime she was around anyone sick or in pain. Not knowing what to do, she would just stick her hands out and hope the energy would reach the person who needed it. She still wasn't embracing the idea of being a healer, but like me, she was becoming a little more open-minded.

I started seeing colors around people. At first, I didn't know what they were. The colors would change on different parts of their bodies. They would usually surround the person I was looking at. They were stronger at the head, then faded as I looked down. It would only happen once in a while, so at first I thought I was just seeing things. But then, when I started to see them all the time, I checked it out with my mom. Of course, she got all excited and told me she'd been reading about exactly what I was going through.

She said the colors around people were called auras and that each color meant something. Red meant that the person might be angry. Or green meant that the person was going through a growing process. To me, they were just colors. I didn't feel the hand of God behind it. I didn't get any deep messages when I saw them. I just saw colors and sometimes just small areas of color, like around a person's head or stomach.

It excited my mother that I was showing some signs of psychic ability and if it made her happy, then I figured what the hell, it wasn't hurting me in any way. I was just seeing colors.

My mother wanted me to tell her when I saw an aura so she could interpret what that person was going through by my description of the colors around the person. To me, that seemed ridiculous. If she really wanted to know what the person was going through, she could just ask them. But she felt that knowing what a person was feeling before they told you was an important tool, a part of my learning process.

Away from the house, we were a normal family. We went to the boat on weekends, we went to movies and out to dinner, and when we went out, there was never any talk about ghosts or auras. My parents were careful about talking to anybody about what was happening to our family. It wasn't worth the hassle of trying to explain what was going on. Plus, I think we wanted to at least pretend we were normal some of the time. I know I never said anything to my friends—except my best friend John Jordan.

I met J.J. in kindergarten. He was the kind of guy you could tell anything to and he wouldn't go blabbing it all over the place. He didn't judge me, and he didn't make me feel like I was crazy. He knew I was crazy. That's why we got along so well. I was the crazy one, he was the logical one. It worked.

J.J. was always into finding out things. So, the first time he heard the *noises* when he slept over, he asked me what they were. I told him some of the stuff that was happening around the house and he paused for a second. Then he said, "So, you have ghosts, huh? How'd that happen?"

I told him everything. I told him about Mrs. Olsen, the Ouija board, and my aura thing.

"Wow, when do I get to see a ghost?" he said, when I was done.

J.J. was great. The next day, he started asking my mother everything he could about ghosts and being psychic. My mother saw J.J. as one of the family, so it didn't bother her. And the cool thing about J.J. was that he wasn't afraid.

One time he was sleeping over and he couldn't sleep, so he went downstairs to the living room and decided to sleep on the couch. He started getting comfortable and the TV started going on and off. Instead of freaking out, he came back upstairs, woke me up and told me he just had an *experience*—like it was no big deal.

Another time, he was sitting in the living room and as happened from time to time, a little ceramic statue of a lion got up and moved across the table. Again, J.J. just thought it was interesting. That was helpful for me as a kid. So much of how you feel about yourself comes from how others see you. J.J. didn't judge me or choose to distance himself from me. He chose to be my friend and stick by me. That made it easier to accept myself and my family, and what we were going through. This wasn't the case with my other friends.

I remember a sleepover I had one time. I was about ten or eleven years old and at that age, it's important to be *cool*. I had these guys over from elementary school and I was worried that one of our *dead friends* would show up and embarrass me. I could just imagine these guys running out the door screaming in the middle of the night. I would be branded Eddie Munster and my social life would be over.

As I feared, the typing started and the guys start wondering what was going on. I could understand. It was midnight, nobody was awake except us, so why the typing? I first tried telling them that it was an old house and that old houses make noise, but then one of them said, "I thought your dad had this house built." That was true. There went the old-house theory. Then I tried telling them that it was probably mice, but I seemed too eager to come up with an explanation, so they weren't buying the mice deal.

Then they became convinced I had a secret going on and it started to become an issue. It also didn't help that the typing was getting louder and louder. I didn't know if they were going to put it together and start screaming *Devil boy, Devil boy,* and run out of the house. But J.J. could tell I was getting nervous, so he decided to start a pillow fight. Before long, the guys forgot about the noises, which by that time had died down to a low thumping.

J.J. saved my butt. He knew I was in trouble, and he knew I couldn't do anything to get myself out of it. The cool thing about it is that he didn't make it a big deal. He fell asleep with everyone else and didn't mention it until a couple days later when no one was around. He was my best friend and I was grateful he was in my life.

Our lives kept going and things kept happening around the house. Because of that, the tension was building between my mother and dad. I'm not sure if my father had a harder time with my mother's new interests, empowerment, and independence, or all the floating objects and ghosts.

I felt bad for my father. Not only was his family changing, the whole world was changing. Men's and women's roles were changing, and my father had a hard time figuring out what his role was. Sure, he was the man of the house, the breadwinner, but he wasn't the one we went to anymore when we were afraid—at least when it came to the things happening around the house. He wasn't the one who had all the answers.

My mother was waking up and coming into her own. My father did well when my mother looked to him as the main person in her life, but that wasn't the case anymore. His stock had fallen, yet, I had to give him credit. He was trying to understand and change with it all. He even started asking Mrs. Olsen questions about his business, but even that was becoming a source of frustration for my dad because like most psychic advice, it could be a tad vague.

He was now making more money than he ever had. He was setting up franchises all over the country. He could buy anything he wanted, and he usually did. We would fly two states away just to have dinner. Everything was first class and we always had the latest toys. It was what he thought was success, what he thought would make him happy. And when it came down to it, he thought it was his job.

But now, just being successful wasn't enough. He felt he needed to be spiritually evolved as well as successful, and for him it was happening way too fast. It bugged him because he should be able to control how fast he grew spiritually, but he couldn't.

My father's solution to any problem at home was to spend more time at work. The more time he spent at work, the more time my mother worked on developing our psychic abilities. Everything she learned, she tried to teach us. For my mother, it was just as important to know what a chakra was as it was to know how to do algebra.

When my father was home, my mother tried to stick to a normal routine. But after a while, it started to become less and less important to her to meet his needs. Her needs were starting to take precedence. When she wasn't around, she was leaving him fewer love notes and more notes on where dinner was and how to cook it. Besides the psychic world, I don't think my father was as totally uncomfortable anywhere else as he was working in the kitchen. That man could burn water. My mother knew this, and he knew that she knew, but her interest in taking care of him was minimal. The tension was starting to build.

I stayed out of it. I had my own problems. I'd decided to be more open-minded, but I still wasn't ready to embrace this whole way of life like my mother did. I wanted my life to be normal. I knew we would never be the *Waltons*, but we didn't have to be the *Addams Family*. And even though I thought we were doing a good job of keeping it in-house, the word was starting to get around. Echo and Lance's friends were asking questions. My friends were wondering why odd things were happening at the house. Even the neighbors started saying things.

I remember my next-door neighbor Bobby coming over to our house once, asking me if I could show him a ghost. He heard from some people at school about the Ouija board story and finally got the nerve to ask. I liked Bobby. He was like my little brother, and he was curious about everything. If you wanted to try something and you didn't want to get in trouble for it, you could always get Bobby to do it. All you'd have to do was phrase it to Bobby in the form of a question and he'd do it. Like I wonder what would happen if I threw this apple at that car. He eventually caught on, but those early years were fun. Anyway, he came over because he wanted to see a ghost. It's not like ghosts are trained seals. I never knew when one might show up, and if you stand around asking a ghost to come, not only do they not show up, but you end up looking stupid—which in some cases is what a ghost gets off on.

A part of me was insulted that Bobby thought I was *dial a ghost*. For one thing, I couldn't just conjure up a ghost, or at least I didn't think I could. And I wasn't going to wait around for a ghost to show up so Bobby could get freaked out and soil himself. I decided this would be a good opportunity to teach him another lesson and scare the bejesus out of him. I figured that after he wet his pants, he would find out I did it and think it was all a bunch of crap, and he would never bring up the subject again.

I set up a little séance in the bathroom. It was the only place I could find that was completely dark (there weren't any windows and it was the middle of the day). So, we went into the bathroom—the candles are burning, the lights are out. Bobby sat on the tub facing the mirror. I sat facing him with my back to the mirror and told Bobby to start concentrating and ask for a spirit to come. We both became quiet, and the air seemed to stand still. I could feel the atmosphere getting colder and creepy. I told myself, it was because I was sitting in my bathroom with another guy with the lights out and the door closed, but the tension seemed to be getting worse. Now I was getting nervous. The quiet was deafening, the hair was standing on the back of my neck, and I was thinking it was time I yelled boo and got the hell out of there.

All of a sudden, Bobby's face turned white and his chin hit the floor. I looked at him as he was staring at the mirror. I turned around to see what he was looking at and there was a disfigured head staring back at us from the other side of the mirror. I froze, I could not believe what I was seeing. This was a truly ugly face.

As I was standing with my mouth wide open, the only thing that broke my trance was the sound of Bobby screaming as he ran out the door and halfway to China. I was alone with the head, frozen and unable to move. A dozen things raced through my mind in that two seconds I stood there. The two main things being I was going to die, and it was my punishment for trying to scare Bobby. I prayed for my feet to move, and like a miracle they did. I took off like a rocket after the now completely gone Bobby.

I had two major problems. One, what was I going to say to Bobby when I finally caught up to him? Bobby wasn't shy when it came to talking about people and their shortcomings. When word got out that we had the elephant man in my bathroom, we'd have to start charging admission. Two, how was I going to explain this to my mother? Surely when she went to the bathroom, she'd want some explanation for the floating head. She took this stuff seriously and if she found out I brought this guy to the house just to scare Bobby, she'd kill me.

I caught up to Bobby and struggled with what to say. I thought I might try and explain what I thought happened, but it hit me that I'd probably make things worse, so I gave him the old stand-by answer—swamp gas. I told him that even though we didn't live by a swamp, it possibly came from the sink drain. Or maybe it was the jet stream forcing the pressure down from Canada and we both know how weird those Canadians look. I went on and on, and as I was lying my brains out, I looked at Bobby to see if he was buying any of it and he wasn't even listening.

Bobby was out to lunch. He didn't want to talk about it. He didn't want to hear about it. He didn't want to even think about it. As far as Bobby was concerned, it didn't happen. I tried to ask him if he was okay, but he just talked about school and how he needed to get home to do his homework.

The first thing I thought was that I was off the hook. Bobby didn't want to deal with it. Sure, he was a mental case, but if he didn't want to talk about it, I didn't want to talk about it. Maybe by tomorrow it would all blow over and life would be good. But I still had to deal with the floating head.

When I got home, I immediately went upstairs to the bathroom. I blew out the still-lit candles and turned on the lights. I slowly looked in the mirror, but there was nothing. Whatever had been there was gone. That weird feeling was gone and the place felt okay. I was never going to take a bath in there again, but at least the head was gone.

I called Bobby to make sure he hadn't lost his mind and was drooling in some corner somewhere, but he was fine. Or he acted like he was fine. He had decided to push whatever damage had been done to his psyche deep down inside himself.

I felt guilty about what had happened. I liked Bobby. He was fun to hang out with and we did a lot together. But after this little episode, it would be a while before he invited me over for a game of Twister.

Not that I didn't understand his wanting to forget the whole thing. I knew what that was like. I'd been trying to do that for years. Actually, he was lucky. This would probably be the first and last time Bobby had an experience like this. After a week, he'd forget the whole thing happened, or try to, and his life would return to normal. Maybe he'd have the occasional nightmare, but he'd be okay. I didn't have that luxury of denial anymore. If anything, things were getting worse.

I didn't try to bring that head into the bathroom. I don't like floating heads or any parts of a body floating around. It was supposed to be a pretend séance, not a real one. If I really thought it was going to work, I would have done it in Nikki's room. Kill two birds with one stone.

The unnerving thing for me was the ease with which that face appeared. Boom! There it was. I wasn't sure if that meant my psychic powers were getting stronger or the dead guys were getting bolder. Neither choice was a good thing. With the environment in the house already uncomfortable, this little experiment made it even worse.

It was like going down a dark, creepy staircase, step by step, each one feeling worse than the last. The possibility of going back upstairs seemed improbable, so the only way out was to continue down. I tried to make light of it all, like Don Knotts in *The Ghost and Mr. Chicken*, but it felt like it was getting away from me. I was already becoming more afraid, especially at night. The feeling that came over me when Lance first saw that the ghost was with me every night. I would lay there and think how lucky I was before all this happened.

Four

The Church

"I hate all of my friends, I just want to start over and get all new ones." "Well, you're about to," I said, "and it's happening pretty quick." "Wow, even though I can't stand them, I can't imagine my life without 'Noodles and Zit'." "Well," I said, "the good news is, 'they' can."

The idea of returning to a stable life was shot to hell when my mother received a telephone call from a minister named Birdie.

Birdie was the General Patton of the psychic community, such as it was back then. She ran what they called an *alternative church* in the poor part of town where she would teach classes on how to develop your psychic abilities. She would choose the people she felt had the gift—and only those people she chose were allowed to attend her classes. Control wasn't a problem for Birdie; she was a master at it.

But Birdie was exactly what my mother needed—a strong, extremely psychic teacher who would push her learning process and expose her to other people who were also learning to open up psychically.

Mrs. Olsen was more of an independent study type of teacher. If you had questions, she would help you with them, but she felt that you needed to go down your own path at your own pace—a sensible approach, if you ask me. If I could've picked my own pace, I'd have been ready to go down my psychic path in about fifty years, but my mother was ready now. So, when Birdie called out of the blue and told her about this dream where her spirit guides told her that she had to call my mother and have her come with Echo to the church, my mother jumped at the chance.

I didn't find out about Birdie and her *church* until my mother and Echo had come back from their first so-called *service*. At first when she told me about what it was like, I wasn't concerned. I figured it was just another kook that my mom went to see, and with a name like *Birdie*, I wondered how seriously you could take her. But as she continued describing her experience at the church and I saw a look of excitement on her face, I got the impression this might not be a short-term deal.

My mother was pumped, really pumped, and the more excited she became, the more depressed I became. Somewhere in the back of my mind, I was thinking (or hoping) that all this psychic interest was a phase, like bell-bottoms or white lipstick. I believed my mother would get sick of all of this stuff and move on—to landscaping or bowling, like my normal buddies' parents would do. But now with the introduction of this Birdie person, my mother's passion was building again. And as my mother went, so did the family.

My father wasn't thrilled with my mother's increasing excitement either. Mrs. Olsen was one thing. She was a hands-off teacher and therefore, not a threat to my father. But this Birdie woman was a different story. If you were to create the person most likely to incite my father, it was Birdie. She was controlling, possessive, overbearing, and could give a rip what other people thought of her—a female version of himself.

My father didn't know how to compete with a person like Birdie. He couldn't match wits with her on an intellectual level. As far as he was concerned, she was from a different planet. He couldn't beat her up because she might turn him into a carrot. And since she was a minister, he wasn't a match spiritually. He was too prideful to change his way of thinking and Birdie had no reason to change hers, so he knew that—perhaps for the first time in his life—he faced real competition for my mother.

The first time I met Birdie, she scared the hell out of me. She had to be at least 120 years old and the only way I knew she was female was by the blue dress she wore. As it turns out, she wore the same blue dress the whole time I knew her. Her hair was obviously done in a blender and when she laughed, she cackled.

But I can't say it was her appearance that scared me. My sister Nikki wasn't Doris Day in the morning, so I could handle ugly. I was afraid of meeting Birdie because of something that happened to my mother the night they first met.

My mother said right before she was introduced to Birdie that she was thinking about the moon and how beautiful it was. Birdie came over, extended her hand to shake my mother's, and introduced herself. My mother said hello. The next thing to come out of Birdie's mouth was, "It is a beautiful moon tonight, isn't it?"

My mother told me if she hadn't been warned prior to meeting Birdie that Birdie had this ability to read other people's thoughts, she might have considered it a coincidence. But my mother knew that it wasn't. She suggested that I be careful about my thinking when I was around Birdie.

My mother also told me how extremely spiritual Birdie was. She said she didn't just talk the talk, she walked it. She felt that God provided everything for her (except teeth and a hair brush) and she'd make sure everybody knew that God was her provider. He put gas in her car, paid for her food and rent, and helped her help other people financially. If you challenged her on it, questioned the validity of God being her source, you were in for an eye-drying lecture on the power of God and the shortcomings of skepticism.

But just knowing she might be able to pick up on my thoughts set me off, because I really didn't want to offend a person who could potentially turn me into a grape. When I walked into the church, my mother introduced us. I was determined to think something nice about Birdie. But sometimes, the harder you try not to do something, the faster you do it. The first thing that crossed my mind when I saw her was, *oh my God, she looks like the sea hag*, because she really did look like the sea hag. I quickly realized what I was doing and tried to change my thoughts. *She's not the sea hag, she's not the sea hag*. But as I was doing this, it hit me that the theme was still sea hag and my goose was probably cooked.

As Birdie got closer, I knew that life as I knew it might be over. Not only was I unable to stop thinking she was the sea hag, but now in my head I had her chasing Popeye and beating up Olive Oyl.

If she was upset with me, she showed no sign. In fact, when she looked at me, it was with a soft, caring, honest look that I could feel in my stomach. She bent down to me and said, "You're a gifted boy. I can see that Jesus walks in your heart." Then she pointed to my chest and started to walk away.

It wasn't the most personal thing to say, but I felt it. I also felt badly for being so judgmental. So what if she wasn't burdened with the trappings of beauty, she was much more than that. She wasn't spooky or overpowering. She was sweet and caring.

Even though I felt like an idiot for my near-sighted thinking, I was glad the initial meeting was over. I felt confident our next encounter would be better and looked around the room for someone else to judge. Out of the corner of my eye, I saw Birdie turning around and walking back toward me. I straightened myself out, and prepared to greet her with more love in my heart.

She walked over to me, leaned in toward my ear, and whispered, "The sea hag had more teeth." She then stepped back, smiled like she was very happy with herself and sure enough, had only one tooth in her whole head. As she cackled and walked away, the only thing I could do was smile like I just stepped in dog crap and think to myself, *oh crap*. I decided to spend the rest of the night in the car.

Things started to heat up once my mother began attending *the church* on a regular basis. From what I could see, it wasn't a church at all. It was more like a basement with folding chairs facing a small stage with a single chair and a stand-up mike. There weren't any stained glass windows or fancy organs, and the people there didn't dress up and try to look their Sunday best. Most of the people looked liked they had been hit by the ugly stick. Some were downright spooky looking. They were nice enough—even loving—but not slaves to fashion. And the funny thing was, it didn't matter.

They were there because this was the only place they wanted to be. These were the people who didn't fit. They were the folks we *normal* people used to pray for in regular church. But here, these people had found a home. They came from all walks of life, from different lifestyles, and all seemed to have that one thing in common. Their eyes had been opened and here they found a place where they wouldn't be judged or ridiculed for having those experiences (at least not until I showed up).

Some were even ministers themselves who would sneak over and check out the service because they knew that there was more going on than what they had been taught in the more traditional church. They prayed and sang. Man, did they sing, and it just didn't matter what kind of car you drove or the clothes you wore, or the people you knew, it was all about talking and learning from Spirit and being part of the church. Sure, it was a spiritually alternative church, and back then just below communism as far as acceptability, but it didn't matter. They were happy and some were close to finding answers to questions that they'd had their whole lives.

That's why my mother was there. She wanted answers, just like everybody else there. Like, *Why are we here? Where do we go when we die? Why was our poodle floating around in the living room?* And they were more than willing to talk to my mother. Maybe because she was pretty or because her shoes matched or her hair was clean. Or maybe because she carried herself with a certain style and they knew that a woman like her, a cake-eater from the burbs, wouldn't be in a place like that unless she had to be. Plus, and more importantly, they all needed each other. They had a bond.

It was 1967. If you heard voices or saw floating people, you kept your mouth shut or ended up in a psyche ward. It wasn't hip, it wasn't cool, and if people did talk about ghosts or noises in the night, they did so *under the covers* (where, if you'd asked me then, you should keep this stuff).

Psychic stuff wasn't kept undercover at Birdie's church. That's all they talked about. And as weird as the people were and the place felt, my mom loved it. She started to get close to some of the regulars and they got close with her. They supported each other and they all seemed to make each other feel good (a little *too good*, if you ask me). My mother was spending more time socially with these people. They'd go out to dinner, meet for lunch, go to each other's houses—including ours—and it didn't take long to figure out that our house had *heat*. Soon, the little group, the niche of churchgoers, was constantly hanging out at our house. And you couldn't find a stranger group of people.

There was Nonette. She stood about four-eleven, with dark red hair and piercing black eyes, and had the disposition of a Tasmanian Devil. She was a street-smart ex-prostitute who didn't care much for people, especially not men. She did, however, like my mom and she loved my sister. She was convinced that Echo was her daughter from a past life. She hung out at the house because she felt comfortable there. She was in ill health and I think she wanted her last years on earth to be gentle ones. I remember a story Birdie told us about Nonette.

One night, Nonette was giving readings in a downtown hotel. In the room next to her was a rather loud rock-and-roll band and Nonette was having trouble concentrating on her readings. She couldn't ask the manager to tell them to turn it down because she would have been kicked out for giving readings, so she went next door herself and as nicely as Nonette could, she asked the boys to please turn it down.

The response was less than cooperative. When Nonette was leaving, she warned the boys that if they didn't turn down their speakers, they'd be sorry. Unimpressed, the lead singer suggested she simply speak louder, laughed, and walked away. Sure enough, when they started playing again, all their amps blew, their guitar strings broke from their guitars, and the drummer's foot went through his bass drum.

The lead singer ran over to Nonette's room and accused Nonette of causing these things to happen. Nonette just looked at the kid, asked him if anybody got hurt (as if to suggest the next time you bug me, somebody will), smiled, and went back to doing her readings. From then on, she didn't have any more problems.

Another time, Nonette wanted two weeks off from probably the one legitimate job she ever had. Her boss, a traditionalist, had no problem with the two weeks. However, this being only her third day on the job, he felt vacation time was premature. She continued to ask him, but the man wouldn't budge.

Nonette decided to make her vacation plans anyway. She set everything up and on the day she was scheduled to leave, her boss developed a mysterious illness. Nobody could figure out what it was. It put the poor slob in the hospital for two weeks while they ran tests. Meanwhile, Nonette went on vacation and when she returned, he got better. Maybe it was just coincidence, but I doubt it. She'd never admit to doing this stuff; if you asked her, she'd look at you like it was none of your business and walk away. But if she liked you, she wasn't shy about sharing her *gift* with you.

Once, I was complaining to my mother about this kid at school who kept bugging me. Nonette was there helping my mother fold clothes and overheard our conversation. "You just get Nonette a piece of his hair, honey, and I'll take care of it for you," Nonette said in her deep, crackly voice.

The room suddenly got chilly. I looked over at my mom with an excited look on my face. But just when I was going to ask her where the scissors were, she gave me one of those *don't you dare* looks and I had to tell Nonette that *I could take care of it*. I don't know exactly what would have happened if I had taken Nonette up on her offer (a part of me was dying to know). The spooky thing for me was how genuinely disappointed Nonette was in not being able to do whatever she was going to do. Thank God she liked me.

Then there was Roy. Roy was the last person you'd find in a white upper-middle-class neighborhood. He was huge, about six-foot-eight. He was black and he was angry. He was angry about a lot of things— the obvious racial tensions of the times, the high expectations put on him most of his life (he was a high school and college basketball star), and that he was born with the gift of healing, and like a mechanic with a tutu, didn't know what to do with it.

He found Birdie's church and started working on developing his gift, but was still uneasy with the whole deal. One reason I liked Roy was that he questioned everything. You couldn't just tell Roy a ghost story, he'd want to see photos and get hair samples. He was blunt, cold, and didn't give a rip if you didn't like him. He did like my mother though, and because of that, he tolerated me. My mother liked him because she saw the sensitive side to him. She saw how hard it was for him to deal with his gifts, and knew if he could come to terms with it, maybe there was hope for the rest of us.

Tony was another regular. He was the first professional male psychic I'd ever met. For that matter, the first professional gay psychic I'd ever met. He was tall, lean, and far more interested in performing the readings than just saying them. He had that *more comfortable on stage* feeling to him and I think all he ever wanted to be was a channeler for Judy Garland. He was colorful and funny and one of the top psychics of that time.

Everybody wanted Tony to do a reading for them and Tony knew it. He was bored with being a psychic. He'd done all the things a successful psychic did back then. He kept a low profile, but not too low. He went to the places where people had heard of him and he dazzled them with his abilities. He'd been to New York and LA, and as much as Tony liked being the center of attention, now he just wanted to try other things, simpler things, like healings or levitation.

He liked our place because we treated him like everybody else. He was Tony, the psychic, who just happened to have a thing for show tunes. Once in a while, his ego would kick in and he'd go off on one of those wild dramatic readings, usually to impress some strapping buck. But my mom or Birdie or somebody would tell him to get a grip and Tony would eventually settle down. Underneath all of those layers of psychosis, Tony was a sweet guy.

With my mother's newfound friends coming over all the time, the house had a different feeling to it. There was an excitement in the air because there was a sense of discovery. But there was also the feeling that our house was no longer just our house. It was like we had a dinosaur fossil in the living room and all these scientists were walking around checking it out. I got the sense that they thought they were doing us a favor and we shouldn't look a gift horse in the mouth.

Since they all had this single-minded purpose to learn everything they possibly could about the world of the supernatural, they would try every different exercise they could to help develop their psychic abilities.

One of the first exercises was called *Billets*. Billets is an exercise that helps you use your intuition as opposed to your intellect. Several people would write a question (usually to someone in spirit) on a piece of paper, fold the paper a few times, put the question in a bowl, and then pass them out. When you pick a question, you hold it in your hand and then try to open up psychically to get a feel for what the note is about. You don't look at the question, and there's no way you can figure out what the note says, so you have to learn to trust your feelings.

Billets was a great way to learn to trust yourself, but it also came with some responsibility. You have to know what you're doing, something my mother and sister found out when they were practicing with a group of my cousin's friends.

For some reason, they thought it would be fun to see how other people reacted to trying Billets. So, they asked my cousin's friends, about seven of them, to write a note to someone who was dead and ask a question, fold it up, and put all the questions into a hat. Well, they all did this and then took turns choosing a note and holding it in their left hands.

Everybody was nervous and giddy so they didn't notice that one of the guys, Keith, was getting pale and sweaty as he was holding his note. Suddenly, Keith started saying *make it stop, make it stop!* My mother looked at him, not sure if he was upset or joking, and said *make what stop, dear?* With fear in his eyes and anguish in his voice, Keith turned to my mom again and said, *the pain, the pain, make it stop.* Neither my mother nor sister knew what to do.

What little my mother was taught at that time was to say the Lord's Prayer any time she felt afraid, and this was definitely one of those times. So my mother went over to Keith and started saying the Lord's Prayer over him. By this time, Keith was rolled up in the fetal position screaming *my hands are on fire, my arms, make it stop!* My mother then took the note from Keith's hands and as soon as she did, he stopped screaming, calmed down, and the color came back to his face.

Everybody else, however, was still shaken up. They all wanted to know what was going on and what had caused Keith to freak out like that. My mother especially wanted to know what was going on. This was the first time she had seen a reaction to Billets like this. She opened the note that was in Keith's hands and the person it was written to was a guy named Frosty McGinn. My mom asked if anybody knew who that person was. The group looked at each other and got quiet. Finally, my cousin said *that was the kid who climbed up the electric high wires and died last month.*

Keith turned to my mother and said *that's what it felt like, like I was being electrocuted.* The rest of the group looked at each other, tossed their Billets on the floor, and walked away. Having gone through weird stuff like that, I could appreciate what they must have felt.

My mother told me that story because she wanted me to understand just how dangerous it can be to screw around with something if you don't know what you're doing. Even if you think you know what you're doing, like my mother thought, strange stuff can happen.

There was another exercise called reading of faces. Reading of faces is when you hold a photograph upside down in your hand and without looking at it, you describe the people or persons in the photograph and whatever emotional feelings they were going through at the time the photograph was taken. Again, it was hard because you had to trust your intuition.

They would practice these exercises all the time and when I'd walk by the kitchen, they would invite me in to practice with them. This wasn't to scare or tease me, as they felt I had a natural ability and I should practice it. For me, it was just too weird, too heavy. Ghosts, spirits, intuition—I didn't want to sit around talking about that crap all day. If this is what they wanted to do their whole day, it was fine with me, but just leave me out of it. Problem was, I didn't want to hurt their feelings. It was nice that they were asking, but it only made me have to come up with some excuse to not join their little group. Since they were all practicing their psychic abilities, it was hard deceiving them, but I managed.

They also practiced other things, like using their minds to move objects or disciplined exercises like levitation. This was making things more difficult for me because as they were getting better at the exercises and learning more, their need to tone it down was diminishing. They were more out in the open. And because they were more out in the open, it was difficult to hide things from my friends.

I remember bringing one buddy, Tommy, home from school with me one day. Tommy was one of the more popular kids at school. He could run like the wind, he was smart, and he had one of those leader-type personalities that people like. Both of his parents had jobs, which was unusual back then, and that strong work ethic seemed to rub off on Tommy. I liked him because nothing seemed to bother him and that personality trait made it easier to invite him over.

We walked into the kitchen and there was Tony, meditating, trying his best to levitate. I decided the best thing to do was to ignore what was going on and get both of us something to eat. I walked past the chanting Tony and went to the refrigerator. I asked Tommy if he was hungry, but he seemed more interested in what Tony was doing. I was put out because now I had to try to explain to him why the gay guy was floating in the kitchen. I tried to brush it off by telling him he was with the circus, but the way he looked at me suggested this was his last visit to the house. Probably just as well. Tommy had a tendency to be jittery. Nonette would have turned his hair white.

Meanwhile, my mother was starting to get a name for herself in the neighborhood as a witch. With all the people coming and going (sometimes in the blink of an eye), it made sense that the neighbors were wondering what the hell was going on. The rumors really started flying on the next Halloween when Echo suggested that since everybody already thought my mother was a witch, she should get some tarot cards, dress up like a witch, and do readings at a Halloween party. Echo was in college at the time and was always looking for a party.

What started out as a fun idea turned into a career for my mother. She blew people away with how accurate she was. It was as though the cards were talking to her and with every reading she gave, her confidence grew. Her confidence grew so much that Tony was concerned she might develop an ego. Back then, humility was very important. So just to make sure her head didn't get too big, he started calling her Madame Zonk, and the name stuck.

Slowly, non-psychic people began sneaking in through the back door to ask my mother questions about ghosts and other strange phenomenon. She was becoming the go-to girl when it came to psychic information. God would tell Birdie, Birdie would tell my mom, and my mom would tell the neighbors. It was that simple. Birdie didn't have exclusive rights to God, but everybody thought she did or at least wanted to think she did. Anyway, the word was out and now even the mailman was hanging out in the kitchen.

The whole thing started to consume our family and as it did, we all reacted to it in different ways. Whether it was the weird stuff at home or just being in college, my sister Echo started drinking heavily and that created a whole new set of problems for her, like possession. If you mix the two—alcohol and psychic exploration—you have a good chance of getting possessed.

Some people believe that when you drink or do drugs you open up that natural protection you have around you, which sometimes allows earthbound spirits to pop inside you. In Hollywood, possession was dramatic, and since what came out of Hollywood was my only reference on the subject, I thought when you were possessed, you threw up pea soup and turned your head 360 degrees. As it turns out, that only happens when you go through menopause. In reality, possession could be as subtle as a person's behavior or the look in their eyes.

My father chose to ignore the whole Echo situation. Being the master of the universe Viking god, any time a female had a problem that meant it was a female problem, and female problems were low on his list of priorities. He hated talking about anything that had to do with the subject. As far as my father was concerned, women were good for only a couple of things and talking about female problems was definitely not one of them.

My sister Nikki was privately dealing with her own issues. She was having a hard time sleeping and sometimes it was hard for her to wake up. She told my mother that when she woke up one time, she couldn't open her eyes, talk, or move. She could hear people around her and feel their presence, but couldn't call out. She was aware of being afraid but not sure what to do. Finally, she got enough energy to force herself to wake up. My mother asked Mrs. Olsen about this, and she told my mother that that sometimes happens when your soul can't get back in your body.

When I heard about this, I felt bad for Nikki. I never thought she was affected by any of this stuff. She always seemed so busy. She was, after all, the most attractive one in the family and seemed to have plenty of other distractions going on, namely boys. I also felt badly for her because as much as she bugged me, I loved her, and the thought of someone I loved having such a scary thing happen to her made me feel even more helpless.

I just wanted it to be normal. I was tired of the people, the church, the noises, the smells, and the things moving around. I didn't want to talk about reincarnation, life after death, or poltergeists. I didn't want to do psychic exercises or read ghost stories. I wanted to go bowling and not have pins drop before you threw the ball. I wanted to look at someone and not see colors all around them. And it would be nice to come home from school and not have one of my family members possessed.

Five

Hello Jerry

"Can't I just keep it around for a little bit longer? It doesn't bother anyone and my friends think it's cool." "You mean like a pet?" I asked. "Yeah, like a pet," he said. "I've always wanted a pet." "But it's not a pet," I said. "It's a ghost." "So," he said, half serious, "what's the difference?" "Well," I asked, "when was the last time you heard of someone getting possessed by anything named 'Fluffy'?"

There were times when I just wanted to pack my bags and leave. Being ten, however, limited my options. Nevertheless, it was a fantasy that helped me cope from time to time. I was locked into this journey and my only two choices were to learn to take it all with a grain of salt or be miserable the rest of my life. I learned to take it with a grain of salt.

On the other hand, my mother was practically in Nirvana. Everything she could get her hands on that had to do with psychic phenomena—books, articles, or tapes—she ate up like Kate Moss eats rice cakes. For her, *hobby* was spelled o-b-s-e-s-s-i-o-n. Even her way of relaxing was to go on road trips to psychic camps or spiritual retreats.

These *camps* weren't advertised at grocery stores or coffee shops like they are now. They were hush-hush and selective. The moral winds of the times dictated the secrecy, but that secrecy only made it more interesting for my mother to go. Wed with the fact that only a few were asked to attend, my mother almost never said no. When they called, she went.

For me, these getaways weren't thrilling. They were on the other end of the spectrum. Spiritualists and psychics aren't party animals. Everything they do—whether it's getting dressed or clipping their toenails—is done with a sense of ceremony. Even laughter, much like a golf clap, is done with restrained enthusiasm. Not the group of people a ten-year-old wants to hang out with.

Now, if you put these people in a church setting, tear down the walls and ceiling, replace the pulpit and pews with trees and bushes and take the words fun and exciting out of the equation, voilà, you've got a spiritual retreat. Somehow these people had a way of making even the trees seem serious. I spent most of my time at these places dreaming up reasons why not to go on another one, but the truth was that even as bad as being stuck in the woods with Peter Lowry wannabes might have been, it was a better alternative than staying in the house without my mom.

I'm not sure if it was just me, or if other people in the house were aware of it, but when my mother was gone, even for a short time, there seemed to be more psychic activity in the house. Things would move around more, noises became louder, the cats and dogs would get jumpy and hiss, or bark at the air. Maybe it was like this all the time and I just didn't notice it as much when she was home, but when she wasn't around everything sure felt weirder.

One day, my mother came into my room and announced we were going on another road trip. I tried launching into my psychic victim monologue, but she stopped me in the middle. She explained that in order to reach this place at the time she wanted to be there, I would have to miss a day of school. This of course made it a lock. We both knew I wasn't going to turn down an excused absence from school, even if it meant visiting the paranormal ponderosa.

Without my confirmation, she told me we were leaving early in the morning and that I needed to get some rest. She thanked me for going with her, which made it difficult to be a jerk, but I did my best. I told her maybe we should go someplace more fun, like the dentist's office, but she just smiled and walked out of the room. The bond between my mother and me made these trips worthwhile.

At the time, I didn't see this trip as being any different than the rest. I figured it would be another gathering of beatnik types looking for answers they couldn't find anywhere else. But this particular trip turned out to be much more interesting than the others. In some ways, this trip changed my life.

We left early in the morning, and on the way there, I fell asleep. I didn't wake up until we arrived. When we drove into this camp, it reminded me of something you'd see in the book *The Hobbit*. It was at the bottom of this heavily wooded valley and as you drove in from the top of the hill, you could see and smell the smoke from the campfires people were burning below. As we drove down into the valley, the sun was just beginning to set. The combination of sunset colors and campfire smoke gave the place a warm feeling.

We got out of the car and, having been in it all day long, my bladder was about to blow. This being a psychic camp with no running water or bathrooms, it was up to me to find a place to relieve myself. These camps were a great place to hang if you were the Jeremiah Johnson type, but not Funland if you're a ten-year-old who likes television.

A tent had been set up for us before we got there. My mother showed me which one it was and told me to meet her back there after I found a place to go. I went in the woods and took care of business. When I came out, there in front of me were twenty tents all set up and no sign of my mother. I was in such a hurry to go to the woods, I didn't bother to pay attention to my mom when she pointed out which tent we had. Discouraged, I went to the nearest tent and sat down. Five minutes in camp and I was already lost, bored, and ready to go home.

I sat there for maybe ten minutes when I looked up and saw this Yoda-like character smiling at me. He couldn't have been more than five feet tall, and the grin on his face suggested that he was either mentally ill or I was sitting on something I shouldn't be. I jumped up to check my pants for physical evidence of dog crap, but I calmed down when I saw there wasn't any.

I gave him a nonverbal *what?* look, but he didn't offer any explanation as to his interest in me. I decided to break the ice and said *hi*. I offered him a seat next to me but he wasn't interested in sitting. Finally, I asked if there was something he wanted. With a Cheshire cat grin on his face he told me he had a present for me.

Having never seen this person before, I was taken aback. I tried to make light of it by asking if he knew my shirt size but he wasn't amused. He gave me a puzzled look, then said that he wanted to draw a picture for me, and to please come by his tent in about an hour. He pointed to where his tent was, smiled again, and then left.

I immediately started looking around for my mother. I couldn't believe I was in camp for ten minutes and the first person I ran into was Chester the molester. *Sure* he had a picture to show me, then he was going to show me some naked etchings, talk karma, and whip out his little elf. The only thing creepier was if he actually thought I was going to his tent.

I saw my mother across the camp so I headed to where she was. She was bugged that I (as she put it) *wandered off* and didn't come back to our tent like I said I would. I explained to her I would have come sooner, but a troll wanted me to come to his tent and see a picture he supposedly had drawn for me. I threw in a little guilt about exposing me to psychotic psychics who like the company of ten-year-old boys.

The stunned look on her face led me to believe I had convinced her to leave. I thought she was so upset with what Chester had said, we were going to pull up stakes and start heading out ASAP. But to my amazement, she seemed more anxious to stay. She asked me again what the little guy told me. I told her again that he wanted to show me a drawing he said he drew for me and emphasized that this was probably illegal in most states. She asked me if he told me his name. I said *no* and then she asked me to describe him to her.

I told her he was about five feet tall with long gray hair, a beard, and a mustache. He had little eyes, but big lips. His eyebrows were so thick you could grow corn in them and I mentioned he wasn't exactly a clotheshorse.

I changed the subject and offered again to help pack, but my mother excitedly said, "No honey, we're staying."

I turned around and faced her. "Mom, the guy's a fruitcake, and if he's *touched*, who's to say the rest of the people here aren't fruitcakes too?"

She gave me an *I'm sure* look, and said in her most understanding motherly love voice, "Honey, the man is not a fruitcake. If this is the guy I think he is, then he's the reason we came on this particular trip to begin with."

She said she heard that this guy had the ability to draw pictures of your guardian angels. She said the only bummer was that it wasn't something you could ask him to do, you had to be chosen. She said that if this was the guy, and she was pretty sure he was, then I had to go because I was chosen. Again, I had that strange mix of feeling special and screwed all at the same time. I told her I would go, but only if she came by his tent in five minutes if I hadn't returned. She agreed and off I went.

I went to his tent and walked in. He was just finishing my picture and was too involved to acknowledge my arrival. As quiet as I was trying to be, he must have known it was me because without turning around he asked me to sit down and said he would be with me in a minute. This time he didn't have that smirk on his face; he seemed more serious than excited.

Before he showed me the picture, he told me that this *boy* came to him in a dream and told him that I was coming to this retreat, and he wanted him to draw a picture for me. He said the boy's name was Gerald, or Jerry, if I preferred. He said he was my age and that he was growing up with me in spirit. Then he turned around and handed me a colored chalk drawing of a ten-year-old boy with sandy brown hair, blue eyes, and a slight smile.

I sat there for a second, not knowing what to say. I didn't want to be rude, but I wasn't one of these androids who believed everything I was told. Unlike everybody else this guy dealt with, this wasn't something that excited me. I stood up and looked more carefully at the drawing. I thought that I might find some artistic value I could comment on, but being ten, even that escaped me.

I looked at Yoda and told him I thought it was great. I didn't mean to sound insincere, but apparently I did, judging by the look on his face. He wanted more from me but nothing came. I didn't know what to say.

I figured the best thing for everybody was for me to just take the drawing and leave. This was starting to feel uncomfortable. Yoda was looking more and more like he was a few fries short of a happy meal and the more I hung around, the better chance of him going off.

I thanked him for his drawing and the time he spent drawing it. I quickly went to open up the flap that acted as the tent door but Yoda stopped me. In an astonished voice he said, "Michael, why don't you say hello?"

I turned around to make sure he was kidding, but the look on his face said he was serious. This was starting to get creepier by the minute. He wanted me to talk to the chalk drawing like it was a real person.

I could feel myself getting anxious and embarrassed. My ears started getting hot and my hands were sweaty. I wanted to run out of the tent and find my mom, but I didn't feel like I could. Like everything else that had been happening around me, I felt like I had to play this out as well. I forced a smiled. As I sheepishly looked at the picture,

I said, "Hello, how ya doin'?" Once again, I looked over at Yoda like, *okay, can I go now?*

As I looked at Yoda, I heard this voice in my head say, "Fine, thank you, how are you?" The voice sounded different from anybody's voice I'd ever heard, but at the same time, it sounded like a normal ten-year-old kid.

Startled, I looked more closely at the troll to make sure he hadn't thrown his voice. I asked him if he heard the same voice that I did and this seemed to make him happy. "The important thing is YOU can hear the voice," he said confidently. Then he told me that I needed to be alone with the picture and he walked out of the tent.

My last remaining speck of normalcy wanted to rip up the stupid picture and run, but my feet wouldn't move. The new part of me, the evolved part, seemed to have other plans. I wanted to know more. As much as I wanted to pretend I didn't hear that voice, I knew I did, and the big surprise was that it didn't scare me.

Again, I stood and looked at the picture, unsure of what to do. I decided that maybe I should be the one to initiate the conversation further, but as I was about to do so, I heard the voice again.

"If you want, I can leave."

The voice sounded sad and disappointed, and it hit me that my reluctance at even being there may have hurt his feelings. Just as I would with a living person, I apologized. I looked around the empty tent and told the voice I would like to know more. I again said I was sorry and that I didn't mean to hurt his feelings. I told him this was all new to me and I wasn't sure what to do, but I was willing to learn.

I stood there for a minute or two with no reply. I started looking around the tent like I was looking for a lost gerbil and found myself wanting to whistle.

I also started thinking this might all be a joke. I mean, really, I'm holding a chalk drawing of some kid I'd never seen before, talking to myself in an empty tent in the middle of the woods and expecting an answer.

I decided it was time to leave. I told whatever might be listening that I was going. I thanked whatever it was for its time and started walking out of the tent. On cue, I heard a loud *Wait* and stopped myself. I turned around and stared at the air as the voice continued.

"You can call me Jerry." He then asked me if I would stay a little longer.

Jerry's voice had a certain vulnerability to it and I could tell he really didn't want me to go. I didn't want to leave either. I wanted to find out what this was all about. I just didn't want to stand there looking like a fool in the process.

I told him I would stay and asked him if he'd mind answering some questions. This perked him right up. He didn't even wait for the questions; he just started talking.

He began by telling me that he had died a few years earlier in a car accident. He didn't give too many details, just that it happened quickly. He said he woke up and the only thing he could see was this big white light. He got the feeling he was supposed to go to the light, but didn't want to go because he wasn't ready. So he said the next thing he knew, he was back here, earthbound.

After a while, he started getting lonely. He missed life on earth and desperately wanted to experience the growing-up process with someone living. That's where I came in. He picked me because our family was opening up psychically and he knew we had a lot of things in common. He said he never believed in this psychic stuff either. When he was aware that he was dead, it was a shock to him. Since then, and despite all the things he didn't like about being dead, there were some cool things to being on the other side.

He told me he could help me with things like schoolwork and girlfriends and that he would educate me on the ins and outs of being a dead guy. In return, all he wanted to do was hang around me and observe my day-to-day life.

As I was listening to him talk, I found myself more and more intrigued. When you're ten, you don't care so much who you play with as long as that person is fun. This Jerry person/thing sounded fun. He didn't have any skin, but the upside seemed much better than the downside.

Jerry finished the conversation by asking me to think about it. I told him I would. I also told him I was going to put his picture up on my bedroom wall when I got home, and he was happy about that. I left the tent and went looking for my mom. It felt good to walk out of the troll's tent intact, like when you survive a doctor visit. I was also excited to talk to my mom. When I found her, I told her about what happened and she looked excited. It was probably because she saw that for the first time, I was actually taking an interest in this stuff.

I never did see Yoda again after I left his tent. We got caught up in other things and we didn't cross paths. With all the weird people in my life back then, it wouldn't have surprised me if he turned out to be a troll. But I suspect he was just one of those people who come in your life for a minute, make an impact, and are gone. I would have liked to thank him, though—from my heart.

In the beginning, Jerry's and my relationship was slow. I would look at his picture hanging on my wall when I came in and think of him. However, we didn't talk on a daily basis. He probably wanted me to get used to him and he probably wanted to get used to being around me. Plus, he was doing what he wanted to do anyway, which was to hang out and observe. He'd pop in for a little bit here and there and we would talk. I'd ask him where he went when he would leave, and he would give me vague answers like *around*, and we'd leave things as they were. I didn't push it at first because I was doing stuff myself with my friends and family. I wasn't totally ready to have a relationship with a dead guy.

A couple of years passed after I was introduced to Jerry and as time went on, we started to become friendlier. Things around the house were certainly getting crazier, so in my quieter times, I'd find myself going to my room and talking to Jerry. As a family, there seemed to be more interest in individual projects and less interest in doing things together, like dinners and movies.

The number of church people coming to the house kept increasing, as did the number of psychics. There were so many people coming and going that you never knew if they were somebody's friend, or just some lost soul looking for an answer.

I was even starting to bend an ear toward all this psychic stuff. I found myself dropping in more and more on the kitchen crew and really trying to understand what they were talking about. This wasn't always the easiest thing to do, especially when they would talk in tongues. As I started to understand what they were saying, my old way of thinking slowly started to change. With the blinders coming off, my perception on life was beginning to change and school was becoming even more intolerable.

I have always had problems in school. Being a hyper little nymph, I had trouble concentrating on one thing for more than two seconds at a time. But being exposed to all the psychic information made it even harder to concentrate, or even care. I started thinking in terms of the big picture. Like *why are we here? Did we ever die? What was our responsibility to other people in our lives?* These were the questions that were important to me.

If you add the dash of emotional instability that goes along with puberty, you can see how unimportant it was to me to be able to figure out what time a train leaving California at six PM and another train leaving Chicago at three PM would meet in Cleveland? As far as I was concerned, maybe their karma was to all die in Barstow.

With the meaning of life becoming more important, and schoolwork becoming less and less important, I took Jerry up on his offer to help me with my studies. And as he had promised in the beginning, he did.

He'd do things like give me answers to questions on tests or point out what to study and what to let go. He'd also warn me when the teacher was coming back in the room so I wouldn't get in trouble for dancing on the desk.

He liked school. He liked the interaction of the students, the noise, and the activities. Of course he was dead, so I could see where he missed that sort of thing, but being dead didn't stop him from being interested in me meeting girls. Personally, I think being dead can make you brave. Meeting girls can be very nerve-racking when you're alive (at least it was for me) but Jerry was pretty gung-ho. The more girls I met, the more he liked it. Hormones can be a powerful thing, even if you're dead.

Having a horny dead friend wasn't such a bad thing. If he wanted to meet girls, I would have to meet girls and if I was going to meet girls, I needed to be in place to do so. Jerry would make sure I was in the best position for doing just that. For instance, if I was out with my buddies and a cute girl was approaching, Jerry would start barking *there's a cute girl coming, there's a cute girl coming.* I would prepare myself as best as I could. I'd usually go for the natural, surprised, indifferent look. The guys I was with wouldn't know what the hell I was doing until it was too late.

They would all be caught off guard getting into their cool poses while I was calm, cool, and collected. This was a definite advantage because there's nothing more embarrassing than having a cute girl round the corner and having your finger halfway up your nose.

It was starting to be fun with Jerry. We were getting along more and more, and he was anxious to be a bigger part of my life. He was also anxious for me to learn about his life. One of the things the kitchen crew had been talking a lot about was a thing called *astral projection.*

The belief was that when you go to sleep, your soul leaves your body, and that sometimes your soul hangs out with other souls. They'd go to other parts of the planet or other parts of the galaxy and just hang, talk about what they're going through or what they're overcoming, maybe even visit someone on the other side. They said your soul would return in the morning and sometimes that was the reason why you'd wake up so tired. If you woke up real heavy, it was because your soul had been out all night visiting.

I asked Jerry about this and he said it was true. He asked me if I'd ever woken up with a start, like someone just shook me or gave me a little jolt of electricity. I told him I had, but I didn't think it was because I was astral projecting. I thought it was because I had a lot of energy and I couldn't wait to get going. He agreed I had a lot of energy, but said the reason my body did that was because sometimes my soul had trouble getting back into my body from being gone all night and I just wasn't aware of it.

Why would I want to be aware of being trapped out of my body? Jerry insisted it was no big deal. He said that getting trapped out of your body rarely, if ever, happened. But, he said, if I did get stuck outside of my body, he would help me get back in.

"Besides, wouldn't it be cool to feel like you were flying?" he asked.

Jerry knew that would interest me. Ever since I was a seed, I've wanted to fly. In our talks, that was one of the things he did that I wished I could do, but that didn't mean I was ready to do this astral projection thing. The whole idea seemed a little far-fetched.

I told Jerry I had two problems with the astral thing. Number one, I wasn't sure that I believed astral projection was real. Maybe all those people who claimed to be astral projecting were just dreaming and making it up in their heads. And number two, if it was real and I did have trouble getting back in my body, how was he going to be any help? Stuff my soul back into my body? Not only did that sound stupid, it also sounded painful.

His first reaction was to pretend that he was hurt by my lack of faith. "I wouldn't tell you I would help you if it wasn't true," he snipped. He then switched gears and became angry. "If you want proof, try being aware of when your soul leaves your body. Go to someone's house you've never been to before and look around. Next time you see that person ask them what their room looks like and see if you're right."

This astral deal started to sound intriguing. I asked him what the requirements were to do this weird thing and he said the only thing I had to do was ask to be aware of everything I did while I was sleeping. I told him I'd think about it and we moved on to other things.

A part of me was interested in doing this. I had always wanted to be the invisible man and this was the perfect opportunity. But even a dipstick like myself knew there had to be a downside to doing this, and not knowing what that was made doing it creepy.

I needed to talk to someone about my decision, but I didn't want that someone to be *in-house*. So I decided to go outside of the kitchen crew for advice. I called Mrs. Olsen.

I hadn't talked with Eve for a while and it was nice to hear her voice. Eve had this sweet little grandmother way of talking that contrasted with the subjects she usually talked about—like when your pastor talks to you about sex. Whenever Eve would talk about parallel universes, it came out sounding funny. I told Eve of my situation and the first thing she did was to warn me how dangerous this *exercise* could be. She said that if I planned on trying it, I should ask Jesus to protect me so no other spirit would enter my body while I was gone. That was a thought that hadn't occurred to me. I was starting to get nervous. I wasn't totally convinced it was possible, but if it was when I tried it, I would ask God for protection and to be surrounded by the white light.

I tossed the astral idea around for a couple of days and finally got the nerve to try it. I told myself I wanted to be aware of my soul when it left my body, and I asked God to protect me. Then I lay there like an astronaut waiting to take off, wondering what my first destination would be and what would happen if something went wrong. When I woke up and it was morning, nothing had happened. A part of me was almost relieved. The second night, I tried it again, but again nothing happened. I was starting to wonder if Jerry knew what he was talking about. Maybe I was right. Maybe this astral thing was just talk.

That day, I told Jerry that nothing was happening. I told him I was doing all the things he told me to do and the only thing I was aware of was that he was full of crap. He told me I needed to be more patient. He said that when it was time, and I wasn't putting so much importance into doing it, it would just happen.

The next night, when I went to bed, I went through my normal routine of asking for protection and so on. At that point, I remember feeling less enthusiastic about the whole deal and more resigned to just going through the motions in case something might happen. I slowly drifted off and started having a dream—or at least it felt like a dream.

I dreamt I was floating over the house of a girl I was dating. I had only been there once, but I could see her last name on the mailbox and her weird steps, so it had to be her place. Then without thinking about it, I was inside the house. It was quiet and dark, and the only sound I heard was the humming of the refrigerator. Even though I had never been to her room, I had a sense of where it was, so I went there. When I got to the door, I just went right through, like it was air. I was amazed. I could see her sleeping, see what she had on, the furniture in her room, everything.

I floated there for a while with no particular plan and then I remember being outside again. I felt the cool air, but I wasn't cold. I could hear the crickets, see the cars on the road, and smell the dewy grass, but I didn't feel wet. It was strange and fun, spooky but liberating. I don't remember being aware of time, but I do remember having a sense that it was time for me to return home, so I did. I don't remember going home or entering my body. I just remember seeing my body and thinking I looked odd in my sleep.

When I woke up, I was groggy, but excited. I wrote down as much as I could remember so I wouldn't forget. I was still buzzing from the experience and I strained to remember as much as I could. I also couldn't wait to see Ann and tell her about what happened.

I went to school and as soon as I saw Ann, I ran up to her with my notes and started to describe to her what I went through the night before. I told her what she had on, where her bed was, and what was hanging on the wall. She was slightly stunned, but I kept going. I told her about the mess of clothes in the corner and the pink and green teddy bear sleeping next to her. I could tell by the blood rushing from her face that everything I was describing to her was true, right down to that strap thing she wore on her head to keep her teeth straight.

I was so excited. I didn't stop to think how this might be affecting her, or how weird I probably sounded. Besides her off-white facial tone, I could see by the way she was holding her crucifix that it was affecting her.

She started asking me questions. She asked me what I meant when I said my soul left my body and she asked why my soul was in her bedroom and how long was I there. These were more rhetorical questions than real ones and before I could answer, or put a spin control on the whole thing, she looked at me like I had suddenly developed leprosy and said maybe we were seeing too much of each other. She suggested that a break was in order, and suddenly realized she was late for her flu shot. This not being the flu season, I realized I was being dumped.

I stood there trying to figure out why Ann wouldn't be excited about my newfound talents. She seemed impressed with my other talents, like my double-jointed elbows and that clay ashtray I made for her in pottery class even though she didn't smoke. This new ability was way more exciting than making an ashtray. I couldn't understand why anybody wouldn't be excited.

Yet as I was watching her watch me, I saw a look in her eyes that I used to get whenever somebody in the kitchen would get possessed or a ghost would just pop up. It was that *oh my god, get me out of here* look. I knew what she was feeling, and I knew what she was thinking.

The reason she didn't embrace my experience and offer me her hand in marriage was because she was a normal person. She had a normal family and a normal house with normal walls that didn't bleed. She didn't live in a haunted house with haunted pets and a kitchen full of psychics. She had normal friends with normal problems, not a dead friend with a hormonal imbalance. The closest she probably came to this stuff was watching Scooby-Doo.

Because I was so caught up with what I was able to do, it didn't hit me that there might be some negative consequences. Ann screaming down the halls for a chaplain was one consequence, but my arrogance in thinking other people wouldn't be affected was another.

When I got home I talked to my mom about the experience. I told her about the dream, Ann, what Mrs. Olsen had to say, and everything. I told her how disappointed I was that Ann wasn't happy about the whole thing, and I told her how cool it felt being out of my body.

My mother sat quietly and listened. I figured she would be excited by what happened because whenever I showed interest in psychic phenomena, she was supportive. I finished my story and asked her what she thought. She looked me in the eye and said, "I don't want you doing that again, at least not for a while."

Her response threw me. I asked her why she didn't want me to do it again. "Because it's rude to just pop over uninvited into someone's room like that, that's why," she said. "You wouldn't like it if some girl did that to you, would you?"

Suddenly I got a visual of Ann coming over and finding me sleeping on my face, wearing Batman pajamas and drooling. I answered no.

"And what if, while you're gone, some strange soul like Lee Harvey Oswald jumps inside your body," she continued. "What am I supposed to do then?"

She was on a roll, so I kept quiet.

"You're not ready to do this yet, Michael. You have a lot to learn about many things. I'm glad you're okay, but no more." She kissed me on the head and walked away.

She was right. I wasn't ready to start leaving my body and go floating all over the place and in a way, it was a relief to know I wasn't allowed to do it anyway. Not that she could stop me. But without her blessing, in case something did go wrong, I'd be screwed.

I ran into Ann a few times and we eventually started talking again, not about what happened but about school or our friends. She chose to handle the situation a lot like Bobby handled the face-in-the-bathroom-mirror thing by pretending it never happened. We got along okay, and even went on a few dates, but things weren't the same. Anything remotely psychic wasn't brought up. This stuff wasn't for everybody.

Jerry may not have been as helpful on the astral projection thing as he first said he would be. I don't recall hearing him or feeling him anywhere when I was floating around, but he was helpful with something else. When I was about eight or nine, I started getting these *feelings* with people. I would look at a person and I'd get this sensation, like when you smell snow or burning leaves or warm bread, and how that evokes a certain feeling in you. Well, that was what would happen when I'd get these feelings. I didn't hear voices or see a spirit, but I would sort of know what the person was feeling or at least it felt like I did because of those sensations.

At the time, I didn't want to admit to myself that I was having these feelings. I saw all the weird stuff happening in the house and the strange people associated with it and I was worried that that would happen to me, like one day I'd wake up and want to do readings and talk like a hypnotist.

Still, a part of me was okay with this feeling because it didn't happen all the time or with everybody I met. When it did happen, it didn't last long. I also didn't go through changes when it happened. It felt natural, not foreign or dramatic. I just got these feelings and, somehow, I could tell what a person was going through.

Another weird thing was that I could almost see the future for people or at least a possible future for them. The only way I can describe it is, I could see a connection coming like a cable coming closer to me. And I knew that one day when the cable and I connected, I would be able to see the future for people and tell them about it. I don't believe that anything is carved in stone, but I do believe that some psychic people can see opportunities coming up for somebody and that person can choose what they want to do.

At that time in my life, I didn't know what to think of all this stuff. Good or bad, I did know I was going to become more psychic some day—I could feel it—so I knew I was going to have to deal with it. I just didn't know how.

One night, the whole family was sitting around the dinner table talking. My parents had read some book that said it was important to *get down* with your kids verbally so you could close the generation gap. The year was 1968, and it was a hip thing to do. We were all obligated to say something, preferably something with a little meaning. Being the oldest male, Lance started. He talked about the burdens of being the coolest person alive, his relationships with his many women, and the football team. Echo went next and talked about the horrors of failing art, working as a waitress at Uncle John's Pancake House, and boys. And Nikki talked about her hair.

The only thing I could think of to talk about was this *feeling*. I figured it was a good time to try and explain it and maybe if I did talk about it, it would go away. I started out the conversation with "I know that Nikki had a bad day at school today." This got everybody's attention, but I'm sure they were expecting me to say something stupid, so my mom cautiously asked me what I meant.

I told them that sometimes I would get sensations when I looked at a person and know what they were feeling. I told them I thought Nikki was having a bad day because when I saw her, I felt sad. It would only last a second or two, but in that time, I just knew. At that point you could hear crickets. I could tell they thought I was kidding. They all looked at me still expecting the punch line. I kept trying to explain the feelings I was having, but I couldn't explain it in a way that wasn't connected to any psychic thing. I didn't want that to be the obvious answer. Plus, I didn't want that to be encouraged any more than it already was.

I kept going on and on, trying to convey what I was feeling, but the more I tried, the worse it got. After a while, I wasn't even making sense myself. I finally ended up making up some story about something else, just so I could get out of the conversation and get out of the kitchen. This didn't meet with much resistance, because by that time everybody was pretty much *Michaeled out*.

I thought about telling Birdie or Mrs. Olsen, but I didn't want the same reaction I got sitting at the dinner table. Or worse, I didn't want either of them to think I was a budding psychic. That would be intolerable. The only one that made sense to talk to about my new feelings was Jerry. Keeping in mind he was only twelve, as was I, I wasn't expecting a whole lot as far as answers go, but I was surprised with what he had to say.

He told me that as far as he could tell, those *feelings* that I was having was my psychic ability trying to come out. He said a lot of people had these feelings, but most just stuffed them and eventually they went away, probably because it was so unacceptable. From where he was, it was pretty natural to have those abilities. But just like developing a musical talent or a physical talent, it would take time to become a true psychic.

He said that some people could *pick up on* past lives or the future, and some were good at finding things like keys or people or talking to the dead. The key to any good psychic was understanding the messages. That's why he thought that the really good psychics were the ones that had been around a while, because you'd have to be exposed to all the symbols and feelings and messages for a long time to totally understand what Spirit was trying to say. He said that when that finally did happen, when it all came together, the time you had left on earth was usually short.

That part about taking a while to understand Spirit didn't make sense. It was pretty easy to understand Spirit. Jerry was a spirit, and if I could understand him, why would it take a lifetime to understand any other spirit, unless they didn't speak English? Jerry said that some spirits, usually the higher forms, tended to be vague when they talked to you. He said those kinds of spirits wanted you to figure out your own solutions instead of relying on them.

Jerry said that from all he gathered from the spirits on the other side, people were here on earth to learn life's lessons, help other people, or deal with their karma.

He also made it clear that psychics were no different than anybody else. He said they could help people with certain things, but weren't put here to answer all life's questions. In fact, they were here to learn as much as, if not more than, everybody else. He also said they were no more special than the guy who empties your trash and if they started thinking they were, most would lose their gift.

As interesting and educational as all of this information was, it was starting to get a little long-winded for my patience. I stopped Jerry before he got onto religion and brought up my original question. *How do I understand these new feelings and what do I do with them?*

Jerry paused for a second. "I think it takes a while to understand what all this stuff means," he said.

Great. I knew the meaning of life, but I had no clue as to what to do with myself.

Jerry did help me with more practical things like telling me about a person's demeanor before I encountered them, so I'd know how to deal with them. If a friend was in a bad mood, Jerry would warn me so I wouldn't say something stupid and get my butt in trouble. On the other hand, if a friend was in a good mood, Jerry would tell me that too so I could borrow money from the guy. I was definitely becoming more comfortable with having a ghost friend.

I remember wishing some of my living friends would be as much fun as Jerry. I never felt alone when Jerry was around, and that was important to me back then because everybody in my family was into their own thing. Even though the house was full of people, I felt separate—like a visitor or a tourist. I can't put my finger on why I felt that way. Maybe everybody in the house felt that way. We all had a common ground in that we were all a part of this stuff, but other people embraced it better than me. It wasn't just because of the psychic stuff. I think I still would have felt odd, but the psychic connection just made it worse.

That was why it was so important to me to try and be normal— because I never felt *normal*. By now, even *normal* was changing. It was normal at one time for my mother to behave as June Cleaver. Now, it was normal for her to behave like Zola, mistress of the night.

Growing up with a powerful psychic in the house could be a challenge, but add the morality of a mother and you can forget about stuff like sneaking out. Whenever I got the nerve to do it, the house would be locked up and a pillow and blanket would be waiting for me on the front lawn when I got home. After a couple of these episodes, I had to seek help from a professional—someone who had been there and figured out how to beat the system. I turned to Lance. (Why learn from your own mistakes when you can learn from your big cousin's?) Lance had been in my predicament a few times and had found a way to override my mother's radar. He said that in order to fool my mother, I had to tell myself I wasn't sneaking out as I was sneaking out.

The theory behind this was that if I wasn't thinking *Oh God, I'm going to get caught sneaking out again* I wouldn't be emitting any stress or fear vibes for her to detect on her psychic radar. If I was thinking *Oh, this bed feels so warm and snuggly* when my mother made her psychic sweep, that's what she'd pick up. Most of the time it worked, but if she suspected *anything,* no matter what you were thinking, you were busted.

Another drawback to having a psychic mother was her ability to size up my friends in a New York minute. She could pick up on whether they were trustworthy, honest, good hearted and caring, or rotten, lying, snakes-in-the-grass. And she wasn't shy about sharing her opinion. Eddie Haskell wouldn't have had a chance with my mother. She saw this as a blessing, but I saw it as embarrassing. When your mother walks in and tells your new *cool* friends to empty their pockets because she knows they've got cigarettes, that's embarrassing.

The same thing happened when I started dating. She could tell if a girl was naughty or nice within fifty feet. In this case, her abilities worked in my favor. I naturally liked the naughty ones, so if my mother liked a girl, I'd stay away from her. If she didn't, I'd fall in love. My mother eventually caught on and gave her approval to the nasty ones. A lot of my teen years were spent trying to stay one step ahead of my mother. It wasn't easy.

Jerry wasn't always Mr. Helpful. Some days, he was a regular pain in the ass. One day, I was playing Little League baseball, a sport I was not very good at to begin with. There's something about a kid with no control throwing a rock-hard sphere at your head that gave me the creeps. Anyway, I was in my usual place in right field, checking out the dandelions and praying for rain, when some doehey had the nerve to hit a high fly ball right to where I was standing.

I immediately positioned myself directly under the ball and waited for what seemed like four hours for it to land in my mitt. As it was about to land harmlessly, I could hear Jerry yelling *you're going to miss it, you're going to miss it*. By then I was stiffer than a wedding dick and the ball hit my glove and popped out.

Some can argue that I was just a bad ball player to begin with, and that was why I missed that ball. Still, others could say it was my self-doubt that was talking and not Jerry's voice. I say there's nothing more difficult than trying to catch a fly ball with a dead guy yelling at you.

Overall, I had to admit that I was becoming more determined to be comfortable with all this psychic stuff. I wanted to learn more, so I could at least learn to protect myself from ghosts, psychics, or my mom. I figured the more I knew, the less I'd be afraid and the stronger I'd become. Not that I was ready to put up a third-eye shingle and start doing readings. No, that was still a recurring nightmare, but at least I didn't have to sleep with the stereo on level 10 anymore. I was learning to flow with it (not that I had a choice).

My father, on the other hand, decided on mutiny. He was barely hanging in there to begin with. The final straw came one night when he and my mother were playing chess. One of the chess pieces rose up, moved across the chessboard, and landed on my father's lap. All the weirdness—the kitchen crew, the ghosts, the moving objects, the people, the freaks, and the floating psychics—were rolled up into that little bishop. My father looked at my mother, stood up and said, "That's it, I'm outta here."

The next day, he was gone.

A part of me didn't blame my father. If Jerry wasn't around, I may have wanted to go with him. Sure, he wasn't father of the year, but he was the last link to the old reality in our house and when he left, I would be just another step closer to the twilight zone. I think I resented him for years for that. It felt like he jumped ship to save his own butt, and he didn't care about mine. He had to know it would get worse when he left. And it did. With my father gone, whatever bit of normalcy that was there was out the window, and the lid to Pandora's Box was about to open.

Six

Pandora's Box

*"I'm sure you get asked this all the time, but what IS the meaning
of life?" His stare suggested he was serious. I paused for dramatic
effect and then said, "I was taught that the meaning of life was to
live it." "Oh, come on, that's it?" he asked. "The meaning of life
is to live it? Geez, I didn't come all the way to hear that. There's
got to be more than just that." "Okay, okay," I said. "I'll tell you
but you have to listen." "Oh, I will," he said, and he leaned in to
hear what I had to say. "The meaning of life is the number 8."
Puzzled, he leaned back to ponder. Then a small smile came to his
face. "Yeah," he said. "That does make sense."*

Things didn't happen right after my father left; it took about twenty
minutes. The most obvious difference was the house had a different
feel to it. It was lighter, easier to be in. There were glimpses of that
feeling whenever my father went on business trips, but the tightness
in the air would return with my father. I would gauge the amount of
trouble I could get into by the length of his trips. If he was gone for
two weeks, I knew the first week was mine and I could relax. I didn't
have to empty the garbage right away—I could let it slide. The dogs
could wait to eat and the beds didn't have to be made. But a three-day

trip meant less room for error. One day tops, and then it was *your father's coming home—you'd better pick up your toys*.

But now, he wasn't coming home, not even to check in. He was starting his new bachelor life. He had perms to get, beanbags to buy, silk sheets to cover whatever heart-shaped bed he bought for his new love grotto. He had moved on, and even though he was only a mile away from the house, it felt like he was in another country. Surprisingly I wasn't sad. It felt good to have that pressure lifted. It felt almost *too* good.

Back then, divorce was still something only whispered about in the dark and after ten. The *victims* associated with divorce were usually described as being overwhelmed with grief and confusion. Unable to function in normal society, they were forced to work in concentration camps and restaurants. Then, only after rigorous therapy and training were they allowed to return to normal society, usually finding work in the hotel/motel industry or real estate. But here I was, unfazed by this devastating event and seemingly unaffected by it all. If I did feel anything it was guilt for not feeling bad.

I knew my attitude wasn't going to be well accepted with my family and friends. I knew that if I walked around with a smile on my face somebody was going to question my ability to cope. Someone might even assume something was wrong with me and the last thing that I wanted was some over-sensitive tree-hugging grownup questioning me about my feelings.

I could tell people the tension in the house had reached such an all-time high that it hadn't been fun coming home when my dad was there anymore. I could say with my father gone I could finally relax and not feel like I was walking on egg shells every time I walked in the door. But those answers would only open the conversation up to more questions.

The best and only approach for me was to play the strong victim, lower my head when asked about the divorce, and change the subject as soon as I could. Being the youngest, I got the most attention regarding my well-being, but a few dramatic *I'm fine* responses and most people left me alone to heal on my own. If someone did pursue the subject further I would look that person in the eye and assure him or her I was okay. This gave the impression I was not only okay, but that I was also a strong little trooper who would eventually be fine. The person felt better for asking and I felt better for being done with that question and that person. Spring was in the air and I was becoming more optimistic.

The second thing that happened shortly after my father left was Tony asked my mother if he could move in. This was the first time we would have someone other than housekeepers or relatives living with us and that in itself was fun. Not that Tony was coming for a slumber party. Being a gay psychic/actor didn't offer much stability then, so he needed a place to stay.

I didn't have a problem with Tony moving in. He was always nice to me; he was always nice to everybody. What I didn't know, but later found out, was Tony didn't travel alone. Like most psychics, he had an entourage of dead people who were always around him. Some psychics had only a few spirits around them, while others like Tony had a lot. And Tony's spirit friends were not the quiet, shy types most people wouldn't even know existed. They were the loud, bang-on-the-walls type that everyone could hear.

Some said that Tony had those particular kinds of spirit with him because some spirits appreciated his dramatic flare for life while others said it was his powerful psychic energy that caused these loud spirits to hang out with him. I assumed just his profession alone would attract other similar spirits to him. If you're an actor and you have the ability to talk to dead people, how can you not attract spirits with flare? Whatever the reason, they all came, and with them came a definite surge of paranormal activity.

Before Tony came, you might feel one or two spirits in the house, but when Tony moved in it was more like ten to fifteen. His room felt particularly crowded, like a Turkish prison. And everywhere he went in the house, his entourage went with him—like Pigpen, only with dead people instead of dirt. Personally, I didn't mind his little posse as long as they didn't make their way up to my room, but it did take some getting used to.

When my mother okayed the Tony deal, it opened the floodgates to other people staying at the house. Lance's friends, Echo's friends, anybody that needed a place to stay ended up at the house. With my father gone, there wasn't anything stopping people from coming. And as far as my mother was concerned, it wasn't a problem. She felt we'd had it so good for so long it was our obligation to help other people. It was part of the karma thing she'd been reading so much about.

Everybody came from different backgrounds and everybody had a story, usually a mish-mash of drama and necessity. There was Chris, who got kicked out of his house because he hated his rich and controlling father. Or Jean, who ran away because she got pregnant. Or Scott, who was running from the law because he stole his uncle's car in Illinois. We had people from all walks of life and mental capabilities staying at our house, and for the most part everybody got along. Some stayed only a night while others stayed for months. The weekends seemed particularly busy with people who just needed a place to crash. After a while I stopped asking who was who and went with the flow. It all seemed too big to try to care.

My father's absence also meant the psychic embargo was lifted. There were more people practicing Billets, more séances, more readings, more everything. People were meditating, chanting, humming. Anything that might bring them closer to spirit or answers about spirits (short of sacrificing goats), people were doing.

With the increased activity around the house, the hours of operation also changed. B.P. (before psychics) a typical day for me started with my mother, usually chipper and full of pep, making her first attempt at waking me up around 7 AM. Her monotone pitch and continual delivery was the same tone and method used to break American GIs in World War II. Despite this torture, I was usually able to stay half asleep until the pitch changed to the *I'm not screwing around* tone that meant I either got up or died. I would then make my way down to the kitchen, where a quick bowl of oatmeal, sugar, and red dye number three would jolt me back to reality and on to seize the day.

But now, she and her friends had discovered it was easier to do their business between twelve and three in the morning. (Something about the world being quieter—no electricity, telephones, TVs. Machines in general were less active at that time and that had an effect on spirits' ability to be seen, or for people to see spirit.) My mother and her friends would stay up all hours of the night doing their little spirit chats. This meant her tolerance for my ignoring her in the morning was minimal. If I didn't get up the first time she told me, June Cleaver became Roseanne Barr on crack and I had two minutes to move.

My mother's response to the one time I complained about this new schedule was, *nobody wants to hold a séance at eight in the morning, dear—get over it*. She then proceeded to pat me on the head and walk away. Normally at this point I would follow her and argue my point with the intention of some sort of compromise. But as I fixed my hair and thought about what she had to say, I had to agree she was right. Dealing with Mr. Rogers at eight in the morning was hard enough. But dealing with a bunch of Kumbaya-chanting nomads whose main goal was to reach enlightenment through conversations with the dead at that time of the day would have been way too much to handle. Once again I shut my mouth and went with the flow.

The problem with going with the flow is you don't always have control of where it takes you. Ideally this is where a Higher Power is supposed to come in and help guide you through the rapids that creep up from time to time—be the rudder of your ship. But if you don't have a rudder or you had rudders but didn't use them, then the rapids could get hairy. I believed in God. I knew all about Jesus. I just didn't apply them to my life. I didn't think they were around for that purpose. I always thought God and Jesus were my *get out of jail free cards* type of deals. If I got in over my head or needed a break legally, then in theory I would call on them to get me out of trouble. But day-to-day stuff I always thought was up to me to get through. I was having a hard time figuring it all out. Because of all the new faces and activity in the house and all the weirdness that came with it, there was a stronger sense of that *out-of-control feeling* I felt in the beginning. I hated that feeling—a heavy mixture of fear, anxiety, and dread.

All the drama that the new people brought in also attracted ghosts. It was like party central for dead people. If I heard a knock on the door there was a fifty-fifty chance there was nobody there. If I saw someone standing in the hall or in the kitchen or anywhere else in the house I'd have to do a double take to make sure whatever it was had skin. And if I saw something move out of the corner of my eye, I'd just roll my eyes and let it go.

It felt as though the ghosts had taken over the house, and it wasn't ours anymore. And even though we now had Birdie and Mrs. Olsen to answer some questions, we still didn't totally know how to protect ourselves.

I was being told by just about everybody that it was important for me to adjust to all this new stuff and to accept change and grow from it. I was being taught that life was a series of lessons and by accepting and learning from these lessons, we would ourselves then grow and help other people who needed help. This, I'm sure, was the same speech Hitler told the French when he *borrowed* their country. My situation wasn't nearly as dramatic as what went on in Europe and my mother wasn't Hitler, but I could relate to the whole *occupied* thing that went on over there. I felt like I had little control over my fate. I was resigned to going with the flow. But now I was also being asked to embrace the passions and depths of the serious subjects that were being tossed around on a daily basis. The truth was, I wasn't that much into becoming a deep thinker with designs on helping the world. I was twelve.

And like most theories, it was much simpler to say it than to do it. If you just keep accepting change and accepting it and accepting it, soon you lose sight of who you are and what you are. At least that was the way I saw it. I was losing my bearings. I didn't know if I was coming or going and with my home being ground zero as far as changes were concerned, it was difficult to hang on to who I used to be.

Mrs. Olsen referred to this as *the learning process*—part of the Pandora's Box effect we would experience when we opened up more psychically. She said there was good and bad when it came to exploring something as complicated as the occult. She said as fun as one aspect of what we were learning was, there would be other parts that would be equally as hard and confusing. She said we needed to be able to handle both good and bad aspects of the whole psychic experience; otherwise, we needn't bother exploring it at all.

Mrs. Olsen also said something that stuck with me the rest of my life. She said, "It isn't the problems in life that matter. It's how we handle the problems that makes the difference." The reason this theory made such an impact on me back then was it gave me the impression that even if I couldn't control the problems I was dealing with, at least I could control how I dealt with them. It made me feel better knowing I could control something in my life. So far, the only way I knew how to handle things was to stay in my room and try to block it all out.

But even going to my room didn't mean I was without weirdness. My roommate was a dead guy. Jerry didn't have a bed or dresser like a normal roommate and he wasn't in my room all the time, just enough for me not to be shocked by his presence when he appeared. But he was more or less my roommate. The good news for me was, in the conversations we had he seemed just as bewildered by all the action in the house as I was. Like me, he couldn't seem to *get* why everyone was so into learning about the dead. Like me, he found the living to be way more interesting.

As life became more intense, so did the kitchen discussions. In the beginning, whenever the kitchen crew got together their discussions tended to be lighter—more about the excitement of what they were about to discover. But as they learned more and formed their own opinions and new people joined the group and challenged those opinions, tempers could run high.

I started going to the *little talks* when I was twelve. Consciously it was never my intention to join the group. I wasn't led by some hunger for knowledge; I was just hungry.

When you walked in the front door of our house, the first door to your right was one of three to the kitchen. The kitchen itself was shaped like a diner—long and wide. As you entered that door, the large kitchen table where everybody sat was the first thing you saw. Then as you went further into the kitchen, a little island with a knickknack shelf separated the eating area from the cooking area. The electric stove was in that part of the kitchen and was surrounded by a counter, which we used mostly for breakfast and quick meals. The two other doors were also located in that part of the kitchen. One led to the garage and the other led to the formal dining room, which was used as often as I used the word *plethora*.

Every day I would come home from school and they would all be around the kitchen table, hammering out the deep, dark secrets of the universe. I would creep as quietly as I could past the group and make my way to the refrigerator and the cupboard, which were at the other end of the kitchen. I would then get my snack and slowly sneak away. I probably could have come through the formal dinning room door and been less noticeable, but a part of me wanted to know what they were talking about.

When I did hear something that piqued my attention, I'd find myself taking more time, pouring my milk into the cereal bowl or staring at the cupboards, while I did my best to act invisible and eavesdrop. I believed that if I kept my back to the group and appeared uninterested, I could stay undetected for up to five or ten minutes.

But being blessed with the *clod gene*, I would inevitably draw attention to myself by spilling the milk or knocking over a jar filled with something *loud*. The group would then notice my presence, lose patience with my being there, stop their discussion, and wait for me to leave. The combination of embarrassment and frustration would propel me out the door so fast I'd sometimes forget my food.

One day I walked in and as usual, ten to twelve people were sitting around the big kitchen table. Their conversation grew quiet, as it always did whenever I walked in, but picked up as they realized it was only me, *Mr. Thumbs*. I went to the cupboard, opened it, and as I did, everything inside came spilling out like someone was pushing it from the other side. I closed my eyes as tightly as I could and stood as stiff as an imperial guard while cereal and crackers poured over me and onto the floor. I could feel every eye in the room on my back and I knew my days of coming in the kitchen after school were numbered. If I had a gun, I would have shot myself to a standing ovation. I could not believe this just happened.

With my eyes still shut and my back to the group and the deafening sound of total humiliation about to overtake me, I heard a familiar and friendly voice asking me if I was okay. It was my mother.

The pitch of her voice suggested I wasn't in as much trouble as I originally thought. She sounded worried. At this point turning around to address her was not an option. My ears were on fire and my face was beet red. I answered back as casually as I could, trying to pretend nothing had happened. But any attempt I made to move was amplified by the grinding sound of Captain Crunch with crunch berries. When I responded that I was fine, I was just looking for the sugar, the worry tone in her voice changed to pity and she immediately jumped up and offered to help.

The group went back to their discussion, knowing the walking time bomb was being policed, at least for the moment. As they did, my mother and I cleaned up the mess and I took the opportunity to apologize and explain how unintentional it all was. I even offered to not come into the kitchen anymore after school until after their afternoon meeting was over—something I was more than willing to do at that point. But as my mother was often capable of doing those days, she surprised me by asking me to join the group instead. She did so in a way that made me think she had given this idea some thought. And when I turned around and saw an empty chair and an *if you can't beat them, join them* expression on the rest of the kitchen crew, I knew that they had also given some thought to my joining the group. I was surprised, but glad.

I dusted myself off and meekly walked to the chair and sat down. A plate of food was already prepared in front of me and I thought to myself how nice everyone was for being so patient and kind. Not wanting to be rude, and being hungry, I dug in and grabbed the first thing I saw on the plate—a piece of Monterey Jack cheese—and proceeded to stick it in my mouth. As I was doing so I noticed the group again get suddenly quiet.

For a brief second I thought I might be doing something wrong, but then it hit me—these people were always saying some sort of prayer—surely they were just about to say one when I sat down. I stopped myself from chewing the cheese and lowered my eyes. I casually put my hands together thinking the traditional way was the right way, but with this group you never knew—they might pray with one hand over their heads. I waited for the prayer to begin. But nobody said a word. I started getting that sinking feeling again like somehow I was doing something wrong. Sure enough, as I slowly opened one eye, I saw everyone at the table glaring at me. I quickly went through the sequence of events from the time I sat down. Should I have said *please*? Did I make too much noise when I pulled in my chair? Was the Monterey Jack poisoned, leaving me only seconds to live? With my mouth full of cheese and unable to open it, I gave the universal *what* look to the group, hoping someone would explain what I had just done. About that time my mother, aware of the group's sudden silence, turned around from her Captain Crunch duties, saw me sitting in the chair, and screamed, *Michael what are you doing?*

I didn't know what to think. I'd gone from frustration to embarrassment to serenity to fear to confusion, all within five minutes. Suddenly I was Alice at the tea party and I started to wonder if everyone else was crazy. I grabbed a napkin that someone had politely thrown at me and spat out the cheese. I looked at my mother and with complete sincerity and fervor asked her, *what did I do?*

Exasperated, my mother looked at me, then the napkin with the spat-out cheese, and with the same tone as Vivien Leigh in *Gone with the Wind* she said, *that food is for your grandpa Boyd.* She then stared at me like I was supposed to know what she was talking about and went back to the refrigerator, grabbed some more cheese, and angrily started slicing. (I missed the dead grandfather coming for lunch memo.)

The room again became painfully silent. I would have felt worse but I was too busy being confused. I knew at that point I couldn't ask my mother what the hell I just did, so I did what I thought any logical person would do and pleaded my case to the group.

"Grandpa Boyd has been dead longer than Lincoln," I said. "So I really don't think he's coming for tea." I did my best to avoid eye contact because I knew any one of them would have burned holes in my head for saying such a stupid thing.

With kindness and a condescending chaser, Birdie turned to me. "Yes, dear. We know your grandfather has passed," she said. "But that doesn't mean he can't join us for lunch now and then and smell our food." She then smiled, exposing her one tooth, and asked me nonverbally if I *got* it.

I really hated it when Birdie smiled. It brought up that sea hag issue, and being on such thin ice as it was, I didn't want my life to be over before I had a chance to live it. So I focused. I focused on the chair with the food and I focused on my mom. I looked around the room and really tried to grasp what they were suggesting. And even though a two-year-old would have gotten it by then, I didn't want to believe I was sitting in a chair with my dead grandfather, eating food that he had been sniffing for God knows how long. But as it slowly registered on my face and the nodding heads around the table confirmed what was obvious, I closed my eyes as tightly as I could and tried to go to my happy place.

My happy place didn't have a dead grandparent sitting at the dinner table or a one-toothed super psychic who could read your thoughts. In my happy place it was a cool fall night. I have just intercepted a pass from an opposing quarterback and I'm running full speed, almost the entire length of a football field for a touchdown in the waning seconds of a championship game. I can smell the grass in my happy place. I can feel the rush of adrenalin as I run for glory and I hear the crowd as they cheer my heroic effort.

But now, those cheers turned to shrieks as I hear my mother's voice screaming at me to get up. I opened my eyes to see her motioning and yelling that I'm sitting on my grandfather's lap, my grandfather-who's-been-dead-for-ten-years' lap.

I jumped up like my pants were on fire. Goose bumps popped up all over my body and I shook myself from the inside out hoping to clear myself of the *Dead Guy* vibe that covered me like a bad smell.

As I brushed off my entire body, I asked my mother why somebody didn't tell me earlier that the seat that looked like it was set up for me was in reality reserved for my dead grandfather. I reminded her this was my first time in her group and I didn't know all the ins and outs of what went on. Not only did I believe I was entitled to these answers, but finally something was coming out of my mouth that made sense. And my mother knew it.

In chess this would be considered a draw. We both had valid points and both of us were wrong. Any attempt to gain an advantage at this point would be a waste of time—or worse, dangerous—and we both knew it. So my mother pointed to an empty chair and I sat down. The group was bored with me and resumed their discussion. And I was glad to not be the topic of conversation. If I could just get through the rest of the meeting without a mishap or misunderstanding I would be a happy kid. But life isn't always about being happy.

I grabbed some unsniffed cheese from the center of the table, along with crackers and some grapes. I looked around at the other people at the table to make sure I wasn't eating from some sacred altar and it was then that for the first time I got a good look at who was there. When you're making an ass of yourself it's funny how you don't notice people.

I watched and listened as they got into a debate over a thing called *the Akashic records.* Like so many things I overheard when I'd stop in for chow, the Akashic records was just another thing I'd never heard of before, and frankly I wasn't that interested. I was just glad to be part of the group and not setting the table on fire. But as they raved on and the debate started to heat up, and words like *karma, responsibility,* and *life lessons* were mentioned, it dawned on me there might be more to what they were talking about than songs on a record. I started to become interested in what they were talking about.

But what the hell were they talking about? Finding out what *an Acacia record* was would mean speaking up and possibly again making a fool out of myself. And since I was enjoying my anonymity so much, I wasn't sure I wanted to surface and be noticed again. But what was the point of being in the group if it wasn't to learn something? And how could I learn something if I didn't know what we were talking about? I composed myself and opened my mouth. When my mouth opened everybody else's shut. Not because they respected my opinion. They were just impressed with my ignorance.

"Are you guys talking about actual records like the kind you put on the stereo?" I asked sincerely.

"No," replied Roy in his *Barry White* voice. Then he turned his attention back to the group.

"Well then, what are you talking about?" I asked, this time with a little more urgency.

"I said the Acacia records," Roy retorted. "Just sit and listen." A quick glance around the table supported his instructions, so I shut up.

As soon as I did, the conversation resumed. Roy started it, then he looked at the group. "How do I look at these records?" he asked. "And if they do exist, what's the point of having them if I can't see 'em?"

"They're for our souls when we pass on," Birdie said.

"When we pass on? That's what I'm saying," Roy barked. "What good are they if I can't use them when I'm alive?"

"I've seen my records," Tony chimed in. "I was a dancer for the sheik of Iran in my last life, then the queen of England. Then Cleopatra."

Everyone in the room rolled their eyes, and Roy jumped in again. "See! That's another thing. Anybody can make up whatever they want to about where they've been and where they're going."

The group mumbled like groups do when they think about stuff. I took that opportunity to ask again. "I know you said the Acacia records. And you want me to shut up and listen. But I still have no idea what an Acacia record is."

I didn't ask like a sarcastic boy or a condescending fool. I asked like I really wanted to know and because of that, Birdie became the one to educate me. "The Acacia records are records of all the lives we've had and all the things we've done in those lives our whole existence," she said. "They are who we are, what we are, what we've learned, and need to learn."

I said something deep like *Wow* and the conversation continued.

I didn't have a lot to offer in those early conversations. I wasn't a deep guy; I was twelve. I liked being part of them because I felt, as they all probably did, that we weren't just talking—we were trying to find the answers to the meaning of life. Maybe if I managed to keep my mouth shut and learn something I might be able to become a deep guy. Not that I wanted to become Gandhi. I was still going to be a professional football player. Just a *deep* football player.

That conversation carried on for what seemed like hours, as did most of them. I don't know that we ever did find the answers or come to any real conclusions or get the meaning of life, but we tried. Some of those conversations were so deep even Jack Kerouac would have gotten lost. But it seemed like the more we learned, the less we knew. There was just so much out there and so many ways to look at things, there was no *one* answer. Some of us tried to intellectualize things, put them in categories, while others thought only with their hearts. I figured it was somewhere in between. And why look for something you won't ever find? So after a while, for me the groups became a study of human nature rather than the *find the meaning of life* group I originally thought it was. Watching the personal interactions was just as interesting as the subjects we were talking about.

Not that I didn't always like the subject matter. It was fun to learn stuff about things my peers wouldn't know about and in some cases it was downright helpful. But it was in those early groups that I learned the most about people.

Learning some of this stuff gave me an edge. If I needed a comeback to an insult a schoolmate might give me, I could always say, *that's some bad karma, Bob,* and he wouldn't know what the hell to say.

This may sound trivial but at that age, you need all the ammo you can get. Kids are sadistic, mean, and quick. If you can come up with something that will shut a kid up long enough to give you time to retort properly, you've got an edge.

I didn't like school. I wasn't popular; I wasn't the fastest runner or the smartest kid. I was tall and thin, with a cereal bowl haircut. I had a tendency to be either too shy or too aggressive. I was funny, but I was awkward. I was sensitive, and like everybody else, I just wanted people to like me.

But with all the psychic stuff I was being exposed to, I was starting to put things in a different perspective. I was starting to think that maybe it wasn't so important to have people like me or to be cool or popular. And the funny thing was, the less important I saw those things, the more people started to notice me. Birdie used to talk about that. She said if you wanted something, you had to let it go. You had to make yourself not want it. At the time I didn't know what the hell she was talking about but now I was starting to get it.

With more people paying attention to me, my confidence improved and going to school wasn't such a drag anymore.

The year I turned twelve turned out to be one of the best years of my early life for a lot of different reasons. One, Jerry and I had now become as close as brothers. (We even had nicknames for each other. He called me *breather* and I called him *floater*.) And he filled a void. The only other male in my life was my cousin and we weren't close. Lance was a teenager, a cool teenager. The last thing a cool teenager wanted around was a little cousin.

Jerry and I spent so much time in my room we ended up having discussions about everything under the sun, and beyond. We agreed that the kitchen crew was taking all this psychic crap way too seriously and just how stupid that was. And we would sit and laugh about the different personalities and how everyone thought they knew *the answer*. I thought this was funny because I didn't think it was possible, but Jerry thought it was funny because he didn't think anyone living could know the real answers to life. Since I wasn't dead I couldn't argue with him, but his *I know more than you because I'm dead* attitude was starting to bug me.

Then a guy came over to the house that put some holes into that theory. *That guy* was a channel, or channeler. (Channelers are people who let a spirit come into their bodies and speak through them.) He came over to show us the power of channeling, and also the danger in underestimating the power of spirit.

He was a normal-looking guy, brown hair, brown eyes, maybe five foot five, 150 pounds, probably in his forties. He wasn't the kind of guy that stood out, let alone someone you'd think was a channeler. He sat down and said he had to prepare himself by concentrating on letting go of something (what I'm not sure, but nobody wanted to hurt his feelings so we let him do whatever). Then, like Mrs. Olsen, he asked spirit to come and speak. Unlike Mrs. Olsen, he asked the spirit to speak though him.

He became real quiet, and suddenly his face started to change. The skin around his eyes started to stretch, his lips became thin, and his nose began to shrink. He took on the appearance of a Chinese man. I sat and stared in amazement. What I was looking at and what I thought was possible were on opposite sides of my head. It was also scary. When he spoke, he spoke in Chinese, fluent Chinese! It didn't matter what he said, we couldn't understand him anyway. That he looked and sounded Chinese was so amazing. Then he became quiet again, put his head down, closed his eyes, and his face returned to normal. He lifted his head and with eyes still closed took a deep breath and lowered his head again.

Again his appearance started to change. This time the color of his face changed. There was a red tint to his hair and freckles started to appear around his nose. When he lifted his head to speak he had a strong Irish accent—so strong that it was just as hard to understand him then as it was to understand him when he was the Chinese man. He talked for a minute or so and then he put his head down again and returned to normal.

I had never seen anything like that before—and judging by the looks on the faces of the people in the room neither had they. The man asked for a drink of water, which we gave him, and then he said he had to leave. He said he was tired and he hoped what he did was helpful. We all thanked him for coming over, said our goodbyes, and away he went.

The group could hardly contain their eagerness to discuss what had just happened. When he left, the conversation erupted. We talked about how important the experience was, how we could see with our own eyes the power of spirit, and the ease in which the spirits jumped in and out of the man. We also talked about how impressed we were with the realness of the whole experience. It wasn't just talk; it was action—proof that what we had been talking about for so long was real.

I was impressed with the group's excitement. The experience validated the reason for being there, much like a bleeding statue might validate a church, or a vision might validate a shaman. This guy was it, our crying Virgin Mary, and just as we were ready to announce the little guy as the Second Coming, Birdie interrupted by angrily asking us why were we so impressed.

"Haven't you people learned anything I taught you about spirit?" she asked.

The room became silent (Birdie had the ability to suck the life out of a room).

"Well?" she asked.

The best we could do was look at each other like *I don't know what you're talking about*. Somebody, I'm not sure who, said *Birdie, that was amazing, didn't you see his face change? Didn't you hear his voice change? Didn't that just blow you away?*

The room again became quiet.

"Yes, dear. I saw it all," Birdie calmly said. "But tell me what his message was. What did he say that enhanced or educated your lives?"

She looked around the room. Nobody said a word.

"What I saw was a spirit enter another person's body," she continued. "This spirit talked gibberish, and then another spirit entered his body. I suppose it was interesting to watch, but it was certainly no value to me."

"If you're impressed with dramatics, then go to the circus. What you just saw was all show. You have to see beyond that. Did any of you understand what he said?"

None of us did, so she continued.

"Don't assume, just because someone has passed on, that they have more knowledge than you. If a spirit comes to you who died three hundred years ago he has learned only what he was taught three hundred years ago. If I were to tell you, you must learn to love more and trust in God more, would it mean more if it came from a spirit who has been dead for three hundred years, and if it does, ask your-self *why?*

"Yes, spirit can help you with life after death and support or debate decisions you may have," Birdie said. "But it's the living and their ex-periences where you would want to get most of your counsel."

We all agreed because Birdie did have a good point—we were all taken in by the dramatics and the man didn't have anything of value to say. And I suppose it is important to not be taken by flash, but damn, what a show! To this day I still think that was amazing.

Whenever I would remind Jerry of this guy, it would drive him nuts. Not only did it throw a monkey wrench in his *I-know-more-about-life-because-I'm-dead* theory, but he got jealous every time he heard about spirits entering other people's bodies.

Jerry was starting to become more and more interested in being alive. He wanted to experience and learn all the stuff he couldn't on the other side. He missed the growing-up process and because of that he was asking me more and more questions about being alive. Not that the questions bothered me, but it was the beginning of what would be a bad trend.

Another reason 1970 was such a good year for me was because I was getting more comfortable with my home life too. The house had a carnival atmosphere to it, and because I was learning more, I was feeling more empowered. It was still filled with weird ghosts and there was still that feeling in the air of being out of control, but I was learning to take care of myself, and I was also learning to look at the positive side of things.

Another reason it was a great year for me was that one of the last things my father did before he left was to buy the family a trampoline. Actually, he bought it for Nikki, but we all used it. So did our friends, the neighbors, the football team, France. There were people at our house all the time—day and night.

Ignoring my discomfort with the psychic stuff was easier with the house full of people. There was always a distraction, so I had less time to remind myself just how scared and helpless I felt. Even when I was alone, I wasn't alone. Where I resented that in the past, I welcomed it now—anything to get me through all of this was fine with me.

But because of the increased hubbub, hiding our psychic ways was now useless. With everybody coming and going and talking and staying up all night, there was no way for it not to get out. But it was becoming so big it didn't matter. My mother was now full speed ahead and if people had a problem with her lifestyle, well maybe she had a problem with theirs. This philosophy was especially clear when a reborn Christian would come to the door.

For a right-wing fanatic reborn Christian, our house was the Super Bowl. As far as they were concerned the place was lousy with people who needed to be saved and if they managed to save only a few, their place in heaven was secured or they won a box of steak knives. Either way, they were determined to change who we were.

My mother, on the other hand, felt that these well-dressed people were the ones who needed to be saved. She felt that everybody had a right to worship whomever they wanted. For instance, Birdie and Mrs. Olsen loved Jesus, loved him more than life itself. Roy leaned more toward Mohammed. Nonette, well I don't think we really wanted to know what she put her faith in. And Tony, he believed in the teachings of Buddha and Marilyn Monroe.

It was always part of their discussions and sometimes it would get heated, but they all agreed that whatever name you used, there was a Higher Power involved and we all had the ability to access it. Where they would run into problems was when someone wouldn't have an open mind and insist that his or her way was the only way.

So my mother didn't have a problem with a reborner's religious beliefs; it was their inability to accept the religious beliefs of others that seemed to set her off—that and their obsession with the Devil.

The first time I dealt with a Bible thumper was when I made the mistake of answering the door instead of letting someone else get it. A man in his twenties wearing a tie introduced himself and then asked me if this was the house where the psychics lived. I'd heard worse descriptions of the place, so I wasn't offended. I told him *yes*. And then like a tired salesman he clicked into his machine-like, prerecorded sales pitch.

At first I didn't have a problem with his approach. I figured anything to do with Jesus couldn't be all that bad. Even when he told me the only thing I needed to do to join the group was to give my life over to the care of Jesus Christ, I thought *now how hard can that be?* After all, I was a big fan of J. C. (If you talked to Mrs. Olsen for more than two minutes you'd have to be.) But then, it started to get a little creepy. Maybe because he sensed I was actually listening, his pitch became more personal.

"You want to go to heaven, don't you?" he asked.

"Sure," I replied.

"You don't want to burn in hell, do you?"

"No," I said.

"Well, did you know that in the Bible it says those who dabble in the occult go to Hell?"

"Really?" I said. "I wonder why it would say that."

"It just does," he replied matter-of-factly. "But if you get down on your knees right now and accept Jesus Christ as your personal savior and renounce the occult and all that dwell in it, you can be saved." Then he stared directly into my eyes.

I was at a loss, on one hand, why this shiny happy person would lie to me about my soul. He seemed genuinely concerned and he was quoting the Bible. On the other hand, we were standing in the front hall and it hardly seemed like the right place to get down on my knees. And I really didn't want to renounce my mother and all her friends.

I asked him if I could be excused for a second and I went into the kitchen where, as usual, everybody was sitting around. I told them my dilemma, that there was a man out there worried about my soul. That I was possibly going to burn in Hell and there wasn't anything I could do about it except to renounce them all as demons and kick them out of the house. They asked me to please invite *my friend* into the kitchen and maybe they could help straighten things out.

When I brought him into the kitchen he suddenly took on the appearance of a twenty-ounce porterhouse steak surrounded by a pack of lions. For a second I almost felt sorry for the guy, but not after he started talking. He introduced himself, and went right into his sales pitch. He started quoting scripture and as he talked, his eyes seemed fixed on some point in the room, like he was in a trance. He avoided making eye contact, which made it harder to take him seriously. He was scared but determined.

The kitchen crew just let him talk. Nobody seemed bugged or upset. They all sat quietly while he rambled on about the Devil. He seemed obsessed with Satan. He talked about the power of Satan, the range of Satan, the many disguises of Satan. I was starting to wonder if that was who this guy was working for. As his confidence grew, he talked about how doomed we all were if we didn't change our ways. He said God would punish us. He mentioned salvation, but in order for us to receive that salvation we must come to his way of thinking. When he was done he asked us all to pray so we could be saved.

But nobody moved. I assumed this meant the show was about to start. Any minute somebody was going to speak up and rip this guy a new halo, but everybody was quiet. Some people were obviously uncomfortable with the whole thing. Tony kept humming the song "Oh come, all ye faithful," and Nonette was asking everybody for a scissors so she could get a lock of the guy's hair. But overall, everybody was non-reactive.

Finally Birdie asked him if he was referring to the Old or the New Testament, and then she asked if he'd ever read Corinthians and she mentioned a verse in which it talks about the gifts of the spirit. She went on to talk about all the other things it says in the Bible—and other places—about psychics and healers. She talked about the good things psychics and healers have been known to do. She even brought up that since some of the Bible was written forty years after the fact and sometimes longer, that maybe spirit had a lot more to do with writing the Bible than it is given credit for. She then said something that has stuck with me through the years. She looked him in the eyes and said, "Son, if you're going to sell Coke, don't talk about how powerful and strong Pepsi is. Talk about how wonderful and beautiful Coke is. You'll get more business."

When she talked, she talked like a teacher would talk to a student and she was amused by his ignorance. She asked him to try to go through life a little less afraid and thanked him for coming by. She also welcomed him and his friends back anytime, only they had to keep an open mind.

I was a tad disappointed. Mr. Clean comes onto our turf, starts ripping apart our way of thinking, and the only thing she can say is *try to keep an open mind*? What was that? He wasn't going to have an open mind. The Jaws of Life couldn't open that boy's mind.

He looked at us, not sure what to think, and opened his mouth to say something, but Roy stopped him before he spoke. "Don't embarrass yourself," Roy said.

The man then backed his way out to the door, afraid to turn his back on a room full of heathens. When he left, the group talked about what was said, and as they talked it was clear other people felt the same way I did. But it was also clear that to attack him, as I wanted to do, would only be doing the same thing he was doing to us—trying to force beliefs down the throat of someone else. Birdie again talked about evolving, seeing the love in a person, no matter what their beliefs, and using that as common ground to build a relationship on. She also talked about the ability to see people in different learning stages in their lives. That way, there'd be less chance to be judgmental—something Birdie saw as a weakness.

The reborners took Birdie up on her offer to come back and started dropping by on a regular basis. For a time it seemed like our house was a rite of passage for the young Christian in training. When Birdie wasn't there, the discussions became heated and intense. Putting my two cents in was becoming fun.

I was surprised at how confident I felt about what I believed. The more I talked, the better I felt. The better I felt, the stronger my arguments became.

But that was it. The discussions started to become more about who could argue the best, and less about the content of the argument. Sometimes we would argue about the same thing over and over, forgetting our original points. We weren't changing their way of thinking and they weren't changing ours. It was a pissing contest that finally ended for me when I realized what Birdie had said was true. If you felt strongly about your beliefs, you didn't have to argue for them. You just live them, stay open to other people's thinking, but don't slam yours down their throat.

As much as I was evolving in the kitchen, life outside was proving to be more difficult. The biggest problem for me was school. I was already hyper, but all the stimulation I was getting at home was making the other parts of my life appear incredibly boring. I was restless, my hormones were popping up all over the place, girls were looking cuter and cuter. My body was starting to change and I felt like the Incredible Hulk when he went through that thing right before he beat the crap out of everybody. I just wanted to bust out. And I didn't necessarily want to do the right thing. Maybe it was Jerry's influence or maybe it was just that time in my life. I wanted to stir the pot a little, or even a lot, depending on the situation.

And I got that chance in the spring of that wonderful year, while eating lunch in the cafeteria with my buddies. An apple crisp dessert cup went flying by my face. Now the old me would have thought it was funny, maybe whooped and hollered a bit, but ultimately would have let it go and finished my lunch. But the new restless, bored me saw this flying object as an invitation from God to let loose, have a little fun. And that's exactly what I did. I picked up everything that wasn't nailed down and threw it at everybody else who was throwing stuff.

It only lasted a minute or two, but it sure felt good hitting Tiger Johnson in the face with mashed potatoes. With the festivities going full bore, I decided to get out of the lunchroom before everybody else and go out to recess as usual. I went to the bathroom and got the green beans out of my hair and checked for a stray carrot or two. Everything seemed fine until I walked out of the bathroom and headed outside. In the hall, I heard Jerry say *mix in, MIX IN* with an urgency in his tone. This seemed dumb to me because as far as I could see, I wasn't in trouble. Nobody was looking for me, and if anybody was screwed it was the people who started it, not me. When I got outside, little Bobby Delaney, the school busybody, told me that some teachers were looking for the riff-raff that started the food fight, and they were going to look for them behind the hockey rink.

In hindsight, the hockey rink should have been the last place I went but, feeling invincible, I decided to warn whoever was there not to be there. All the time, Jerry was telling me to go back and blend in. Sure enough, when I got to the ice rinks, there were three teachers and Carl the janitor waiting for the supposed trouble-maker and guess who was the only one stupid enough to show.

Suddenly I'm Al Capone. They escort me to the principal's office and announce they got the guy who destroyed the lunchroom over the loud speaker. You could almost hear the collective gasp from the student body as they announced my name. I tried to explain that it wasn't just me, but my unwillingness to name anyone else and my clean appearance said to them I was the lone gunman. I was kicked out of the lunchroom for the rest of my life and had to walk home to have lunch, which was about a mile away.

To make matters worse, every time I walked home for lunch I could hear Jerry saying, *I told you so*. Jerry was not going to let me forget how he tried to help me that day and I wouldn't listen because

I didn't trust him. Trust, as Birdie would say, was part of evolving. Evolving, as I would say, sucked.

But Jerry wasn't always the captain of good. He may have been watching out for me on that occasion, but there were times he liked the idea of me getting into trouble. It was his suggestion I forge my mother's handwriting so I could write a note and get out of school early. And he didn't stop me when I put tacks on my teacher's chair or a fish in the teacher's lounge water cooler. (I saw the principal more than he saw his wife.) Or the time Jerry convinced me to jump out of the third-story window (he insisted I would love the feeling of flight).

It was difficult to distinguish the difference between my thoughts and Jerry's because I did have this need to get into trouble. But Jerry's influence wasn't helping. It was making things worse. With every negative step I took, I could feel Jerry's excitement growing.

Somehow I got through the spring quarter without being expelled and graduated from elementary school. At times it was touch and go, but I did it. And I was feeling good about everything. Summer was coming, our trampoline was up, and in some ways, I was growing up. You wouldn't think so by my actions, but I was making a name for myself. My cousin was super jock, wonder boy, lady-killer, and I was crazy. It felt good to have an identity, such as it was. With school behind me, my confidence growing, and no real consequences for my bad behavior, I just needed one more thing to make for a wild and complete summer: Alcohol.

Seven
Drugs, Sex, and Getting Possessed

"So what's the big deal if you get stoned once in a while? It's not like you're going to get possessed or anything." "Maybe," I replied to the twenty-one-year-old male, "but when you get drunk or stoned and people tell you the next day you didn't seem yourself, who do you suppose you were?"

With all the people coming and going and the overall party atmosphere surrounding the house, it made sense that there would be actual parties. That spring and summer there were. Between my cousin and sisters, we were having parties every night. At my age, I was naturally curious about that sort of thing. I didn't want to miss out on *any* new experiences.

Growing up, drinking wasn't an issue around our house. We just didn't do it. Both of my parents had stopped drinking when I was five, so the closest thing I came to drinking was Catawba juice on New Year's Eve. I wondered about drinking and getting high, but I hadn't had the chance to explore it. Especially with Dad in the house, if I were to experiment and he was to catch me, my life as I knew it would be over. But with him gone and normal life a thing of the past, I figured it would only be a matter of time before I checked it out.

But then there was my mother. Granted, she was less of a threat on a physical level than my father, but the damage she could inflict on a shame and guilt level was much more devastating. I'd rather have her break my leg than me break her heart. So even with my father gone, it was still going to take a miracle for me to get my hands on anything stronger than root beer.

Well, thank God for miracles. Good things come to those who wait, and I had waited long enough. One night my cousin was having a party, and as usual I was eating dinner and trying not to think of all the fun everybody else was having. My mother was doing her usual thing, which was clearing the table, bringing more food, and fussing. It was still light outside, kids were laughing and playing, the robins were starting to sing and you could feel the magic in the air. I would have given anything to be partying with the big boys. Normally at this time I would ask my mother if I could go downstairs and she would give me a dirty look and send me outside for an exciting game of kick ball. But for some reason this night, she said, "Make sure you eat some bread to soak up the alcohol."

I looked at her to make sure she wasn't high, but when she smiled at me I thought, *Hallelujah, there is a God.* I later found out she was speaking to my cousin, who just happened to walk in behind me at that time.

Armed with what I thought was my mother's permission, and eager to learn what *blotto* meant, I parked myself next to the nearest kegger and started drinking. I remember not particularly liking the taste of the beer—I remember actually hating it—but I wasn't there to enjoy myself. I was there to get drunk. And I was going to do so even if I had to hold my nose while I drank it. I drank and drank until my body said enough, which in real time came to about thirty minutes. The next thing I knew I was face down in the toilet.

If projectile vomiting were an Olympic event, I would have brought home the gold. Everything, including my liver, came up. I was amazed at how passionately my body didn't want that beer in me. A passing-by partygoer suggested that since this was probably my first time (he must have been psychic), I should probably reintroduce the alcohol I just threw up so my body could adjust.

This somehow made sense and I promised myself as soon as I stopped barfing that was exactly what I was going to do. I picked myself up from the porcelain altar and wobbled toward the kegger. With the walls tossing me around like a ping-pong ball, I only managed to make it a few yards before one of them threw me face first at the feet of someone wearing black pumps. That someone turned out to be my mother. She had been told that I was a little under the weather and she came looking for me. When she pulled my head up and saw the look on my face, she wasn't that happy to see me. The look on her face almost sobered me up. She told me to get up to my room and stay there. She said she wouldn't deal with me until I was sober and then my ass was hers. She looked so disgusted I didn't dare say a word. She stared at me just long enough to make me feel even more like a worm and then finally walked away. I was relieved.

I started to crawl my way up to my room when I felt two arms pull me up and drag me up the stairs. It was Lance.

"Hey thanks, pal," I said, as if suddenly we were friends.

"Sure," he said somewhat surprised and amused. "But Mae's going to blame me for this, you know."

"Relax," I slurred back. "I got Mom right where I want her."

He looked at me and for a second I thought he might be impressed. Then his face changed and he said, "Yeah. We're all very proud. Now try and be cool until tomorrow." He threw me on my bed, said *stay here*, and shut the door.

I lay on the bed, listening to people laughing and music playing. Because it was still light outside I wanted to get up and make my way back down to the keg, but the bed was spinning so fast it was all I could do to hang on. This drunken feeling gave me a new confidence and strength. I actually called my cousin *pal*. If I even looked at him wrong, he'd whip out the BB gun and give me five seconds to run. But not only was he not mad, he had even smiled at me. This was the beginning of something good. I could feel it. If I could just get past the taste and the need to throw up every time I drank, I'd have it made.

There were a couple hitches to my plans of becoming the world's best drinker and one was the guilt. I felt badly about disappointing my mom and as pissed as she looked, I knew she was hurt. And the prospect of hurting her more seemed wrong. But how could she keep me away from something that felt so good? Another problem was the consequences. I could only imagine the horrors that awaited me when I woke up.

I was still groggy the next morning and pretty sure one of the dogs had thrown up in my mouth while I was sleeping. Nevertheless I forced myself out of bed and hurried to get dressed before everybody woke up. My plan was to sneak to J.J.'s, spend most of the day there, and when I returned tell my mother I was too drunk to remember her telling me to stay in my room. The plan was flawed—mainly the part about me admitting I was drunk—but I wasn't thinking long term. I just wanted to get out of the house before my mother woke up. I crept downstairs and opened the door and just when sweet freedom was about to embrace me, I heard my mother's voice ask me to come to the kitchen. I appreciate the ironies of life so much more at those moments. The birds were singing, the sun was shining, the grass, still fresh from the morning dew, begged to be walked on. If I had just oiled that door two days ago like my mother had asked, I could have slipped out and been halfway to J.J.'s by now. As it was, the window of opportunity passed.

When I walked into the kitchen my mother was sitting at the table with her cigarettes and coffee. She had a determined look on her face, one that I rarely saw. She asked me to sit and judging by her voice, I knew my only hope was to plead insanity and promise to never do it again. She started out the conversation by telling me that she was worried for me. She told me our family had a history of alcoholism and I had a fifty/fifty chance of becoming one myself. She told me she didn't want me to drink any more and if I did and I got into trouble because of my drinking, that she would hold me accountable and she wouldn't bail me out.

She told me how drinking attracted negative spirits and that if I kept drinking I would bring in bad spirits—the kind that wouldn't go away. As she spoke, she seemed to be holding herself back. I could tell part of her wanted to shake me and scream in my face *what the hell do you think you're doing,* but she didn't. She wanted me to hear everything she was saying. So I listened.

She went on to remind me we were under a microscope. People around the neighborhood and school were watching us. Most of them, she said, already thought we were the Devil family. They didn't need to think we were also the alcoholic Devil family. She stopped for a second to gather herself and then told me she loved me. She asked me if I felt okay, and I assured her I did. She suggested I go back to bed, but I told her I was going to J.J.'s. I could almost see the icicles form as she told me I was not going to J.J.'s because I was grounded for a week. One more wrong word from me and it would be a month. I said okay. She got up from the table, grabbed her coffee and cigarettes, and left.

I didn't realize how intense the conversation was until I felt drops of perspiration dripping from underneath my arms. This was not what I expected and harder to process than if she went ballistic on me. I understood what she was doing but it made me feel worse. My mother hadn't gone soft or suddenly become indifferent; she was attempting to evolve. She was trying to apply what she had been learning to our relationship. We had been studying *The Prophet* and one of the things discussed was the chapters on children. Kahlil Gibran, the author, believed that parents were not to force their dogma on their children. "Your children are not your children; they are the sons and daughters of life's longing for itself," he wrote. "You may give them your love, but not your thoughts." My mother seemed to be affected by that and she talked about it often.

What she was telling me was if I was going to act like an adult I was going to be punished as an adult. She was telling me she trusted me to make the right decisions and if I made the wrong decision, I was responsible. What I heard was, *do whatever you want, but don't get caught. Don't make a fool out of yourself or do something stupid just for the sake of doing it.* What I heard was, *I know I can't stop you so be careful.* I could live with that.

Our relationship changed that day. I was no longer clean and shiny. My mother saw in my face the night before how much I loved the feeling of being high. She recognized I was starting to separate myself from her and rather than help push me out faster she opted to stand on the sidelines until it was time to stop me.

We both knew I was going to continue—and I did. Even after our talk and the trust she gave me I couldn't wait to feel that feeling again. It was warm, comfortable, safe, strong—something I hadn't ever felt. But I knew if I was going to drink and get away with it I was going to have to learn how to do it better. My cousin seemed the logical choice as teacher. You could never tell if he was drunk or stoned and he was always one or the other. Plus it seemed like a good bonding tool. We had never connected on other levels, but we were both interested in getting high.

At first I rationalized getting high as a form of celebration—the end of school, the beginning of summer. But after a while just waking up was reason enough to celebrate.

The way I saw it, this was my time. I had paid my dues, I had read all the books, I went to all the camps, I witnessed enough bizarre flying dead people to last a whole lifetime, and not because I wanted to. I had to. I handled the divorce, and I rolled with it all (sort of) and I was almost a teenager. I could drink any twelve-year-old under the table. If I wanted to party, so be it!

I wasn't the only one wanting to celebrate every time we needed to change the light bulbs. Jerry was becoming more and more interested in my drug and alcohol use. At first he acted put off, almost prudish, but as time went on and he saw how much fun I was having, he wanted to join in.

Jerry and I had talked about letting him jump inside me on a few occasions. I always chickened because it seemed like a creepy thing to do. What if he wouldn't let me back in or did something weird when he was in me? And I didn't know what it would feel like to have him inside me. Plus Birdie and Mrs. Olsen told me it was a bad idea. They said letting anybody in your body was just inviting trouble. Who was I to argue with those guys?

But the more I got high, the more determined Jerry became. He started doing the guilt thing on me. He would bring up how he was always there for me and how he had never asked me for anything until then. He told me I didn't trust him and then he'd go on and on about how rotten that was. It was starting to get on my nerves. Although a small part of me was curious to know what it felt like to have him inside me, I wasn't going to do it the way he was asking.

Then one day as I was sucking on the better half of a bottle of Mad Dog 20/20, Jerry showed up with a different pitch. He promised he would only do it once and if I felt strange he would just pop right back out. He apologized for being such a jerk and then asked me one more time.

Maybe it was the wine or the way he asked, or all the things he said to me earlier, but I thought *what the hell, why not get possessed*. I closed my eyes and envisioned Jerry walking into my body and my body allowing it to happen.

I felt a presence inside my body—like being in a small closet and someone joining you. It felt cramped and odd. I could feel Jerry's excitement and I could tell he wanted to take me out for a spin and I remember feeling scared and saying *no*. I closed my eyes and demanded he get out and I saw myself rejecting him. I felt him go and I slumped on the floor. I was numb.

"Geez. I was only in you for a second," he said. "Come on. Let me try it again, this time a little longer."

"Forget it," I said. "That's too fricken weird."

"Oh, you baby. Try being dead," he replied.

I didn't say a word. He was right. I was being a baby. Even drunk it freaked me out. I knew if I let him stay in me longer, he wouldn't have gotten out. I grabbed the wine and drank what was left.

The next few weeks Jerry stayed away, which was fine, because I didn't want to hear it. The parties continued, as did the kitchen discussions. And the difference between the two groups was becoming obvious. Like my mother had warned, the drinking and drugs had brought a darker influence as far as spirits were concerned. The basement, which was my cousin's room, had a particularly strange feeling to it. When you were downstairs you felt like getting high, you felt wild. It was a party room. Everybody easily saw ghosts and nobody cared. Every dead alcoholic or junkie within a fifty-mile radius hung out in the basement.

On the other end of the spectrum was the kitchen. It was quiet, more sacred. People went there to study, expand, grow. It was better to be there but harder. I found myself drawn to the fun and excitement of the basement. The two worlds didn't meet. Like oil and vinegar, they were cosmically unable to mix. As far as I saw it, I benefited from both.

The one drawback to my summer of fun was that none of my friends drank or got high. I told J.J., but he wasn't much interested. I was afraid to tell anybody else I hung out with, because they already thought I was strange. People were noticing there was something different about me, but with most of us going through puberty, who wasn't acting strange? Privately I was noticing myself saying things that I wouldn't normally say. I would speak my mind more and feel comfortable doing it. I remember in fifth grade one of the popular kids and I were laughing about something and he looked at me and said, *ya know, Bodine, if you weren't so dumb you'd be a fun guy.*

I smiled and took it as a compliment because that's the way I felt. I didn't like myself much. But that was changing and I started liking myself for knowing the things I knew and the things I was willing to try. Plus even my cousin was thinking I was cool.

The fall of 1971, I turned thirteen, and life for me couldn't have been better. I was excited about starting the seventh grade, because it was a bigger school with all new people. A guy could get lost in a junior high. It was a chance for me to start over and with my new sense of self-confidence and desire for adventure, I figured I couldn't lose.

About a month before we started junior high, J.J. and I went to a little circus by our new junior high school. This was exciting for us because this wasn't our regular turf. We had heard of this guy named Bill Baitmen for a couple years. He was supposed to be the big dog, the star athlete, and the guy who started shaving when he was in fifth grade. A kid who transferred from another elementary school had told us about him. He was supposed to be really tough. The rumor was he had gotten into a fight with some ninth grader, and won.

As we were walking around the circus, we saw a bunch of people playing in the moonwalk and decided that was the place to be. While we were bouncing all over the place, Jerry showed up and told me to go over to where this guy was bouncing with his buddies and start giving them crap—not in a mean way but in a fun way, like a normal adolescent kid would do. I wasn't sure if Jerry was setting me up or not, but because of our troubles earlier in the summer we were both trying to be nice to each other. I motioned to J.J. to come with me and we both went over. I started giving these guys crap. J.J. soon followed my lead (between the two of us we could dish out a lot of crap). They returned the insults as most boys will do, and soon we were being friendly.

In the course of our bonding ritual, they asked us what school we went to. We told them Cornelia, but we were going to Southview in the fall. They said they were also starting at Southview, but had gone to Concord.

"Did you say Cornelia?" one of them asked.

"Yeah, why?" I said.

"Isn't that the school that witch kid goes to?" he said.

J.J. looked at me. "What do you mean witch kid?" J.J. said.

Then the leader of the group said, "We heard there was a kid who went to Cornelia whose family is a bunch of witches. His name is something like Bowdin or bindene?"

I looked at J.J. "Oh, you mean Mike Bodine?" I said. "Oh yeah. J.J. knows him."

By this time everybody had stopped bouncing and the guy who ran the thing kicked us out for the next batch. As we were walking out, they brought it up again and asked J.J. if he really knew this guy, Mike Bodine. J.J. looked at me with a half smile and said, "Yeah, I know him. Pretty scary guy. I've even been to his house, seen stuff happen there that would turn your hair white."

The leader jumped in. "Bullshit. It's all a bunch of lies. People just make that crap up!"

I didn't say a thing. I was ready to change the subject but J.J. wasn't ready to let it go. "No, I'm not kidding," J.J. said. "I had to deliver a paper there one time and when I got there, the door opened by itself." (That was true, but the spirits always did that to J.J.)

The guys stood there, not sure what to say. J.J. was loving it.

I decided to change the subject. "Say, any of you guys heard of Bill Baitmen?" I asked.

They looked at the leader guy like we're a couple of idiots and said, "Yeah, why?"

"I just heard some stuff about him and wanted to know if it was true," I said.

"Like what?" they asked.

"Well we heard he was this tough guy who beat up some ninth grader and started shaving when he was five," I said. "Probably a bunch of crap. You know how rumors start."

They smiled. "Yeah, rumors are weird," one of them said.

Finally it was time to go. "Hey you never finished telling us about that witch kid," one of them said as we were leaving.

"Maybe some other time," J.J. yelled back. "By the way, what's your names?"

As cocky as they could, they yelled back, "I'm Coleman. This is Burgy. And this (pointing to the leader) is Baitmen."

Without missing a beat, J.J. answered back. "Oh, well I'm J.J. and this is Mike Bodine, the witch kid."

Their eyes widened and their mouths opened, all except Bill's. He looked impressed with our deception. I could tell by the smirk on his face that we were going to be friends.

In the weeks that followed, Bill and I did become friends. I spent a lot of time at his house, mainly because he wasn't sure about coming to mine. Even though he said he didn't believe all the stories, I sensed that he was uncomfortable with the whole subject. Bill was a meat-and-potatoes kind of guy. His father had died when he was young so his mother and sister raised him. He was afraid of being considered a mamma's boy so he became a man at age nine. Anything to do with intuition or spirituality could be considered *feminine* and Bill wanted none of that. Plus, if it was true and there were ghosts flying all over the place, it might scare the hell out of him and he definitely didn't want that—not with his major reputation.

I liked Bill. He was cool. He carried himself with a lot of confidence and people treated him differently than they would a normal guy. Birdie once told me that we were attracted to people because there were things about them we wanted. That was true with Bill. I wanted his confidence. He just knew he was important and he didn't care what other people thought.

It took awhile, but eventually he got up the nerve and started coming to the house. Once he did, like everybody else, he didn't want to leave. Our house was an adolescent Disneyland. We had the trampoline, the parties, the floating psychics. We had the bands (my cousin pursued his drumming and had become so good, bands would come over and jam with him). We had the drinking, and the girls (mostly my sisters' friends), and we had the basement.

The basement was where everybody hung out. It was huge, and divided into three sections. The bedroom had three king-sized beds, a huge stereo, and the wall was painted with this big Martian landscape. The ceiling was painted black with fluorescent stars and planets. Then there was the sitting room with huge hash pipes and chairs we had taken from a haunted house (you could literally see spirits sitting in the chairs). There was the band section where bands from all over would come to jam with my cousin.

The centerpiece of the basement was a thing called *the box*. My cousin had a wild imagination and one day after a dream he had made this box about five feet long surrounded by five speakers. You could crawl inside, where it was lined with carpeting and pillows. You could shut the door and crank up the music. It had just enough room for two if you took your clothes off, and he had built it about five feet off the ground and into the wall so when you shut the door you couldn't see it from the outside. It was the perfect make-out room, or it was great if you just wanted to be alone.

Bill's friends started coming over, and soon the place was filled with people my age who thought my house and I were cool. Maybe they just thought my house was cool. Either way, I was set because I was about to start junior high school and I was already established in the upper pecking order. For a thirteen-year-old, it was hard to think of anything being more important. Life was good.

Junior high started out calmly for me. Being in a bigger school was just what the doctor ordered. There were so many people running around, so many distractions. Rarely, if ever, did I run into people

I knew from my old school. But a month into the program, things heated up. I had let my hair grow during the summer and for some reason, that seemed to piss some people off—namely the older jocks who thought long hair meant you were gay.

For me, football was everything. It was the one constant in my life and I loved it. I loved the smells, the sounds, the emotions, and I loved that it had nothing to do with ghosts, psychics, or haunted houses. When I was playing or practicing football, that life didn't exist for me—it was a million miles away.

I made first string my first year and some of the older brutes had a problem with that, especially with my hair flowing out the back of my helmet. I liked that it bothered some guys. The ones with the lower IQs would be stumbling over themselves just to nail me, but knowing their weakness, I would just move. If the coach had asked me to cut my hair I would have. I loved playing that much. But he never said a word. He was probably worried I'd go off the deep end the way I went around smashing people. Because of the way I played, some people referred to me as a crazy freak. No matter what I did, I always had a label.

I didn't help matters with my mouth. The way I could spread the crap you'd think I was running for office. But I didn't feel I had a choice. In junior high school, if you showed any weakness, you were screwed. I'm sure it had a lot to do with the alcohol and the parties happening at the house. But between being labeled the witch kid and the crazy freak, I needed a publicist to hold my reputation together.

I got along with just about everybody. I liked the nerds because they were odd and sensitive. I liked some of the jocks because they were talented and under a lot of pressure to succeed. I liked some of the popular kids; even though most of them tried so hard to be perfect—some of them were really good people. And I liked the freaks because like me, they were lost.

In junior high, it feels like you're going over the rapids and it's all you can do to hang on and not fall off. I saw some people have a hard time adjusting and it was difficult deciding to let go of your paddle to help someone else. I couldn't see the advantage to alienating any one group. You never knew when you might need support. There was one person, however, I was told to stay away from even before I started school—his name was Bucky McClung.

The guy that Bill had gotten in that fight with was Bucky. Only thing was, Bill didn't win. He hit Bucky with everything he had and when Bucky stood there with a smile on his face, like now it's my turn, Bill managed to run to his house before Bucky caught up to him. I guess you could call it a moral victory. He was the only guy Bill was afraid of. The whole school was afraid of Bucky McClung. Bill didn't describe Bucky as a bully, he just loved fighting like I loved football.

Nobody fucked with Bucky and if you stayed out of his way he wouldn't screw with you—usually. Everybody knew of him and the stories passed on about his antics grew with each person. Some said he killed a guy in the school next to ours and the only reason he wasn't caught was because he chopped up the body and fed it to his dog. Some said he almost killed his father. Some even said if you looked at him, like Medusa, you'd turn to stone.

He was two years older than me, so running into him in class wasn't a possibility, and socially we ran in different circles. I had Bill and J.J.; he had the people you see on the walls of the post office. The only way I figured I would see him was in the halls.

But whenever I did see him in the halls and people whispered *that's Bucky McClung*, there was something about him—not his face, just his presence. He had a definite charisma to him, like a celebrity, but unlike his dark reputation, in person, he was always smiling, always talking.

It hit me that maybe people were making him out to be something that he wasn't, like with me. I wasn't a witch, freakazoid kid. I was a normal hyperactive spaz like everybody else at school. And if people could be wrong about me, maybe they could be wrong about Bucky.

And really how can a guy named Bucky be so tough, especially the way he smiles and laughs all the time? This is the question I would ask every time someone would say how tough he was.

I should have known better than to openly question his reputation. You tell one kid you like raspberries, within a week it comes back you're a communist. But I honestly wasn't believing this guy was the antichrist everybody was saying he was. Too bad they didn't have a class in being wrong. I would have aced it. Not long after I made my little comments about Bucky, a friend came up to me and told me not to go out the back door after school because Bucky was waiting for me. I asked my friend why he was waiting for me.

"Because you called him a fag," he said.

"Hey, I didn't call him a fag," I said.

"Yes, you did," my friend said. "I even heard you say he was a pussy because his name is Bucky."

I looked at my friend like he was crazy. "Why would I say Bucky McClung was a pussy?" I asked.

"Hey, you're the crazy one, not me," he replied and I realized I was screwed. If my friend thought I said those things, then God knows what Bucky must have thought. It also occurred to me that that was why people had been pointing at me and whispering to their friends all week long. I thought maybe I'd spilled something on my shirt and that was the reason for the stares and the pointing. But they weren't pointing at a stain, they were pointing at a nimrod who was about to get his ass kicked.

I told my friend thanks for the warning, even though I suspected by his conversation that he might have been one of the people spreading stuff about what I said, and I went through my options. Catching the bus wasn't possible because I'd heard the last one pull out while my friend gave me the bad news. Even with the heightened adrenalin I couldn't run home because, unlike Bill, I lived two miles from school.

It was too late to move, or call in sick, and probably too late to work on a better relationship with God.

If I had a choice between being a man and getting my ass kicked or losing my pride and running away, give me some Keds and a ten-second head start and I'm yesterday's news. But for some reason, I found myself walking toward the back door. Even as I was walking, I was amazed at my feet and the direction they were going. I kept telling myself to stop and run the other way, but I just kept on going.

I turned a corner and headed toward the steps leading outside to certain death. I felt like I was out of my body and the only thing running through my head was the whistling tune from "Bridge On the River Kwai."

But then I heard a familiar voice. "Dead man walking," it said, and a smile came on my face.

"Jerry," I said. "Where the hell have you've been?"

He talked fast—he told me not to worry that he would be with me. He said he had some information that would help me, but in the meantime I should trust that everything was going to work out and then he left.

It's not that I didn't totally believe Jerry. I wanted to believe Jerry, but he wasn't always that helpful, and a part of me wondered—if I did die at the hands of Bucky, it would probably work out better for him because we'd have more time to play.

I decided to rethink my options for a second. I stopped walking and leaned against a locker. At home, one of the things the kitchen crew was tossing around was a thing called *positive visualization*. The theory was, you visualize something coming in your life—like a job opportunity or a relationship—and eventually it's supposed to happen. If it doesn't happen right away, just the process of believing is supposed to make you feel better.

Not having a lot of choices, I decided to give it a shot. With the sense of urgency surrounding this, I figured the gods might speed up my order. I closed my eyes and in my mind's eye I imagined everything being okay. I saw myself walking out, seeing Bucky, and Bucky calmly asking me if there was a misunderstanding. I saw myself explaining to Bucky it was all a big mistake, and going our separate ways.

As I was running this fantasy through my head, I slowly got the sense it was going to be okay. I started walking again and with every step that feeling got stronger. If I was going to die at least I would die wearing rose-colored glasses.

Jerry showed up again, only this time he seemed excited, like he had a surprise for me. He even thanked me for trusting him, which could only mean I was in trouble. I asked him what made him think I did trust him, but he was too focused to play.

He told me he had someone with him in spirit who knew Bucky—Bucky's Uncle Harry. Bucky and his uncle had been close when Harry was alive, so close that, when Harry died, part of Bucky died with him. Bucky became cold and lost, and that bothered Harry. Harry wanted to tell Bucky (whose real name was Marc) not to give up, that Harry was around him all the time.

I stopped for a second and gave it some thought. As touching as all this sounded, if Jerry was making this up, Bucky was going to chop me up in such small pieces his gerbil could eat me.

When I finally made it outside, I was surprised at the crowd that had gathered to watch the carnage. They looked at me with a mixture of curiosity, apathy, and excitement. It was clear nobody was going to step in and save my skinny butt. Then I saw Bucky, but unlike in my visualization, he wasn't smiling. And this time I wasn't in the audience, I was center stage.

Looking at Bucky through the eyes of one of his prey gave me a different perspective on him. Bucky was huge—not physically, but in his presence. He had taken off his jean jacket and was wearing only a T-shirt and jeans. At six feet, 175 pounds, he was lean and muscular. Even through his white T-shirt, I could see the muscle bands in his shoulder expand at his slightest movement.

His facial features alone were intimidating—steel-blue eyes, thick blonde, slightly long hair, a sculptured face, handsome but hard. He stood with his legs apart, his arms to his side, and his head slightly cocked. He was neither swayed nor influenced by the crowd. It was like he was alone. He was a professional and I was dead.

If there was an upside to all this drama, it was the rushes I was going through. I was both terrified and excited—terrified because I knew he could do some serious damage to me. I got visuals of walking away all bloody, with my teeth falling out and my testicles dangling from my broken nose. I was excited because there was a slim possibility I might walk away from this intact, and if that happened, I'd be a legend.

When Bucky saw me he smirked, like he was glad I showed up and then started walking toward me. As he did I heard Jerry yell at me *don't look down* and I found myself straightening up. Bucky asked me if I was the guy who called him a fag. Instead of answering him, I asked him very sincerely how in the world he got a name like *Bucky*. I remembered Jerry telling me his real name was Marc so I truly wanted to know. But the question excited Bucky, as well as some people in the crowd.

Normally, Bucky had a little foreplay before he devoured his victims, but this gave him permission to bypass all that.

"Bucky, huh?" I continued. "I bet it was your uncle's idea to give you that name."

Bucky stopped coming at me.

"What was his name? Terry? Larry? Harry. That's it. Harry. Did he give you that name? I bet he did. He seemed like a nice guy, that Uncle Harry."

Nobody but Bucky knew what I was talking about, and suddenly he looked very small to me. The flare in his eyes disappeared and I knew I had him.

He looked at me and in his deep voice said, "Hey, you're the kid who talks to ghosts."

I paused and looked cockeyed at his mouth. "Could I just look at your teeth?" I said. Then I walked up to him. "Your uncle wants me to tell you he's with you all the time," I whispered into his ear. Then I backed away.

He stared at me with curiosity for what seemed like an hour and then smiled. I could feel the tension fade. So could the people watching. They were genuinely disappointed.

Bucky came up to me and put his arm around my neck. I could feel how solid his forearm muscles were by the way he was cutting off my oxygen supply. He said he wanted to talk to me some more and then smiled and walked away.

Later, as we were becoming friends, I asked him why he didn't just start beating me up when he first saw me. He said he was curious because I didn't look down.

I asked what difference that made and he said, "When you look down that means you're afraid, and if you're afraid, you're weak."

He said he was curious why I wasn't afraid. Then he said that when I started talking about his Uncle Harry he figured it would be bad luck to hit me. I could hear Jerry in the background screaming *yeah, you're welcome.*

I was taught that people come into your life for a reason, that no one was unimportant. J.J., for instance, was my best friend. I shared my dreams, my hopes, my fears—everything—with J.J. He was the first guy I called whenever I wanted to do something, and I trusted him with my deepest secrets. J.J. even saved my life.

We were riding our bikes all day in 100-degree weather and 200 percent humidity. I hadn't eaten yet, so we stopped at my father's office to get some money and then we were going to get food. I went into my father's office and suddenly I started seeing all these colors. The walls start melting and then everything went dark and I passed out. I started going into convulsions. My dad wasn't sure what to do, so he brought me to the bathroom and tried to cool me down. Meanwhile, J.J. ran three blocks to a shopping mall, flagged a cop, and they took me to the hospital before I died. When I woke up a few hours later, the doctor told me if I had arrived at the hospital five minutes later, I would have died.

Then there were people like Bill. Even though I'd only known Bill a short time, he had already elevated my social status to the point where people came to me for friendship, as opposed to me having to go to them. In turn, I introduced Bill to drugs and alcohol, so our relationship was mutually beneficial.

There were people like Tom who taught me how to hold a hockey stick, and Johnny, Kate, Patti, Bobby, Mary Jo. All these people and more had a big impact on my life. But I have to say that no one had the impact on me emotionally, physically, spiritually, and socially that Bucky did—especially given the short time we spent together.

The day after we had our little chat, Bucky came up to me and told me he wanted to come to my house after school. He told me he wanted to continue our conversation about his uncle.

Bucky wasn't the kind of guy you say no to, but figuring we all need to brush up on our manners, I said *sure, you can come over—if you say please.* The guy next to me who was getting something from his locker suddenly stopped what he was doing and looked at me like I was about to die.

Bucky stared at me for a second, and then smiled.

"I like you, Bodine. I'll see you after school," he said. Then he turned around and started walking away.

"Wait," I said. "You don't know where I live."

Without looking around, he said, "Everybody knows where you live." He kept on walking. I wasn't sure if I should be flattered or paranoid.

I started feeling nervous about Bucky's upcoming visit. As odd as the atmosphere around the house was, it was still my house. Sure it made Amityville Horror look like Queen Ann Kiddy Land, but I grew up there. It was where I lost my first tooth, where I got my first kiss, where I learned to walk. The first time I got possessed happened while I was living in that house. It was home, and I felt protective of it.

The thought of bringing killer Bucky home was unsettling. I knew it was stupid to feel that way. After all, the place had so much riff-raff living there the police had listed it as a *hot house* (actually it was more like a *Hell house*). But still, for some reason, I was uncomfortable with the whole thing.

Maybe it didn't have anything to do with the house. Maybe it was me; maybe I was afraid to bring Bucky into my life. He was the Don Corleone of my school and maybe too much for me to handle. But I had to admit I liked him. I saw something in him the first time I met him, a certain vulnerability that made him human. He had flair, strength, but also an unpredictable side to him. I think that was what was unsettling to me, that part of him that could go off at any time. I think I was afraid that all the weird stuff going on at home would somehow make him lose it and if he did lose it, my life would be hell at school. Whatever I thought didn't matter anyway, because he was coming over whether I liked it or not. Like everything else I had to deal with it.

When Bucky got to my house, as usual I was jumping on the tramp with some people from the neighborhood. He brought some buddies of his with him, and one of the guys he brought was a guy named Mark Warner. This guy scared me almost as much as Bucky. The first time I met Mark Warner, I was at a freshman dance at this big church.

I was waiting for J.J. outside of the church when J.J. came running up to me, out of breath and scared to death. About thirty feet behind him were three guys, chasing after him. As soon as he got to the church they stopped, knowing a teacher or an adult of some kind would be inside.

"You little #@*%*#&, you're dead! You got to come out of there sometime and when you do, we're gonna kill you," they yelled at J.J. From what I could tell they were pissed—especially the leader, Mark Warner. He had a hard look to him. His eyes were wild and intense, and his smile was more of a psychotic stare. He had dark brown hair, a jean jacket with a black T-shirt, and black jeans. He was lean, mean, and by the way he was acting, crazy,

I asked J.J. what he did to piss these guys off, and J.J. said he had no idea. He said he was just walking to the dance and these guys started chasing after him. He said he started running because he got scared. He kept screaming *what did I do, what did I do, what did I do* as he was running, but they just kept coming after him.

Now, J.J. had a tendency to be a smart-ass. He was, after all, my best friend, and that stuff is bound to rub off. But he wasn't stupid—he wouldn't start something with a group of guys unless they knew he was kidding or they were two feet shorter than he was. The last thing he would do would be to give these guys crap—especially being alone and especially wearing that flowered shirt. So I believed him when he said he didn't know why they were so mad.

I decided to see if I could ease the tension a little, or at least ask them why they were so mad. I went outside and into the parking lot where they were. As soon as they saw me, they started coming after me like bees. They were running at me and saying stuff like, *oh you want some too, you little @%&*%$!#*. I barely made it back to the steps before they caught me. For some reason these guys were pissed and they weren't the kind of guys you negotiated with.

I remember feeling totally afraid. Someone I didn't know was going to beat me up for no reason, and there wasn't a thing I could do about it. I couldn't go tell a teacher; this was the big league. You might as well stick a pacifier in my mouth and make me wear a diaper. I'd be called the biggest baby in school and they'd still beat me up, only later and with good reason.

My friends weren't any help. They all stayed away from J.J. and me like we were condemned men. Even Bill came up to me and said *I heard Mark Warner's going to beat the crap out of you and J.J. Man, I wouldn't want to be in your shoes,* and then he just disappeared. And Bill was supposed to be the tough guy.

I was thirteen. This was my first mixer. Inside there was music and dancing and girls, and outside there was pain, humiliation, and death.

Jerry eventually showed up and I'd never been so happy to see a ghost in my life. I asked him what he would do if he was in my position and he said he would throw up. Then I asked him again, this time with a little more urgency in my voice.

He didn't say anything for a second and then he brought up Birdie. "Didn't Birdie tell Roy to surround the people he was angry at with white light? Maybe you could try something like that with these guys," he said.

I reminded Jerry I wasn't angry with these guys, I was terrified of them and they were pissed at me. Was he suggesting I go out to them and ask them to surround me with white light so they wouldn't be angry at me? What, was he nuts?

"I came here to help you out and all you do is give me crap. Go ahead and get yourself beat up. It won't hurt me a bit," he said. Then he left.

I knew what he was talking about. I was supposed to surround these guys with white light and I'd be fine. The only problem was, it was a stupid idea. These guys wouldn't respond to white light. Hookers and guns maybe, but not white light.

My options were limited. I didn't have a lot to lose so I thought what the hell, I might as well try it. I closed my eyes and as best as I could I visualized Mark and the boys under this white light—like a flashlight. As I was doing this, Jerry came back and interrupted me.

"Don't forget the unconditional love," he said. (He meant you have to fill your heart with unconditional love toward the person you're covering with the white light.)

Now this part can be trickier, especially if the people you're thinking about hate you unconditionally. What you have to do is think of a person you love, or a thing you love, and transfer those feelings to the people you're dealing with. This is supposed to calm you and the other people down and help defuse any tense situations.

As I was doing this, J.J. came running up to me and told me his dad was there to pick us up and so we were saved. I was extremely relieved, but also a little disappointed; I wanted to see if my white light experiment worked.

That was the last time I saw Mark Warner until there he was, in my back yard. For a second, I thought maybe all this stuff with Bucky was a trap, an elaborate scheme these guys cooked up to get me alone so they could beat the hell out of me. My fears were somewhat tempered when I saw a smile on Mark Warner's face. He extended his hand to shake mine and said *how you doing, man.*

A little nervously I said *fine* and then he asked me if he could jump on the trampoline. Not expecting that question, I excitedly said *sure, go ahead.*

He was still mean looking, but he didn't feel mean. He seemed pretty nice. From that point on we started to become friends. And he turned out to be one of the most honest, sensitive, caring guys I had ever met—somebody you'd do anything for. It's weird how life is. This guy could have terrorized me for years, but because of my association with Bucky, we were suddenly friends. I was even more convinced I had some sort of light around me, and my confidence grew.

Mark Warner and I never talked about that first night and I'm not convinced the white light thing had any effect on our relationship. He could have forgotten who I was, or now that I was Bucky's friend, maybe he had decided that I wasn't such a dweeb after all. I don't know. I do know his attitude was like night and day from that first night I saw him and the second time I saw him.

Don't get me wrong. He didn't turn into a saint. You still did not want to be on the wrong side of this guy. I saw him go after guys with the same intensity as Grant took Richmond. But with me, he was great. Maybe there was more than I thought to this *power of love* theory Birdie and Mrs. Olsen shoved down our throats.

Bucky was a different story. You could surround him with all the white light and love you could find and he'd probably punch you for making him squint. He was a lot like my father in that he was physically and mentally stronger than most people, and for both of them, control was the only way to go. Vulnerability was a tool, used only as a last resort for getting their way—say for instance getting a woman to sleep with them. Bucky, however, had a chance to be different than my father.

When he showed up with his pals, he was eager to finish our talk. He suggested that while his friends were on the trampoline, we could go inside and talk. I had no problem with that. As usual, people were all over the place—Nikki's friends, Lance's friends, some of the kitchen crew—and almost all of them looked a little spooky.

When we walked in the back door, Bucky had a look on his face that suggested he knew he was about to see a freak show. To make matters worse, as we came in we ran into one of my cousin's friends who was living with us. His name may have been Keith, but there was no mistaking—this guy was the antichrist.

Keith was about six-foot-six, had a beard and mustache, and was probably one of the most unstable people you could meet. He also had somewhat the same reputation as Bucky did when he was in school—except Keith's was worse.

Keith turned to me, looked out the window, and said, "Hey asshole, do you know those guys?" Then he pointed through the window and out toward where Mark and his buddy were jumping on the tramp. "Because if you don't I'll just ask the rebels without a clue to leave," he continued.

What he meant was that he just wanted to go outside and kick the boys around.

Normally Keith wouldn't even have asked. He would have just blown past me and run outside like a greyhound after a rabbit. But he was already in Dutch with my mom, and he couldn't afford to get into any more trouble (something about a shoplifting charge).

"Yeah, I know them," I said. "We were in the Cub Scouts together and after they get done jumping on the tramp, we're going on our first cookie drive."

Keith looked at me like he just ate cold milk toast, grabbed his crotch, and said, "Yeah? Well I got your merit badge right here."

Bucky liked that. He started to smile, which meant he got Keith's attention. Keith made eye contact with him and said, "Oh, Mikey, I'm sorry. You brought home a friend. How nice. Will you be conducting experiments with his soul, or is this a personal call?"

"Okay Keith, you can beat up my friends. But when my mom finds out—and she will find out—I get your car," I said, just wanting to get out of the conversation. I grabbed Bucky and we proceeded upstairs, leaving Keith standing there considering the possibilities.

"Do you know who the hell that was?" Bucky said.

"Yeah, that's Keith," I said. "He's actually a pretty good guy, if you throw him a raw steak from time to time."

"Maybe to you he's nice," Bucky said, "but that's Keith Schwartz. I've heard stories about that guy for three years."

I was surprised at Bucky's admiration. He wasn't the type.

"Well they're all probably true," I said. "But don't worry about your friends. I'm pretty sure he won't beat them up. We can talk in here," I said, pointing to a door that was shut. We walked in and sat down.

This was the den, the room where my cousin first saw that ghost so many years ago. It was where we showed all our family slides and where my father kept his gun collection. It was a comfortable looking room. Books and paintings lined the walls, an overstuffed couch with pillows all over the place took up most of the space, and the colors were soft green and blue.

However, as comfortable as it looked, the room felt uncomfortable to me—probably because I attributed it to the origin of all this ghost stuff. Even though most of the activity had switched to other parts of the house and hardly anything ever happened in this room anymore, it still gave me the creeps.

It must have given Bucky the creeps as well, because when we went in the room he put his arms around himself and shivered. "Weird. It's cold in this room, man," he said, checking out the place. "You gotta have a ghost in here."

Maybe he was hoping I would put to rest all those rumors he'd heard about us by saying *no, of course we don't have ghosts*. But when I looked at him and as serious as a heart attack said, *yeah, we do*, it only agitated him. I don't think he wanted to go there.

We started talking. He asked how I knew about his uncle. I told him about Jerry and what he had said to me. He looked at me like I was a little off.

"You have a spirit friend named Jerry, and he told you about my uncle?" he said.

"Yes, I do. Would you like to see a picture of him?" I said sarcastically.

Trying to show interest, Bucky said *yes* and we went upstairs to my bedroom. On the way up, we could hear Bucky's friends screaming their heads off in the back yard. Keith had decided to have some fun with them after all. Bucky was worried about his friends. He was the leader and as the leader, he was the protector. He said he wanted to go outside to check on them but I told him not to bother, that I thought they were just having fun with Keith.

Bucky didn't seem convinced, but came upstairs with me anyway. We got up to my room and when I showed him the picture of Jerry he seemed to forget his concerns about his friends. He was immediately drawn to the picture.

"Man, this thing looks so real," he said.

"Who's the jerk calling me a *thing*?" I could hear Jerry say. For the first time the thought crossed my mind that maybe it wasn't such a good idea to introduce these two powder kegs to each other.

As Bucky was holding the picture and talking about how real it looked, his eyes suddenly got wide and he threw the picture on the bed.

"The fucking eyes moved. Did you see that? The fucking eyes moved," he said, half-scared, half-pissed.

Well I didn't see it, but I didn't have to. I believed him.

Anytime Jerry didn't like someone or he was bored, he'd move his eyes in the picture. It was something he learned a long time ago and we used to have fun with it, but this wasn't fun. This was starting to turn out like I was afraid it was going to turn out. I could tell Jerry didn't like Bucky, and any minute I thought Bucky was going to freak out. I looked at Bucky.

"Yeah, he does that sometimes," I said, as calmly as I could. "But don't let it bother you. He's just bored."

Bucky wasn't calmed. "Bored? You got a bored dead guy as a friend who can make his eyes move on a picture? That's pretty creepy," he said, like I was out of my mind.

"You think that's bad, you should see what happens when he sneezes," I said, thinking levity might help.

It did. Bucky studied my face for a second. "So, I finally met someone who likes to play with people as much as I do," he said. "That's good." He smiled and stared at me for another second or two.

The screaming of Bucky's friends in the back yard interrupted us. He said he thought he better go check it out. Judging by their pitch, I agreed. On the way downstairs we ran into my mom. I introduced Bucky to her.

"Nice to meet you, dear," she said. "Will you be staying for a while?"

"Ma, he just came by to say hi," I said, giving her the *please don't embarrass me* look.

She didn't bite. "No," she said. "I'm pretty sure you're going to be staying with us."

She looked at Bucky for a second and then turned her attention back to me. "Anyway I have to talk to you about something, Michael, so come and get me when you get a chance. Nice to meet you, Marc." And with that, she left.

"How'd she know my real name?" Bucky asked. I told him it was probably a wild guess, but he didn't believe me.

When we got back outside, sure enough Keith had tied up both of Bucky's friends, and was bouncing them all over the tramp. Bucky normally would have gotten pissed and retaliated but with all that had just happened—the room, the picture, my mom—I think he just wanted to get out of there and think on it for a while. So, he politely asked Keith if he would untie them because they had to go. As embarrassed as I felt for the way Keith treated those guys, I also felt it was payback for what they did to J.J.

Keith, who was great at being a asshole, turned to me. "Naw, I gotta go too. But thanks for playing with me, boys," he said. Then he bounced them one last time as high as he could. He jumped off the tramp, leaving both of them bouncing out of control all over the place and nearly off the tramp and, since they couldn't move their feet or hands, all they could do was scream. He looked at Bucky. "They do have a good set of lungs," he said. Then he went inside.

Bucky didn't know what to think. The whole experience seemed too much for him. He went over to his friends and asked them if they were all right as he was untying them. I tried to calm them down, but they didn't want me to touch them. What remaining pride they had left had to be saved.

I started explaining that Keith was only kidding, and he was probably feeling really bad about it right this minute, but that only made them want to hurt me. They started to complain about how weird it was around the house when Roy came out the door, all six-feet-eight of him and a voice like God, and told me my mom was looking for me, and I needed to send my friends home because we had to talk.

They looked at each other and decided it was time to go. They started to leave, when Bucky turned around and came back over to me. "I'll see you tomorrow," he said, looking at me with expectation in his eyes.

I said okay. He looked at me for a second, then walked away, and went back to being the hard ass I met at school. "Hey boys, let's go steal a car," he said as he walked out of the yard. They started yelling *shot gun*, then they left.

I stood there for a second, thinking about Bucky and how there was something about the guy that I really liked. Then my mom came out.

"Oh, there you are, honey," she said. "Come up to the kitchen. We have to talk to you."

She asked me if my friends had left and I said *yes*. I followed her into the house and upstairs to the kitchen. I asked her how she knew Bucky's real name and she said I told her. We both knew that wasn't true, but it was easier for my mother to pooh-pooh her abilities than to face the fact that she was so right on. It freaked her out.

Eight
The Black Door Room

"A lot of people are afraid of the dark, sometimes for the same reason they're afraid of death, the whole unknown thing," I said. "But it's the same room with the lights on as it is with the lights off, only darker." "I'm not afraid of death, Dad," my seven-year-old son replied. "But in the dark you got your ghouls and monsters and weird things under your bed that crawl up and choke you." "Oh, that's not true," I said, trying to be funny. "They don't choke you, they suck your brains out." We looked at each other and I got up. "So, all the lights this time?" "Yup," he said as he rolled over. "And don't forget the hall light."

We went to the kitchen and, as usual, everybody was there. They seemed excited, which made me nervous. As I sat down and looked around the room, the feeling I got from their expressions was I was about to be told something I didn't want to hear. I was right. My mother looked at me with an understanding teacher look and asked me to have an open mind. At that point I should have hit the door running, but I stayed. She told me there was a haunted house a little ways away and my cousin and a friend of his were going with her to check

147

it out. They wanted me to go with them. She said a girl had supposedly been murdered there and her spirit was active.

I looked around the room, thinking there had to be a catch. If I wasn't mistaken we were sitting in a haunted house. The place was lousy with ghosts and some of them were pretty darn active. Why go to someone else's house to see a dead person if there was a party of five hanging out in the basement? Plus and more importantly, why was I even being asked? I hated ghosts, everybody knew I hated ghosts, and since I didn't like ghosts at my house, why would I like them at somebody else's?

I brought these questions up to the group, hoping they'd get this crazy idea out of their heads. I also felt that if they were going to control my life they should at least be aware of my reservations. But they didn't care. They (the group as a whole) felt I needed to learn how to deal with spirits and my fear of them. They felt I was at an age when it was time and they weren't going to buy into my fears.

There were a couple of flaws in that theory. If they wanted to talk to dead people, make things move, and have people speak through them—that was fine. But it wasn't for me. I was a normal kid in an odd house. Yes, I had become more comfortable with the psychic stuff. Some of it was interesting and I was getting used to seeing dead people in the basement. But I wasn't going to make this psychic jazz my career. And if I wasn't going to make this my career, why would I need to *deal* with my very normal fear.

And if this was a manhood issue and they felt I needed one of those rites-of-passage deals, then just get me a hooker and a six-pack and we could get on with life. But bringing me to a haunted house to talk to a dead girl wasn't going to make me any more—or less—a man.

When I shared these feelings with the group, Roy barked in and said it didn't have anything to do with being a man. He suggested that I had a long way to go before that would happen. (Roy didn't like me much.) I countered by again asking them why it was so important for me to go. Birdie chirped in and told me to relax. She said I wasn't getting the point of all of this, and I needed to listen. This meant a lecture.

She started by asking me if I was really afraid of spirit. This was a loaded question and she knew it. If I said no, I was a liar. If I said yes, I was a wimp. My nervousness dictated levity, so I told her I wasn't afraid of spirit, but Nonette scared the hell out of me. Nobody thought it was funny, and Birdie grew impatient.

"Michael, whether you like it or not, you were given a gift and you have to come to terms with it," Birdie said. She collected herself and directed her next thoughts more toward the group. "The benefit of going to some other place that is haunted as opposed to dealing with the spirits here is that you're used to the spirits in this house."

Not quite, I thought.

"And ghosts can sometimes appear more hostile in unfamiliar environments," Birdie continued. "That's why you need to go—so you can learn how not to give any spirits too much power."

In theory this made sense, but it was also bordering on child abuse. I looked around the room and gathered myself. "Okay," I said. "You all want me to go to a haunted house, filled with who knows what, and get the living crap scared out of me. Then, as a result of this *experience*, I will find that ghosts and spirits are really no big deal and my fear will go away. Is that about right?"

I looked around the table and nobody said a word.

"If you all think that spirits and ghosts are no big deal, then why can't I just take your word for it?" I said. "Why do I have to go to this place?" It was clear I didn't want to go and it was also clear the people in the group were tired of me fighting.

The group looked ready to just let it go, when some guy named Larry stood up. "Ya know Mikey, if this scares you so much, then just don't go," he said. He looked around the room and everybody agreed.

I wanted to punch the guy. Now I had to go whether I wanted to or not. If I said I wasn't afraid, but still insisted on not going, I would have lost the tiny sliver of credibility I had left. I gave in.

I looked at the group. "Fine, I'd love to go," I said. "But if I get possessed, and I will, I'm coming over to your house, Larry, and I'm throwing up on your couch." I looked again at the group and I walked out of the room.

I wasn't really that upset. I could have just said *no*, but I had been sitting on the fence with all this psychic crap for so long it was time for me to go one direction or the other. Besides, I had run out of excuses. I couldn't keep saying no to their little adventures and still hang out in the kitchen. Plus, if I had any chance of convincing these people that this supposed gift I had was better suited for someone else, I needed to show them—and myself.

It was about a thirty-minute drive from our house and on the way we talked about why we were going to this place. My cousin's buddy Tom said his mom was a realtor and she had been trying to sell this house for years, but with all the rumors and gossip surrounding the place, it just sat empty. She said people she brought out to look at the property either hated the place right away, or immediately when they went inside, and some didn't even get out of their cars.

He said there was a murder in the house some years back and people reported that each year on the anniversary of the murder strange things happened there. You could hear people crying or yelling, he said. Neighbors of the house said that most of the strange activity would happen between midnight and three AM.

This wasn't the conversation you want to have before you go to a haunted house. I thought I was sitting on a joy buzzer until I realized it was my pulse. I looked at the dashboard clock. It was 11:45 PM.

My anxiety level increased when we pulled off the main road and onto what looked like the Waltons' driveway. We drove down a long, narrow dirt road surrounded by tall trees and no streetlights. As we drove deeper and deeper down the road, I felt trapped. The only place

I felt comfortable was the car and it was driving me to a haunted house. Finally, we rounded a bend and there, in the middle of God knows where, was the ugliest house I'd ever seen.

As we finally drove up, it looked like everything I imagined it would—and more. Grass and shrubbery had overgrown most of the yard. The dark brown paint was peeling badly from years of neglect. The upstairs windows were all broken out and a weathered *Do Not Enter* sign was hanging by a thread on the boarded-up front door.

The only apparent access to the house was to go through the back door, which meant you had to walk to the back yard. I was not getting out of the car. I wasn't going to walk to the back of this creepy house in the middle of the night, through overgrown trees and wood ticks, so we could get to the back door where who knows what would be waiting for us. At least that's what I kept telling myself as I walked to the back yard.

As we got closer to the door you could barely see a run-down tennis court overgrown with years of weeds and vines. I remember thinking that at one time this place must have had some good times. And the contrast between then and now gave me the willies. I wondered what had happened inside the house to change it.

My mother was downright giddy. To her this was Disneyland, just one big adventure. She tapped me on the shoulder and asked me what I thought so far. I told her not to tap me on the shoulder again because I thought I had just soiled myself, and I asked her if she had a Kleenex. She laughed.

"Oh, come on, honey. Try to not be afraid," she said. "Remember you have a lot of protection around you. And please keep an open mind and learn something."

"You mean like how to break and enter?" I said. She gave me a dirty look and said *Michael*—which meant put a sock in it and follow her—so I did, and we proceeded into the house.

Since there was no running water or electricity, we brought candles, flashlights, and a portable radio. As we walked inside the house there was a large room. To the left, a couch and a chair covered by a sheet were sitting, obviously undisturbed for years. Directly in front was a large hall leading to the front entry where a large winding staircase led upstairs. To the right was a black painted door, with no handle or lock. Behind the door was a six-by-eight-foot room with a small closet to the right and a small window to the left. There were high ceilings with faded and torn wallpaper on the walls.

We set up in the room closest to the back door. We lit our candles, turned on the radio, and talked about what we might expect. It wasn't a long conversation because nobody knew what to expect. I started getting more nervous. The conversation had ignited my imagination and for me that was a dangerous thing. It helped having the radio on. Hearing "Sugar, Sugar" by the Archies took the edge off.

Tom started asking my mother questions about ghosts and psychics. Both he and my cousin seemed to be enjoying themselves, which struck me as a little weird. I guess I was the only one with sense enough to be scared to death. My mother went into her beliefs and philosophies about psychic phenomena, As she did, I looked around the room and like I do with the dentist, I tried to convince myself that it wasn't so bad after all.

The song ended and the D.J. announced that it was now twelve o'clock. Thinking all hell was about to break loose, I braced myself for something huge but all I felt was a cold chill in the room. I asked if anybody else felt it and to my surprise they said they did. I got that weird feeling again—the one I had in the kitchen the first time Lance came running upstairs and told us about the drummer ghost.

I felt like something was about to happen, but I didn't know what. We all started looking around the room. My mother grabbed the flashlight and started to walk toward the front entry. I said *Mom, where are you going?* and suddenly the candles blew out. I yelled at Lance, thinking he was trying to scare me, but he was nowhere near the candles. We relit the candles and I felt a little better, but I could still feel that bone-chilling cold.

About that time, there was a loud slam. We looked over and saw the black door had slammed shut. My mother ran to the door and tried to reopen it, but it wouldn't budge. Since there was no handle or lock, it obviously wasn't the wind. It was like someone on the other side was holding it shut. As we were focusing our attention on the black door room, we heard heavy footsteps upstairs that sounded like there was someone coming toward the top of the stairs.

Meanwhile, inside the black door room, we heard a little girl crying and asking for her mommy. The overall feeling in the house was like we were caught on the tracks and a train was coming. The air pressure was different. It was getting harder to breathe, and I could hear a buzzing sound getting louder and louder.

My mother, sensing my anxiety level was reaching an all time high, looked at me. "Honey, take your candle and come with me. It's okay," she said. She had a calmness about her. She told me to look in her eyes and try to calm down.

I tried. It was either that or throw up.

By now, even my cousin and his friend looked nervous. My mother told them to check out the front entryway and we'd check the outside of the black door room. They didn't bolt for the front room. My mother looked at them, realized they were hesitant, and told them it was okay, that nothing would hurt us. But this was like nothing we had ever experienced before. As much as we wanted to believe her, I, for one, was having serious doubts.

The pressure in the house was now becoming worse, and it felt like it does right before a big storm hits, when all the air in the room gets sucked out. The buzzing in the house was also getting louder as was the little girl inside crying *Mommy, Mommy.* Suddenly we heard the sound of breaking glass inside the room.

"What was that?" my cousin yelled.

My mother and I ran outside to see if we could look in the black-door room's window.

It felt good to be outside. I was getting numb from all the craziness and the crisp air woke me up. Bummer was, I knew I had to go back in. When we got to the window we looked inside. We could see white flashing lights, almost like fireflies, and the silhouette of a little girl hunched in the corner. We tried to open the window but it wouldn't budge. Frustrated, we went back into the house. As we came in the back we could hear the footsteps upstairs getting louder and closer to the top of the stairs. Tom, who was at the foot of the stairs, yelled, "There's someone up there!"

We ran to the front entry to investigate. The radio was now turning off and on, and getting louder and louder. The air pressure in the house made it feel like I was standing in a room full of balloons. The feeling in the house was one of total panic. We went to the front foyer and looked up at the top of the stairs. There, holding on to the edge of the banister, was a pair of greenish-colored hands. Combined with the noise, the pressure, the temperature, and the heightening feeling that you were about to be hurt, it was all too much.

My mother had had enough. She went back to the big room, stood in the middle, and in a firm angry voice yelled, "In the name of Jesus Christ, I want this to stop!"

And as quickly as it started, it stopped.

The black door opened, the radio stayed on, and the feeling of pressure in the house disappeared. I checked myself to make sure everything was intact. It was, at least physically. Emotionally I was a wreck. I had never been so scared in my life.

My mother, who didn't seem to have any doubts about her ability to stop what was happening, went to the black door room and looked inside. There on the floor was a puddle of water. No broken glass, no little girl, just a small puddle of water in the middle of the floor. Later on Birdie explained that that was a sign of spirit.

We didn't say a lot to each other. We just gathered our stuff and got ready to leave. Maybe the others had some conversation, but I wasn't listening. I was spent. I just wanted to go home to my safe haunted house and go to bed. Looking around, I could tell my cousin and his friend were as ready to go as I was.

As we left the house, that *chill* feeling came over us again. The pressure started changing and the humming returned. The door to the black door room slammed shut and we could hear the little girl crying again. We went outside to the window of the black door room. Sure enough, we could see the white flashing lights and the silhouette of the little girl in the corner. It was starting all over again—this time without us.

I could tell my mother wanted to stay and maybe go back in and find out what was going on, but one look at me and she knew we'd had enough. She also knew that whatever was happening inside that house had nothing to do with us, so she was confident it would happen again. She decided to call it a night. Maybe she and her friends would come back the next night. That was fine with me. I took off for the car like Jesse Owens in Munich. I never wanted to see that place again.

On the way home, I tried to figure out why it was so important for me to go through all of that. I didn't come out feeling more empowered or strong. If anything, my fear of spirits increased.

And as a result of this little experience, I found myself wanting to pull away from the psychic world. Whatever lessons Birdie thought I needed to learn escaped me.

As for the house with the black door room, my mother and her friends did go back and had better luck getting information.

According to them, the father murdered the little girl. He didn't mean to kill her, but had become so angry with his wife that when his little daughter was crying he shook her to make her stop. When she stopped breathing, he freaked out and killed himself. His wife found them both, and either had a nervous breakdown or killed herself. Either way, she didn't live much longer and all three were locked into this pattern of repeating the whole incident.

I don't know if anyone researched what really happened there. My mother was satisfied with their findings so for her it was a done deal, and I didn't have any reason not to believe her. This explanation fit with what went on that night. Still, part of me couldn't totally believe what I saw with my own two eyes. It was so bizarre, so weird. I kept telling myself it was my imagination, that my nerves got the best of me and I went over the deep end. But the problem was I felt the chill, I heard the little girl, I saw the hands. To this day, even after all the haunted houses I've been in (and some much worse than this), the house with the black door room is still the scariest—probably because it was my first.

Another thing that I thought about on the way home was *what about Jerry*. I knew things had started getting weird between us with all the drugs and alcohol. But I never thought he'd leave me hanging at that stinking haunted house the way he did. He was nowhere to be found and he had to know that just his presence would have helped take off some of the edge.

The more I thought about it, the more it hit me just how much our relationship had changed. Jerry was constantly trying to get me to let him jump inside me. Whether I was drunk or sober, he just wanted to feel alive. Sometimes he'd try without even asking, and when I'd get pissed, he'd get mean and do stuff to my friends

He'd tap them on the shoulder or move his eyes in the picture. He'd pull on their hair or blow in their ears, touch the back of their necks or stand so close to someone that the person would get the creeps. He liked provoking negative reactions. If the person got scared or paranoid, he'd laugh and want to torment them even more. He was like that sick kid every neighborhood has, the one who pulls the wings off flies or pours gasoline on cats.

I wasn't immune to his pranks either. I couldn't go on a date without Jerry showing up and finding a way to embarrass me, or worse, set me up like he did with Tammy Rampell.

I had a huge crush on Tammy. It took me three months just to ask her out and when I did, I was so nervous I made a fool out of myself. I was about as suave as an epileptic dentist, but she must have liked something about me because she did say yes and after a month or so we were an item. Jerry took an immediate dislike to Tammy. He thought she was too *perky*. I did too, but that was one of the reasons I liked her—she was perky. Cute, perky, and dumb as a stump when it came to ghosts, psychics, or mediums.

Tammy and I were going along nicely in the relationship and you could tell we were getting close to doing the nasty. We even talked about it a few times on the phone and the only thing holding us back was where to do it. Her place was out because her mother did day care and her father was a Marine. My place was a possibility except for one drawback—psychic mom.

However, my raging libido was willing to take the risk, so I pressed forward. I asked Jerry if he'd help me by warning me if my mother came around during the dance of love. He went through his usual *what's in it for me* routine, but eventually agreed when I threatened to ignore him for six months.

Tammy came over and we immediately went to my room. If my mother did come home I didn't want her coming in and sensing there was someone around. She was like the giant in *Jack and the Beanstalk*. She just knew. We worked through our nervousness and settled in the bed. With every piece of clothing she took off, I knew I had made the right decision by trusting Jerry. She was absolutely beautiful. As clumsy as newborn ponies, we got underneath the sheets and prepared to make history. Slow moaning and sweat replaced nervous laughter. Time stood still and everything felt right with the world. Then, in a voice that can only be described as Satan on crack, I heard my mother say, "Michael, what are you doing?"

I covered Tammy with my body like a soldier would cover a grenade. I lifted the sheets slowly from over my head, turned to face her, and said cheerfully, "Oh hi, Mom." I felt like every cell in my body was embarrassed. But what she did next completely surprised me. My mother pulled up a chair to within two feet of the bed, sat down, and in an even friendlier voice said, "Who do have with you there, hon?"

My eyes widened and my heart sank. She wanted to have a conversation. I moved my arm that was covering Tammy's face and said, "Oh, ah, this is Tammy, Mom. She's a friend from school."

My mother stretched her neck to get a better look at Tammy, who was underneath me. "Oh, there you are, dear," my mother said. "Don't get up, but could you help me with something?"

Tammy who was now scared to death, had little choice except to say *sure*.

"This is the third time this week I've caught Michael in bed with a girl," my mother said matter-of-factly. "Could I ask you, do you find Michael irresistible?"

I put my head in my hands and tried with all my might to pretend I wasn't there. Tammy sat up, pushed me off her, and covered up.

"Did you say three girls this week?" Tammy meekly asked.

"Oh yes," my mother replied. "I think it's a problem."

She waited for what she said to register with Tammy, and then asked Tammy if she knew Carol or Sara or Debbie—all first names of Tammy's best friends.

I knew what my mom was doing; she was picking up psychic information on Tammy and using it to teach me a lesson. The only thing I could do was sit and watch, and take it like a man. Tammy started becoming angrier with me. I tried to get Tammy's attention so I could deny the charges but as far as Tammy was concerned, it was just her and my mom in the room at that point. I'd never touched her friends. I didn't even know them except for seeing them at school. But who was Tammy going to believe—the *caring parent* or the *oversexed, silver-tongued teenager?*

My mother then asked my soon-to-be ex-girlfriend to get dressed and come upstairs. She wanted to discuss in more detail my sexual problems and maybe throw in a danish. My mother got up and looked at me with one of those *I'm not through with you yet* looks and left the room. When she did, Tammy got up and immediately started to get dressed. It was as if I was invisible.

"My mom's just saying that stuff to get me back for being with you," I said.

"Really," she said, adjusting her bra. "How did she know about Sara and Carol, and God, I can't believe you slept with Debbie," she said with a haunted look.

"I didn't sleep with any of them," I said. "My mom, well, she's a psychic."

She paused and looked straight into my eyes. "Fuck you, Michael," she said with more force than she had in bed. "That's your answer?"

I wasn't sure what to do. It was a little late to bring her up to speed as far as all the psychic stuff. And if I did, where would I start? She finished getting dressed and went upstairs. They talked for what seemed like hours, at times even laughing. I wanted to go upstairs and put an end to it, but my place was in the basement with the rest of the bugs. I heard them say goodbye and then the door shut. Then I heard the sound of footsteps coming downstairs. I waited like a death-row inmate for my mother to come into the room. When she did, she had fire in her eyes.

"Don't ever do that again," my mother said with somewhat the same restraint she had with my drinking. "If you have your father's genes, you'll probably get someone pregnant. You don't know about body control—how can I expect you to know about birth control?" She then smiled slightly. "Pretty good, me picking up on those girls' names. No way you're gonna talk your way out of that one."

She snickered and then walked out of the room. "Oh, you're grounded," she said—much calmer than when she came in. "Thank Jerry for me."

I heard the door shut and her footsteps going upstairs.

As I was lying there, pondering my fate, and feeling badly for myself, I started questioning my choice of Jerry for head of security. Because of him, I was grounded for a week and Tammy hated me. I couldn't tell by my mother's comment if Jerry was in on it or not, but either way, he let me down. I told the air I was pissed at Jerry. I dared the jerk to show up, but I felt nothing.

Finally, Jerry made his presence known. In a sarcastic voice he told me to lighten up, and then laughed and said I should have seen the look on my face when my mother came in. I told him he was an ass-hole and that I wanted him to leave.

"First you want me, then you don't. Can't you make up your mind?" he asked.

I told him I was serious when I said I wanted him to leave me alone, and if he didn't listen, I would call in Birdie to kick his ass. The room went quiet and I didn't hear from him for two weeks.

That had happened six months earlier. Things had only kept get-ting worse, and now with this black-door-room experience, not having Jerry in my life was becoming more of an option. When Jerry finally did show up, he was his normal, asshole self. I asked him where he was, why he didn't come out and help me, and he told me to get off his back, that he wasn't my trained monkey and any time I wanted him I couldn't just snap my fingers and expect him to show up.

I told him that was exactly what he was. I reminded him that there were certain rules and guidelines we followed and the main one was he was here to help me. I also reminded him that he came to me, I didn't ask for him, and since he was no longer useful, maybe he should find some other fool and ruin his life.

I went over to where his picture was hanging, ripped it off the wall, and threw it in the closet. I turned around and whether it was because I was so mad or because I was developing more psychically I don't know, but for the first time, I could actually see Jerry.

We both stopped short. It was astounding that after all these years I could finally see him. The ironic thing was it came at the end of our relationship. I was shocked at the clearness of his face, but I could also see that he wasn't the sweet little boy I had met some five or six years ago. His face looked hard and mean. Any innocence that was there when we first met had gone.

He knew I could see him, and at first he was impressed, but it was also an awkward moment. So many times in our relationship I wanted to be able to see Jerry, not just because I was curious, but because it would have made our relationship more real. And now that I could, it brought back all those memories I had of Jerry—the good ones, where we helped each other out, where we cared for each other. And maybe in that split second, kind words by either of us would have changed the direction we were going and stopped the bleeding. But instead, he used the opportunity to smile this petty smile as if to say *who needs you*, and whatever romanticizing was going on in my head disappeared. Too many things had happened and we both knew we could never go back to the way it was.

Then, as more of an insult than a threat, Jerry said, *see ya, breather*, and left. I stood there, not knowing if he was gone for good or just taking a break, but there was a lightness in the air and I was glad he was gone, at least for the time being.

Nine
Two Camps

"I live a pretty good life. I work, I go to church, I have good friends, I care about people in general." "Then why," I asked as we walked briskly out of the store, "are you stealing that camera?" "Because," he said as he checked for security, "sometimes, you just have to be bad."

It was the fall of 1971 when Jerry and I parted company. Things were changing in the house—again. That summer, things started to get out of control. We were having parties all the time, and it was normal to have ten or twenty of my friends sneak in the basement and crash on any given night. I'd wake up to a different girl lying next to me without her clothes on. My mother had given up trying to police all of us and I was too wasted to care.

Like my mother predicted when they first met, Bucky was now living with us, as were several other people. My other friends like Bill and J.J. were scared off by some of Bucky's friends, and I was too busy partying to care.

The kitchen and the basement had become more polarized. As negative as the basement was, the kitchen was positive. As loud and irritating as the basement became, the kitchen became soft and enlightened.

People were still coming to the house to learn about psychic activity, but it was clear there were two camps. Some people preferred the flair and drama of the dark side. They were drawn to the basement. Some people really wanted to learn about spirituality and growth and they would end up in the kitchen. I would hang out in the kitchen from time to time with everybody to not only feel better, but to make sure they knew I wasn't totally swallowed up by the negative. They all knew I was screwed up, but the difference between being there and being in the basement was, in the kitchen the spirits prayed for me, but in the basement they preyed on me.

The feeling in the basement was already becoming dark. But when my cousin and some friends took one of the chairs that was in the black door haunted house and put it into the basement, things got downright creepy.

The chair itself was nice, for a chair from hell, that is. It was an oversized, dark green crushed-velvet lounge chair that looked inviting, but it was one chair you did not want to sit in. Whatever *vibe* was at that house, came home in that chair. Friends of mine would come over to the house and see ghosts sitting in that chair. If you were dumb enough to sit in it (and many people were), you would either get very agitated, depressed, or just ornery. Even if you sat there for a second, it felt like you were sitting in fiberglass, naked.

One time I was going downstairs and a girl came running up from the basement crying, claiming to have seen a dead friend of hers sitting in the chair. I felt badly for her because I'm sure it was a hard thing to experience, but come on. Everybody and their mother knew our basement was quirky. I was becoming jaded.

To me, that chair represented the basement. At one time it was probably elegant and cozy, like our basement, but then because of something it had no control over, it became a magnet for negative spirits and bad vibes. Again like our basement, it was still attractive but now instead of saying *come sit, relax*, it said, *come let me take your soul*. Probably not what they had in mind when they made it, like our house.

What Mrs. Olsen had warned me about so many years earlier had happened, I had let the dark side consume me. I wasn't walking around mumbling *Satan is king*, but I had slowly and surely let it into my life.

It's a funny thing with the dark side. It's easy. It's easy to put your friends down and put down people who aren't like you. It's easy to put yourself down. It's easy to not care about hurting other people, and it's easy not to give a rip. It's easy to hate. It doesn't happen overnight; it slowly creeps in. Every day for me it got worse. I stopped caring. I stopped feeling. I wasn't consciously thinking I was being negative. I just thought I was being tougher, more closed off, cool.

Birdie called what I was doing *dancing with the dark side*, which in a way sounded cool—but she didn't mean it to sound that way. All her experience and all her knowledge was no match for a teenager on drugs. Her only option was to put protection over me whenever she saw me. She wouldn't even say hello; she would just come up to me and move her arms and hands around my head and body, talking to herself as she did. It could get embarrassing when I brought home a date. I did my best to avoid her.

Mrs. Olsen once told me the dark comes to you. And when it does, you become selfish, mean, arrogant, ignorant, and afraid. She said you make the choice to be positive. She said you make that choice every day. You see the beauty and the possibilities. You accept people for who they are and don't judge them. You help people unconditionally and without reward. She said unless you do this every day, you will allow the dark to come to you. She said it's not just a matter of deciding you don't want to be a negative person—you have to work at being a good person.

"There is no fence to sit on," Birdie said. "It's one side or the other."

That fall, when I started school, there wasn't a happy, excited feeling like I'd had the year before. I was having a hard time just staying in school. If I didn't go to school high, I would get high at school. And when I got high, the last place I wanted to be was in class, so I would just leave.

The teachers didn't know what to think about me. They'd try and stop me, but I would just walk outside. If they gave me detention, I wouldn't show up. If they threatened suspension, I'd say *great, I'll take a week*. All I wanted to do was to get high or drunk. I stopped being funny and started being obnoxious. With the way I acted, you would have thought one or two dead alcoholics had jumped inside me. I felt entitled—like if anybody had a right to drink it was me. All of this psychic crap—the strange people, the strange surroundings—who wouldn't be getting high.

I know now, but didn't know then, that I wanted someone to help me—not my mother, but my father. I wanted him to care. I was willing to take it as far as it would go just to see if he even gave a crap. And I didn't care about what other people thought, because I didn't think they cared about me. And if they said they did care, I figured they were lying.

I had little or no time for people who didn't get high and even the people who did get high were wary of me because I was so full of myself. Getting high was the only thing I liked doing. School, friends, the future—all had little importance, except for Lance.

Lance was my role model, the one I wanted to be like, and I would have done anything to show him I was cool. If he told me to take a pill, I'd take it. If he told me to smoke the couch, I would have done it. In my eyes he was strong, decisive, in control—everything I wasn't. He could be cruel one minute and completely supportive the next. One day I walked into the kitchen without my shirt on and whap, a blow dart hit me in the throat. The next week he threw the neighborhood general in the bushes because he came over to beat me up for throwing eggs at his house. He was charismatic and smart, and I blindly trusted him because he was the only one I had.

One of the many drawbacks to living in the dark is, your self-worth takes a beating. For a long time, things were great, my confidence was soaring, I felt strong and excited about the future, and I acted strong and confident. But slowly that started to change. It was the little things that did the biggest damage. In gym, I would strike out playing softball. Or trip over myself when I was running. I hadn't done that in years. My grades starting slipping fast. I started feeling stupid again. I could tell people didn't like me as much.

Self-doubt, fear, insecurity—they all started creeping in. Obviously, the drugs and alcohol had a lot to do with my feelings changing. They say drugs turn on you, and in my case they definitely had, but I was allowing negative thoughts to take me over. For me, the biggest problem was fear.

My father was a Navy boxer—most of the males in the family were tough. I came along and blew the curve. I wasn't a sniveling coward, but I definitely preferred comedy to drama. I loved football and boxing, but I didn't have that killer instinct that both my cousin and my father possessed. Because of that I always felt somewhat less than a man. I made up for it by being funnier than shit but it still bothered me.

When all of this psychic stuff started, it was okay to be afraid. Everybody was, including (although he'd never admit it) my dad. But as time went on and we all started getting used to it, it was expected that we would more or less try to embrace it, or at least get a grip and accept it. Most of the family had. My mother not only embraced it, she married it, and the wedding party was sitting in the kitchen.

Echo seemed okay with it, but she was living in her own place, dating professional football players, and working on her alcoholism. If she was scared, she didn't have time to show it. Lance was so comfortable with the psychic stuff he decorated the basement with possessed chairs. And Nikki, Nikki was different. Satan and Jesus could be battling in the kitchen and she would only notice if one of them were cute. It wasn't that she was shallow, she just didn't care about ghosts or psychics or who might be floating in the kitchen.

I, on the other hand, was still very much afraid. Ghosts, spirits, things that go bump in the night all freaked me out. It felt out of control still, especially since the black door experience. I was embarrassed, ashamed that I couldn't get a grip on my fear, and that made my self-esteem go further down the tubes. It was like Neil Armstrong's kid being afraid of heights. I never imagined being as strong as my mother, and boys my age were supposed to be getting stronger than their mothers.

I felt the best way to overcome my fear of ghosts and all the other stuff that happened at the house was to try to make friends with it, like I did with Bucky. But therein lies the problem. You try and cater to the dark side and it slowly and surely takes away most, if not all, the power that you have.

I remember when *The Exorcist* came out. People were freaking out all over the place. Everybody was so afraid they were going to get possessed and throw up pea soup, that a lot of people went and got baptized. I understood the fear. I wanted to get baptized just about every day. The movie lost me when the girl's skin started scaling and her head turned 360 degrees. If she wasn't possessed, somebody needed to get her to a chiropractor. In real life, possessions are ghost bustings except with people instead of houses. On some occasions things can get hairy, but I haven't had anybody throw up pea soup on me, except my kids.

As a way to combat my weakening sense of myself and my manhood, I started taking more chances and getting into trouble—stealing cars, boats, anything to prove to myself I wasn't afraid and also feel the rush of maybe getting caught. When we stole stuff we didn't sell it, we just used it. The rush came with doing something wrong, not profiting from it. I wasn't a criminal in the real sense of the word, but people were starting to see me that way.

But where I could get away with most of the stuff I did, at least from the law, having my mother not find out was almost impossible. She knew stuff I did before I did it, and like she promised in the beginning, she held me accountable.

One day some friends and I took a joy ride and I accidentally took a bad turn and bam, I hit this old lady in a gigantic baby blue Cadillac. It wasn't a bad accident; we hardly even touched. But since I ended up facing traffic the wrong way we had to stop and exchange numbers. The only problems were I was thirteen, and had no numbers to give, and the car was stolen.

In the two seconds my friends and I had to come up with a plan, we decided to tell the old lady that the driver of our car was a girl and she took off running. I had pretty long hair at the time and we didn't know what else to do. It seemed to work. The women, who seemed nice enough, came up to us and asked us where the young lady driver was. We all said she took off because she was afraid, but it didn't look like there was any damage. I was leaning up against her dented bumper so how could she see any damage. She asked us if we were all okay, and we said yes and then she left. We jumped in the car and took off as fast as we could before the cops got there. We all felt good about ourselves for having talked our way out of a jam.

By the time I made it back home, the excitement of stealing a car and hitting a Caddie had worn off. As I walked in the house and headed up to my room I heard my mother asking me to come to the kitchen. She didn't sound upset so I went with no negative expectations. She asked me to sit, which I did, and then she looked at me with a puzzled expression on her face.

"What?" I said, somewhat confused.

"Do you know the ins and outs of karma?" my mom asked, her eyes slightly squinting.

"Yes. You taught me about karma when I was eight and you bring it up all the time. Why are you asking me?" I said, feeling set up, but truly not knowing what she was talking about.

"Well," she said like Perry Mason right before he exposes the killer, "if you know about karma why would you steal a car, get in a accident, and lie to the person you hit?"

My eyes got wide and my heart went through my throat. It was such a bizarre thing to say that my only option was to try denying it. "What are you talking about?" I said, high pitch and all. "I don't have a clue."

She stopped me from finishing. "Michael, don't make it worse." Her eyes now completely flared. "Tell me how you thought you could get away with this." And then she stared at me like she was looking straight through me. How did she know? Who told her? What did they tell her? How could I defend myself without knowing some of those answers? I was so busted. I just sat there, engulfed with shame, and trying to figure how this could have happened. My mother seemed more disappointed than mad, like a *how many times have I told you not to fall asleep with gum in your mouth* kind of disappointment, only way worse. She then said, "You know this stuff always comes back to you. You cannot screw with karma."

She started to walk out of the kitchen, then she turned around. "By the way, the damage you did to her car came to three hundred and fifty dollars, and you are paying for it. I have her address," she said.

Man, she was good. "Wait," I said. "You talked to her?" (My first acknowledgement that I did it.)

"Yeah, you kids scared the hell out of her. Not nice, Michael," she said and she walked out of the kitchen.

I did know about karma. I'd heard about it so much I got to where I even hated the word. I just figured it didn't apply if you didn't get caught. Yes, in hindsight it was a tad naïve, but I was young and still in the learning process.

I did end up paying for the accident and I stopped driving around in stolen cars. I saw this as a warning. This time I got lucky. The next time I wouldn't be so lucky. To this day I still don't know how Mom found out. Through the years I'd ask how she knew, but like so many things she picked up on, she just shrugged it off as a lucky guess. I learned after a while to leave it alone, but man, she was amazing.

Another strange thing about the dark side is, you know you're doing the wrong thing, but you can't stop yourself from doing it. Take my typing class, for example. The teacher's name was Mrs. Melson; she had been teaching typing 101 ever since Coolidge took office. All those years of hearing loud banging of keyboards had affected her hearing. She only heard you if you waved a flare. She would play a record on how to type over the loud speaker and walk around checking your work. It was a large class and everybody knew when her head was turned you could do anything you wanted.

I had nothing against Mrs. Melson, but having the attention span of a ferret, I was extremely bored most of the time. One day I decided the only thing I could do to break up the horrible pains of boredom was to somehow leave the class and go exploring. I took my typewriter apart and brought the pieces up to Mrs. Melson.

"Uh, excuse me. There's something wrong with my typewriter," I said. I was thinking that she'd take one look at all the parts, freak out, then tell me to go to the library. I would then go to the trees and have a smoke. In theory it was a good plan, one I had used successfully in the past, but for some reason that day she didn't go for it. She somehow grew a spine and told me to put the typewriter back together and catch up to the rest of the class.

I took the pieces of the typewriter, started walking to my desk, and *accidentally* threw them out the third story window. I didn't do it to be mean. I don't think I even wanted to do it. But there I was throwing a typewriter out the window. It somehow seemed like the right thing to do at the time. Mrs. Melson didn't think so.

"Oh my God, what did you do?" she screamed, forcing everyone in the class to stop what they were doing and look my way. "You are an evil child. Just an evil child."

I gave her my best *gee golly* look, but she ran out of the classroom screaming. I stood there for a second in silence as the class, not knowing what to do, stared at me in disbelief. But then Walter Bong screamed *party* and everybody started goofing around. By the time she made it back with the assistant principal, half the class had taken apart their typewriters.

The thing was, I wasn't planning on doing that. It felt wrong and right, all at the same time.

And then there was the time I pretended to slip on some food on the floor in the cafeteria and threw a plate full of chow mein at a teacher named Mr. Gowan. Mr. Gowan was an okay guy. He was very short, very anal, and probably one of the driest people I'd ever meet but so what. We all couldn't be exciting. When I threw the food at him, I wasn't mad at him, I didn't have a grudge against him, I just felt like doing something wrong. Because I made it look like an accident, I didn't get into any real trouble and besides a good dry cleaning he didn't come out any worse for the wear. But because the chow mein hit him in the face and because it was chow mein, everybody from that point on started calling him *La Choy*. Personally I don't think he ever forgave me for that.

There was the time I was on the roof throwing snowballs at my friends when I accidentally hit Mr. Snipes, the gym teacher. When I let that sucker fly, I knew I was probably going to hit him, but to my weird way of thinking, I thought that since I was on the roof when I threw the snowball, he wouldn't catch me. This theory was flawed because just being on the roof was a punishable offense. Luckily I hit him in the face so he couldn't see who hit him.

I just kept doing things that I knew would get me in trouble but I wouldn't stop. I got caught smoking in the girls' bathroom. How dumb is that? I walked into the teacher's lounge and asked if any of them wanted to buy pot. I didn't have any on me; I was just being a jerk. I swore at teachers, I wore T-shirts that read *jocks suck* to gym class. My self-image was so low I pretended I didn't care what people thought, but at the same time I needed some attention and the only way for me to get it was to act stupid.

It was bad, and the gap between the positive and negative side at the house was also becoming much worse. I could feel it when I'd get home from school. The kitchen crew would be sitting there and they'd invite me in, but I was so afraid of being found out that I stayed away. I wanted to live in the light more, but I didn't think I deserved it. I felt guilty for the rotten things I was doing.

Having Bucky as a foster brother didn't help matters any. When we first met, he was already dabbling in the dark side. A few months at our house and he was swimming in it. I loved Bucky. He was more of a big brother than my cousin, even though Lance had lived with us most of my life. In the days Bucky lived with us we got to know each other pretty well. He wasn't a natural born killer, like I originally thought. He was made that way by a lot of bad history in his family.

My mother came into our bedroom one day to tell us she wasn't going to be able to get Bucky up the next morning for summer school because she had appointments early in the morning. In a matter-of-fact way she continued. "Oh, Marc (Bucky), by the way, you'll probably oversleep and in your rush not to be late, you'll want to steal a car. Please don't try it, dear. It won't be successful. Besides it's very bad karma. But I do see you driving the mini-bike down the highway, in which case you'll be stopped by a policeman."

She paused and looked more seriously at Bucky. "Now listen to me, Marc. Do not provoke the policeman. He's going through a hard time right now and if you do, you will go to jail." She smiled at both of us and said, "Hopefully I'll see you both tomorrow." Then she left the room.

We looked at each other like *what the hell was that all about*. At the time we both didn't want to believe she was that good. We wanted to believe she was just keeping us in check. And for an hour or so she did. We vowed to be cool and not do anything stupid. We set the alarm so we wouldn't oversleep and then we went back to the subject of girls and who was the most desirable.

The next thing I knew it was 8:45 in the morning and Bucky has to be at school at 9:00. For some reason the alarm didn't go off, so I woke up Bucky and now we were both in a panic. If Bucky was late, he could get kicked out of school. If he gets kicked out of school, his probation officer sends him to Boys Town. If he goes to Boys Town, I lose my bodyguard.

In two seconds we were dressed and then we had to figure out how to get him there. Bucky decided to hitchhike, but then changed his mind when he saw a car with its keys in the ignition sitting outside our house. He tried and tried but couldn't get the car to start, so he came back into the house and told me he had to take the mini-bike. I reminded him of what my mother said. He looked at me like for the first time it hit him it was all coming true and then he said *okay I won't go on the highway* but as he took off, we both knew he would.

Just as my mother predicted, he took the highway and he got stopped. Because of my mother's warning, he didn't give the cop any problems. Instead he was nice to the cop and told him he knew it was stupid, but he had to get to school. Bucky was never nice to cops. He hated cops and they hated him so this little catharsis was a major deal. The cop ended up taking Bucky to school, Bucky didn't get kicked out, and everything worked out fine.

This would happen on several occasions. When Bucky was about to go and raise hell, my mother would stop him in his tracks and tell him what he was thinking and what he was planning to do. She would warn him if there was going to be any trouble and give him the karma lecture. She tempered it all with concern, but he felt busted even before he did anything. Being the mysterious teenager he was, it scared him that she knew so much about him. At the least it took the wind out of his sails.

Jerry and Bucky never did get along. They both had healthy egos and neither one wanted to admit they were bugged by the other. The real problem was they were both so much alike, if Jerry was alive he would probably be doing the same things that Bucky was doing and vice versa. So with an already touchy relationship, things completely deteriorated when Jerry decided to test Bucky's courage.

One night, Bucky and a friend of his were walking toward his friend's house. They were talking about our house and the odd things that went on when Jerry's name came up. They were about a block away from Bucky's friend's house when they *felt* the presence of someone behind them. They turned around and sure enough, there's this floating head staring at them. They both got so freaked out they didn't bother running home; they flew there. When Bucky told me the story the next day, he was convinced the head was Jerry's. He told me to *keep that thing away from him* and from that time on, he didn't want to talk about Jerry or even look at Jerry's picture. When I asked Jerry about it later, he made a sarcastic comment about Bucky being a mama's boy and I knew he did it.

Even though Bucky may have resented his tough-guy image, he did little to discourage it. Bucky attracted trouble like a preacher attracts cripples. He oozed some weird chemistry that would make people uncomfortable. Girls were attracted to it. Bucky never had to worry about dates, which made it even more advantageous to hang out with him.

Our relationship was mutually beneficial in that I could start trouble with my mouth and he could finish it with his fist. This worked out great because nobody would find out I was a complete wimp when it came to fighting. I liked controlled violence, like football or boxing, but street fighting scared the hell out of me.

I think the dark side was at its strongest when there was uncontrolled violence like that. The fear, anger, hatred—they all came out in street fights and when there was a bunch of people around, you got that mob mentality. Normally passive people would get wild eyed and excited, and wouldn't be satisfied until they saw blood, and when they saw blood, their thirst for it became stronger.

You can't tell me the dark side isn't loving every minute of it. Bucky did. He appreciated being in those positions, and the scary thing about him was that when he was, he became a different person. Sometimes I swear I could see Jerry jump inside him when he was fighting. Bucky even took on a different look.

Maybe it bothered me more because I was growing psychically. I could feel the fear in the people fighting and even if the person was a jerk, I wanted to protect them. There was always this battle going on inside of me between the dark and the light sides. There was compassion and love in the light side, but if I were to suggest to a group of guys who were about to do battle that we sit down and get to know each other first, guess who'd be the first one to get his ass kicked? Me.

There was no question that the dark side was hipper. Just the drama alone was worth watching. But observing Bucky and knowing that being hip had its limitations only made things more disturbing. I found myself wanting the energy and clarity of the light.

Ten
Changes

"I didn't fall asleep, I passed out. I didn't wake up, I came to. One drink was too many, a thousand wasn't enough." He stopped addressing the group and looked down at me with his weathered face and leather eyes. "Damn, boy," he said with a slight smile. "I drank antifreeze older than you."

By the winter of 1971, the teachers and assistant principal at school had enough of my disruptive behavior. I was getting tired of it myself. Just a year earlier I was on top of the world, but now nothing was fun anymore, nothing was exciting. It was all about getting high and not feeling anything.

The day it came to a head was a strange day from the get-go. When I woke up there was hardly anybody around, including my sister Nikki. This had two negative connotations. Nikki went to school earlier because her classes started sooner than mine. When she dropped me off at my school, it gave me time to get high before the regular buses got there. With her gone, not only would I not be able to get high, but I would have to take the dreaded bus. I hadn't taken the bus in months.

If you were cool enough to get your own ride, it separated you from the poor suckers who had to take the bus. You couldn't smoke on the bus. You couldn't listen to music. You had to sit there and wait while the bus driver picked up every retainer-wearing, happy-to-be alive, "oh boy, school" person in the tri-state area. Every seat meant something. The bullies liked to sit in the back. Then the burnouts, the jocks, and the nerds. You could mix and match—the bullies and the burnouts could hang, a burnout with a nerd maybe, but never a nerd with a bully. It wasn't good for morale. As you got closer to the front, your personality became duller.

For me, going back to the bus meant humiliation. I'd rather hitch-hike or even walk the two miles to avoid the humiliation of taking the bus, but that day it was raining cats and dogs, and too cold to be adventurous. I got on the bus to quiet smirks and indifference, and did the unthinkable—I sat near the front. This was a serious breach of bus etiquette. Like a biker at a bake sale, it got everyone talking. I could hear the remarks behind me and the only thing I wanted to do was get off that bus. I got to school ten minutes before eight AM. That meant I had ten whole minutes to get high before my first hour started, and after that horrible bus ride I needed to take the edge off.

I ran to the spot where everyone went to get high—a clump of pine trees by the tennis courts that formed a little cove. But my fears were realized when the place was empty. I was about to leave when someone I had never seen before came through the trees and said, "Anybody here get high?"

My first instincts were that this was bad. Something about the guy was odd. I looked around the place to make sure I wasn't crazy and said, "Yup. We do."

"Cool," he said, without getting my jab. "Ever smoke mush-rooms?" he asked, as if he was going to teach me something.

"Gee. You can actually smoke mushrooms?" I said in my best Don Rickles voice.

He looked at me oddly. "Yeah you can," he said. Then he showed me two dried mushroom caps with a fuzz on them. The guy was a cross between a car salesman and a burnout. Ten more minutes with this guy and I would have gladly re-boarded the bus. I asked him if he knew the time. He said it was almost eight. I grabbed one of the mushrooms from his hand.

"Screw it. Who's got time to smoke 'em?" I said, popping it into my mouth.

The guy's mouth dropped to the floor. "Are you crazy?" he said. "Why'd you do that? You can't do that!"

He was amazed. I was late.

I thanked him for the mushroom and ran off to school. The bell had just rung and I barely made it to homeroom. I sat in my chair and laughed, thinking about the look on his face. I don't think he'd ever seen anything like that. *Maybe this day won't turn out so bad*, I thought. As the teacher explained the fine art of the Dewey Decimal System, I sat back and relaxed, thinking any minute I was about to feel something. Normally I didn't like mushrooms. I didn't like hallucinating that much, but a good shot of booze would take the edge off and I was pretty sure I could find some before second hour. My school had everything you could want; you just had to know the right people. I looked up at the ceiling and noticed the roof had come off. I also noticed the sun and the moon were making out. I started to get nervous. This was a bit too much, too fast. I asked the teacher who was now a lizard if I could be excused, and all I heard was a hiss. This I assumed meant yes. I walked out to the empty hall and everything was spinning like a funhouse ride. The walls were breathing, the floor was moving, and I felt a strange stabbing pain in my stomach. I decided to make my way to the nurse's office. I got down to the first floor and heard a familiar voice behind me. It was my friend Tim.

"Hey, Bodine! Whatever you do, don't smoke any mushrooms today. This guy's got these freaky 'shrooms and they're covered in strychnine."

He then took a step to go downstairs, lost his footing, and slid on his butt like he was going down a slide. He ended up hitting his head on the last step.

"Whoa, are you okay?" I said.

"Yeah," he said dazed. "Did you see that? Frickin' stairs just melted. I hate mushrooms." He grabbed his head and told me he was okay.

I started to laugh, but then realized I had eaten one of those mushrooms. *Oh great*, I thought. *First the bus; now this.* I remember my cousin telling me that some mushrooms have strychnine on them and you have to clean it off, otherwise you get really sick. *What an idiot*, I thought, grabbing my stomach. I knew that guy was bad.

I told Tim I would see him later and to stay away from high places. I then made my way the ten yards or so to the nurse's office.

I remember walking into the nurse's office and I remember her asking me what I was on, but after that everything was a blur until I woke up surrounded by the assistant principal, the school cop, and my mother.

I closed my eyes hoping it was another vision but my mother's voice was too real. "Well sweetie, I'm glad you're alive, but you probably won't think so after our talk," she said.

"Hi, Mom," I said with my eyes half open.

"Hi, honey," she said back pleasantly, like we were meeting for tea. And for the next thirty minutes all three teamed up to give me ultimatums, threats, and limited choices as to how my life was going to go for the next year or so.

Number one, I wasn't allowed back to school until I got some help (not exactly a bummer). And secondly, if I didn't get help on my own, I was going to an all boys' school that was more of a jail than an educational institution (which was a total bummer).

From the beginning, my mother had let me make my own decisions—good or bad. Now she saw an opening to take control of the situation and she ran with it. She grabbed the reins and didn't let go.

With my track record, I had little leeway. The next day I was off to see our family doctor, Dr. Will.

Dr. Will had been my doctor since I was a baby. I felt comfortable around him. He looked like Dr. Welby on the old TV show, and certainly had the same demeanor. He was caring, smart, and old-fashioned. I figured since he was old-fashioned I could tell him I just didn't like school, he would give me a lecture, write me a note, and I could go back to school after a month or two of rest and relaxation.

My plan would have worked if Dr. Will hadn't become educated in the ways of chemical dependency. He had probably just got back from his Youth and Drugs seminar when I came to see him. He was definitely just learning the language. When he asked me if I ever smoked any *Mary Jane,* I really thought he was talking about an old girlfriend.

As I was staring at him, wondering if I wanted to cross that bridge, he jumped up. "Never mind," he said. "Here. Take this test to the waiting room and fill it out." Then he handed me a written test to determine if drugs or alcohol were a problem for me.

My blank stare didn't instill any confidence in him as to my sobriety. I knew the test was the key to my getting out of trouble faster. I thought if I lied a bit here and there, the test would come back normal and I could go back to being unhappy. But because the test had the stupidest questions, I felt obligated to answer the questions the right way. *Did I ever drink alone?* Of course I drank alone. For one thing, it was tough finding people my age to drink hard booze with at eight in the morning; and for another, why would I share if I did know someone who'd drink then? Let them get their own booze. *Did I drink to get drunk?* Now you tell me—how dumb is that question? They didn't make Mad Dog 20/20 for the taste.

I did my best to be as general as I could, finished the test, and took it to the nurse. When her eyes got wide at just a quick glance, the thought occurred to me I might be in trouble. A couple of days later my mother asked me to come into the kitchen. I walked in, sat down and my mother handed me the test results, out of a score of a possible fifteen, I got twenty.

Armed with the results, my mother went about the task of getting me into a treatment center. Problem was, I was fourteen. No one at that age had ever gone through treatment in Minnesota in 1971. The options were narrowed to two choices.

Having little or no idea of what going to treatment meant, I had no preconceived ideas of what I might be in for. When my mother mentioned that one of the places was called *Pharm House*, I got the idea from the name that it was a pleasant place with big trees and rolling hills. I saw horses and cows roaming the lush green pastures, and Grandma Walton on the porch with a bucket of buttermilk. With all the stress I had been under, spending some time in the country would be just what the doctor ordered. I told my mother that was the place for me, and the decision was made. My father, who just happened to be on the Pharm House board of directors, agreed to take me.

When we arrived at Pharm House, I asked my father if this was the right place. It wasn't in the country, it wasn't a farm, and it didn't look friendly. The only Mrs. Walton sitting on a porch was the lady next door, packing a rod and selling cocaine. Pharm House was a hard-core treatment center for junkies and ex-offenders. It was in the worst possible part of town, with the worst paint job, and a vibe to it you cannot describe. Even my father, *Mr. Rugged,* was put off. He turned to me in the car. "Well, why don't we just go in and see what we think," he said.

I already knew what I thought. That haunted house looked good compared to this place.

Inside, we were greeted by a beautiful blonde woman in her early thirties. Her name was Betty and this was her place. She had a look to her that made me think she had been around the block a few times, and from what my father later told me, she had. She had the rare combination back then of being strong, tough, and seductive, and she wielded all her strengths with equal competence. She was fully aware that she could have any man she wanted and *cute* didn't work with

Betty. If you were planning on trying to con Betty, she'd have you for lunch. She'd heard it all and said it all.

She was sweet and kind to me, but I expected that given my father's position on the board. She told us that we had arrived just in time for afternoon group and if I was interested, I could join them. I wasn't sure what else to do, so I said *sure*. A group of about twenty people, mostly in their twenties, were all heading downstairs to a large room with chairs formed into a big circle. Betty gave me a reassuring smile and pointed to a chair where I was supposed to sit. Betty took the notebook she was carrying and sat on the other side of this large circle.

As I sat there feeling a little nervous, I noticed a girl walk in who had this soft, sweet look to her. She seemed out of place and as I watched her sit down and say hi to the guy sitting next to her (who seemed to be ignoring her), I found myself wanting to go over and talk to her. But with the group about to start, I stayed put. I also noticed another thing. Some people who were walking into the group had cups and plates tied around their necks and one guy even had a sign around his neck that read, *I hate myself*. I thought, *to each their own* and watched Betty, who was watching the clock.

As soon as the clock hit four, Betty turned into medusa. Whatever she was when she met us at the door was gone when that meeting started. I should have left right then, but it was too late. She started the meeting by yelling *any asshole that's late gets a con* (short for consequence). This got everybody's attention, including my own.

She looked around the room. "Anybody have any shit to deal with?"

Nobody said anything.

She then turned her attention to the girl I thought was so sweet. "Bunny, why the fuck are you sitting next to Steve?" Betty said. "That's a con."

Bunny stared back at Betty with a disgusted look on her face.

"Group, you decide what the con is," Betty continued.

This biker-looking guy with tattoos on his lips jumped up and started screaming. "I'm sick of this bullshit with Bunny. She knows she's on male stricts (restrictions). Everybody knows she's on male stricts and with the way she's always promoting her pussy, I say kick the bitch out."

Nervously, I cracked a smile. I had never heard the phrase *promoting pussy* before and at the time it was funny, but because I looked around the room to see if anybody else thought it was funny, the guy with the tattooed lips noticed me and turned his rage on me.

"Who the fuck are you and what the fuck do you think is so funny," he said.

I sat there like a deer in headlights.

Until he noticed me, I was a spectator, almost invisible, but suddenly I was part of the show. Everybody was looking at me and I could feel every ounce of my blood rushing to my face. I didn't know what to say. I did know I was way over my head and I would have been ripped to shreds if Betty hadn't rescued me by bringing attention back to the original subject.

Betty looked at *lips*. "He's a visitor," she said. "Now deal with your shit, Antoine."

Antoine looked at Bunny and, like a monster who was put in his place, said in a high-pitched voice, "She pisses me off. She acts like some poor little victim all the time with her little miss sweet tits. Kick her out."

My face as red as a lobster and my butt now starting to squirm, I felt like I had just boarded a roller coaster ride and I had no way to stop it.

Just then a girl who was late came flying in. Betty gave her a look that would scare God. "Get your ass in the middle of the group and stand there," Betty said.

The girl did what she was told and stood in the middle of the circle.

Nobody reacted, and Betty continued matter-of-factly to Bunny. "Well, they want you out, Bunny. How does that make you feel?"

Bunny looked at Betty. "I don't want to leave," she said in a mono-tone voice. "I really don't."

I was convinced, but I was the only one. As soon as she said she wanted to stay, everyone jumped on her.

"That's bullshit," the guy next to me said.

"Fuck you, Bunny," the girl next to him said.

And on and on it went. Each time Bunny said something she'd get crucified.

Finally Betty, looking uninterested, said, "I'm bored with this dialog. Bunny, you're gone." And Betty turned her attention to the woman standing in the circle. "So, precious," Betty said with a conde-scending smile, "you like being the center of attention…"

But before she could finish her attack on the girl, Bunny screamed at the top of her lungs, "Fuck you Betty, and fuck this whole fucking group."

The group got quiet and all eyes were on Betty.

Betty didn't get angry; she stayed calm. She knew she had complete and total control over the group and every movement or inflection she made was for a reason. She looked at Bunny. "Deal with it," she said, giving her a look to suggest she had one more chance to be honest with the group and she'd better not waste the opportunity or she'd be gone.

Bunny took this chance to talk and sometimes scream about her frustrations at being sober. She cried and yelled at the men who ac-cused her of flirting, and finally confessed to having nowhere else to go and no more chances. Everyone in the group was satisfied with her outburst, especially Betty. Betty sat back and watched as the group took over and either supported or confronted Bunny on what she was saying.

I was still getting over the Antoine deal. My hands were white from holding on to the chair. My back was straight, my head was still, and even my eyebrows were sweating. I had *holy shit* written all over me.

Everything I just saw and felt was bad. It was worse than bad, it was insanity. I'd never been in a more intense setting or feared more for my life than I did in that group. I knew subconsciously I probably wasn't in any real physical danger, but I wasn't 100 percent sure. One of these loonies could easily jump me and hit me with one of the cups they had tied around their necks.

But as unwilling as I was to be part of the group, I found myself wanting to protect Bunny from all the verbal abuse. I wanted to tell everyone to stop being so mean to her. I didn't want to die doing it, but there was something about her. I could relate to her defiance and fear, plus she really was cute.

Maybe she was a prick tease like everybody was saying she was. Maybe there was a method to all the ranting and raving. I didn't know. But just by looking at her you wouldn't think she was capable of the evil acts people were accusing her of. I had to know, and in my zest to know what was going on, I opened a door that I would regret opening for years.

I concentrated on her name and asked myself, *what is she really feeling this moment?* I thought I might be able to get a little information like I had in the past whenever I asked the same question. No sooner had I said that when I felt this huge rush of emotion. Fear, sadness, anxiety all came over me like this big wave. I could feel what she was feeling. I almost knew what she was thinking. My psychic abilities had burst open and there I was, picking up on not only Bunny, but on everybody I looked at. My senses were on overdrive, I felt like a deaf person suddenly being able to hear at a Motley Crue concert.

I was overwhelmed with information and feeling. Antoine didn't hate Bunny; he was in love with her and he couldn't deal with her rejection. Betty was never going to kick out Bunny; they were too much alike. Betty was playing her like a fiddle. Most of the men liked Bunny but they were afraid to let anybody know because they didn't want to get put in the *hot seat*.

The girl standing in the middle of the group had been sexually assaulted by a male family member. I knew this because I could feel her shame and it was all directed toward her father. I could also tell she wasn't going to stay sober for too much longer. These feelings came so quickly and clearly, I was amazed. There was a nonjudgmental feeling to it all, a sort of compassion and understanding. For that reason I didn't feel scared. I was more overwhelmed and dizzy from it all.

I put my head down, covered my face with my hands, and told myself I didn't want to know any more. I said I wanted to feel normal again and suddenly, I did.

I looked up, like I just came back from some trance, to find the group staring at me. "Michael, you look a little pale," Betty said. "Why don't you go back upstairs and we can talk after the group."

I didn't know if I said something to get everybody's attention or what but I wasn't going to miss the chance to leave the group. I said okay and went upstairs to where my father was waiting.

"Whoa," he said, when he saw me. "You look a little blue behind the gills. I heard the yelling down there. They weren't yelling at you, were they?"

"No, some girl named Bunny," I said.

"Bunny?" he said. "I met Bunny. She seemed sweet."

"Apparently not," I said. "Boy, that Betty can handle herself," I added.

He laughed. "Yeah. Didn't I tell you about her yet?"

I said *no* and he told me the story of how Betty came to him for money to start up this place.

He said she came right up to his office and said *mister, you are going to help me start a treatment center for kids on drugs.* He said she was this tough New York ex-junkie who was so convincing he started this board to help fund the place. My dad was so smitten with her confidence he even started getting involved in some of the groups.

While he was explaining this to me, we could hear people yelling and screaming in the background. He'd stop talking long enough to rubberneck, but then continue when he'd see me trying to listen too. We were both curious as to who was frying on the hot seat.

I was still feeling a little unnerved by my *opening up psychically* during the group. I'd had some psychic experiences in the past, *picking up* on a person's mood or where my mom might have lost her keys, but I never went through anything like that before. This was intense, and even though I wasn't feeling the vigor of it like when it first happened, I could still feel remnants of it—like the dust was still settling.

My feelings about the people and the place had changed. I felt more tolerance for what they were going through. I wasn't ready to stay there, but I could feel some people's desire to stay straight and the sacrifices they were willing to make to achieve sobriety. I felt vulnerable and humbled by the experience, and I was anxious to get home and ask Birdie what to do.

Betty came into the room where my father and I were waiting. The group was over and she returned to the compassionate host who had met us at the door. She looked at me.

"Boy, you looked like you were going to pass out there for a second. Are you okay?"

"I'm fine," I said. "I just hadn't eaten yet and with all the drama, I got a little lightheaded."

I didn't want to lie to her, especially seeing how she treated people who did, but I really wasn't sure what just happened. Her look suggested she wanted something other than "I'm fine," and the only thing I could think to do was to say something completely off the wall. "It was probably from listening to those assholes downstairs, you sure have a lot of pricks living here."

My father stared at me and Betty smiled. "Yeah, we sure do," she said, knowing that wasn't the issue.

We talked some more and agreed I should come back the following week. I wasn't sure I wanted to come back. I felt so sensitive and open to the people around me and the environment, and I saw Pharm House as the reason for this increased sensitivity. On the way home my father turned to me.

"Where the hell did you learn to talk like that?" he said.

I was taken aback because he knew exactly where I learned to talk like that. "Dad, you taught me how to talk like that," I said.

I stared out the window, wondering why he would ask such a dumb question but I got my answer. "No, I know where you learned how to talk like that," he said. "At those goddamn kitchen meetings. That's where you learned to talk like that."

Now I knew what he was doing. He wanted info on what was happening at the house. And this was his feeble attempt at asking.

"No, Dad. Those meetings are only for casting spells on ex-husbands," I said. I looked back out the window with a smile on my face.

I knew it would bug him. I knew his mind was turning a mile a minute, calculating the possibilities and the probabilities, and I also knew he really didn't want to go there. He chuckled awkwardly and we both went back to what we were doing.

I didn't want to get into it either. Some days it was fun fighting with my dad about psychic stuff and ghosts and goblins, but that day wasn't one of them. I was so flustered by everything that went on that morning—Betty, the group, opening up, still feeling opened—that I was starting to think I could really use one of those kitchen meetings. I turned up the radio and Neil Young's song: "The Needle and the Damage Done," came on. It fit my mood—heavy and sad.

When I got home, I headed for the kitchen. There, as usual, along with a group of other people, was Birdie. I went to talk to her, but she put her hand up to her face as if to stop me, like you would right before you would sneeze. There was some guy talking about reincarnation and I assumed she wanted me to listen. Reincarnation is fine to talk about if you have time on your hands, but I really needed to talk to Birdie. And the last thing I wanted to do was hear some diphead reflect on the joys of being Tokyo Rose in another life. I waited for her to put her hand down, but she kept it up.

Then I remembered. When you talked with Birdie, she preferred you to be calm and centered. I was feeling neither, so I took a deep breath, exhaled, and finally Birdie put her hand down.

"Come here, child, and give me a hug," Birdie said before I could speak.

Stinkin' rituals could also get tiresome when you've got things to talk about. I gave her a hug and she pointed to the chair, so like a dog, I sat. By this time I was losing my tranquil demeanor.

I started to open my mouth, and Birdie again interrupted me. "So you had quite a day. I'm glad," she said in her crackly voice and with a smile on her face. Then she leaned over to me. "I know what happened," she said quietly. "That can be a scary thing when you open up like that. But remember it is a gift from God and a gift from God will never hurt you."

I could see by Birdie's expression that she was pleased that I was *coming out*. It bugged me that she was so thrilled. What she wasn't getting was that I didn't want this gift. I didn't want to walk around *feeling* other people.

When you want to say something and you can't, it can build up, and for me it had. Ever since that day in the nurse's office, I didn't have much say about the decisions in my life, but this was something I had to take control of. I stood up.

"Look, Birdie, I don't want this shit," I said. "This is nothing against you or my mom or anybody else, but I don't want it. If it's a gift then where do I exchange it? If I can't exchange it, show me how to block it out. There's got to be somebody you know who wants it. Give it to them."

I felt my outburst was long overdue. Birdie, my mother, and everyone else in the room didn't agree. I was instructed to sit once again, and as I did, I could feel the tension in the room build. This was the first time I was ever this serious with Birdie.

One of the drawbacks to being an evolved person is you can't just haul off and smack someone when you disagree with them. Such was the burden for Birdie. I could tell by the look she was giving me that she would love, just for a second, to throw me over her knee and start slapping. Fortunately for me, she was an evolved person. Unfortunately, the rest of the people in the room weren't.

Like the four directions of the wind, I got verbally hit from all corners of the room.

"How dare you talk like that to Birdie," Tony said.

"You need to grow up," someone else said.

And the hippie girl in the corner said, "Wow dude, you are so lucky, yet so angry."

With the day I was having, I felt like telling everybody to screw off and die. But instead of causing any more hostility, I opted to just leave.

Birdie stopped me. "Where are you going?" she asked.

"Look, this was a mistake," I told her. "You all don't get it, so I'm going upstairs." I turned to walk away.

"When you have a mouth like yours, you have to have a strong stomach," Birdie said.

I turned to face her. She had a smile on her face and when she had a smile on her face, it was hard not to smile back. The woman didn't have a tooth in her head. How could you keep a straight face? I smiled back and went upstairs.

While I was sitting in my room pondering the day's events, Birdie knocked on the door.

"Come on in," I said, and in she came. She looked at me with indisputable care and love in her eyes.

"I know you don't want this gift, dear, but God does have a plan for you and it does include using your gift," she said. She sat down on the edge of the bed. "I do have some good news for you though," she continued. "You have control over it."

I said *oh really*.

She said *yes*, and then she explained.

She said the reason why I picked up on those people was because I opened the door. She said that as soon as I didn't want to pick up any more, it stopped.

"That's true," I said.

"So if you don't want to pick up on anybody anymore, don't open the door," she said.

Then she smiled, patted me on the knee, and got up to leave. She stopped halfway out of the room and turned around. "By the way, I don't mind the word *shit* so much, but I am glad you didn't tell us all to fuck off," she said. She smiled again and left.

Just when you thought it was safe to have a thought.

In the weeks to come my psychic flashes kept happening, usually out of the blue and usually when I was just thinking about someone, like at Pharm House. People were always going through some life-changing drama, and like with Bunny, I would be curious as to how they were feeling inside. Each time I would pick up on someone, I would feel the intensity like before and sometimes even stronger. It was like stepping into the person's head with all their feelings and fears and anxieties. If I felt uncomfortable, I would tell myself to stop, and it would. But still, it was weird.

I was spending more time at Pharm House. The things I had picked up that first day were turning out to be true. The girl who had to stand in the middle of the group was kicked out for getting high. I'm not totally certain she had a sexual relationship with her father, but one of the group members mentioned something to that effect while they were waiting for her pimp to pick her up.

People were starting to confess to having crushes on Bunny, even the guy who was so pissed off at her. And each time I was proven right, I was glad. It's nice to have natural talent, even if it's something you don't want to do. Even when I was shut down, I was much more sensitive to things than I used to be. Maybe it was my budding psychic ability, or maybe it was because I was staying sober.

It was hard for me at Pharm House. The people who were there were hard core. Most of them were one step from death or prison, and for a kid from the burbs, the urban reality was disheartening.

There were little rays of hope, like Bunny and some of the others, but all in all, even on sunny days it looked dark and gloomy.

I wanted to see Pharm House as an experience instead of a total life change. For me, the idea of staying sober wasn't a problem. I just wasn't going to do it. I would try and do it for a while, but mainly to get everyone off my back and also to prove to them and myself that drugs and alcohol weren't a problem.

Turns out that when you drink a lot, you don't grow emotionally. You stay where you were when you started drinking, and for me that was pre-adolescence. So, all the things that you go through in seventh grade—the insecurities, the awkwardness, and the up-and-down mood swings—were all feelings that I was having now. I felt self-conscious around my schoolmates, like they could see me for the first time and I was naked. I wanted to remind everybody I was still cool, but that's hard to do when you feel like Barney Fife. The problem was, most of my schoolmates were done with that period in their lives. They had overcome it, or if not overcome it, then at least had adjusted to the feelings.

I had absolutely no confidence because without the drugs, I had no idea how I would react to things. I was losing weight because I wasn't eating, and every day I could see my body change from someone with potential to Erkel. Even girls suddenly scared the hell out of me.

Life was turning into a nightmare. If you had asked me a year before what would be my worst-case scenario for my life, this was it. Lose my confidence, but gain every other emotion there is under the sun. Become aware of my conscience, lose my dead friend, and open up psychically.

Naturally there was only one thing I could think of to do to stop my personal hell and bring back my swagger—drink, drink, drink, and pray like hell it worked. It seemed to me that all my problems started when I sobered up. I could admit my using had gotten a little out of hand, but I was sure I could control myself and if I couldn't, I'd just stop again.

I found some old wine downstairs and popped it open. As I drank it down, I started to feel good again. I felt my old confidence come back. That warm fuzzy feeling wrapped itself around me and said hello, and for at least that night, I felt one with the world.

The next day I felt terrible, sick, and guilty. I felt like I blew it and I was freaked out at the idea of someone finding out. I had to admit, though, it sure felt good. This headache wasn't fun and neither was this anxious feeling I was going through. But if it worked once, it could work again. The only thing I needed to do was get my hands on some liquor and I'd be set. I was in luck. It was a school day and there's no better place to find mood-altering drugs than at school.

When I got to school, the first thing I did was to head to *the trees*. I started asking around for some booze. Great place, the trees. You could get anything you wanted there—from cigs to coke. And lucky for me, someone just happened to have a bottle of gin.

I drank what was left as fast as I could and headed back to class. I could feel that warm feeling coming over me and for a second, I thought it was going to be okay. But it wasn't. While I was sitting in homeroom, I realized that drunk wasn't working. I could still feel that sensitive, insecure, scared feeling I was trying to avoid. And the more I thought about it, the more I felt it.

As soon as the bell rang, I ran outside to where a group of people were smoking pot. I didn't have a problem with pot when I drank and at this point even if I did, it wouldn't have mattered. I grabbed a joint from some kid who was obviously nervous about trying it and smoked and smoked till I was practically purple in the face and still nothing. I was just high. The group looked at me like I was crazy, and they were pissed because I smoked all their pot, and all I could think of was *now what am I going to do?*

The bell rang. Going back to class wasn't an option, so I headed home. On the way, I remembered there was a bottle of tequila in the bushes that Bucky and I had hidden a year ago for a special occasion.

When I got home, I dug around for the bottle and found it. I removed the dirt from it to make sure it wasn't paint thinner and when I opened it, I swear a cloud that looked like a skull and crossbones floated from the bottle. I drank it down. I was already a little drunk from school so when I downed this stuff, I could feel it right away. For a second I thought it was going to work, but it still didn't and this scared the hell out of me.

I drank more and more, until I was so drunk I couldn't walk. I finished the bottle and sat there scared, drunk, alone, and lost. This was not the way it was supposed to be. I was fourteen. People my age were just starting to get high. I couldn't stop now. But I also couldn't continue. It didn't work anymore. That magic feeling wasn't there. It was ten o'clock in the morning. I was drunk out of my mind and scared to death because I didn't feel any better, just drunk.

I also remember seeing a ton of spirits around the house, most of them bad. They were hanging over me, watching me like they wanted something from me. Like buzzards. Then, I remembered Mrs. Olsen telling me that when you get drunk, sometimes a spirit will enter your body because your natural defenses are down.

These spirits were usually alcoholics or people who had died from an alcoholic incident, like a car accident or overdose, and who missed the feeling of being drunk or high. Generally, not the kind of folks you want hanging out in your body.

I lay in bed that night and prayed for answers. I was sober and freaked out, but not as freaked as when I was drunk and freaked. I told myself to really try and stop. I told myself I wasn't going to drink for a while, maybe never, and whatever I was going to go through, it was going to have to be sober. I couldn't stand being afraid and drunk at the same time. The next day, May 7, 1972, was my sobriety date, and I have yet to break it. I returned to school the next day to hear how much of an ass I had made of myself the day before. In my rush for a rush, I had said some things to people I probably shouldn't have said, like telling the assistant principal to fuck off. I didn't remember saying

that, but the scowl and the note from my homeroom teacher request-
ing my presence in the principal's office suggested maybe I did.

With Bucky in reform school for stealing a car, and Jerry and I not
talking, I didn't know who my friends were. Even my oldest friend J.J.
was now into drugs, and the last thing he wanted to be around was a
non-using, no-confidence, hyperactive, junior psychic with an eating
disorder.

One night, I was at this park. The park had become my second
home since I sobered up, because going home alone was not an option. Since becoming sober, I seemed to become more aware of spirits. You would think the opposite was true, but in my case whenever
I was home alone I could see and feel so many spirits I would have to
leave. I either ended up at my friend Kate's house or at the park.

On this night I was sitting alone on the swing when I saw a bunch
of guys I met when I first started junior high coming toward me.
These were the guys J.J. and I had met at the circus right before we
started seventh grade. I was glad to see them because they reminded
me of the good times when life was fun. They came up to me, happy
to see me and excited to talk. They were thinking about getting high
and wanted to know what I thought about it. Now, a year ago I would
have loved that question, I could have told them all the wonders and
magic of getting high. But now, when they asked me, all I could think
of was how much it didn't do for me. How much it was all a lie. I told
them it was great in the beginning, but it went bad fast. I told them
I'd never been this unhappy in my life, and I owed it all to drugs and
drinking.

When I told them this, they all looked at me like I was the biggest
drip to walk the planet. Pat Boone wasn't this uncool. I could feel my
hard-earned reputation fading away and I got the sense they wanted
nothing to do with me.

It was ironic to me that the same guys who were looking down at
me because I didn't get high were the same ones who thought I was a

lunatic for being smashed while they played with their GI Joes. Timing is everything—now I was the uncool one.

I looked around at their disenchanted faces, said *hey, I gotta go*, and got up and headed home.

As I was walking away I could hear them saying stuff about me they would never have accused me of in the past—like being square and chicken and how much of a baby I was. I heard one of them say *didn't that guy used to be cool* and then another guy said *yeah, I wonder what happened?*

A part of me wanted to go back and get in their faces, but I would have only looked even more ridiculous. As time went on it got worse. People no longer feared, respected, or even liked me. They just stayed away from me. I was yesterday's news.

Eleven
Karma

"Ya know, if you're nice to people you get a brick in heaven," my mother said as she handed me dinner. "And the more bricks you have, the bigger the house you have in heaven." "What if you're mean to someone?" I asked. "You lose a brick," she said. "So that means Nikki (my sister) will only be able to live in a closet?" "Oops, you just lost a brick," she said. "Now eat your peas."

Every day life got worse. Somebody would make a remark behind my back, I'd walk in a room and people would get quiet, or worse, I was ignored completely. I came home from school one day feeling down and tired of trying to figure out what to do about it all. I went into the kitchen to get something to eat and there all alone sat Birdie. Birdie was never alone and it caught me off guard. It had been a while since our blowout and since then, we chatted maybe a couple of times and always with other people around, but nothing intimate. She looked tired, but glad to see me. She asked how I was, and instead of being flippant, I told her the truth. She probably already knew anyway.

I told her about my lack of friends, lack of identity, lack of confidence. I told her about my fears and insecurities. I told her I didn't know who I was anymore, and I told her my psychic abilities were coming on strong and I didn't know if I could do it anymore. I bared my soul and told her everything, maybe with the hope that she would be able to help with spiritual guidance and love, but again she surprised me.

As I was purging, I noticed Birdie slowly getting a large grin on her face. I gave her the benefit of the doubt, knowing it was probably four hundred years since she had to deal with anything like this, but the grin only grew bigger. Finally, I stopped rambling.

"Birdie, this is serious," I said. "My life has gone down the tubes, and there's nothing I can do to stop it."

Birdie looked at me as though she was embarrassed by my ignorance. "Dear, you have it coming," she said, then waited for my reply.

"I have it coming?" I said. "That's it? I have it coming? Have what coming, Birdie?" I gave her a look that suggested she was mentally ill.

Unimpressed with my look, she said my least favorite word— *karma*.

I rolled my eyes. "Oh please, Birdie. Don't start with me about karma," I said. "I know about karma. This is different. This is…"

She mercifully stopped me from saying anything else. "You know very little, but you're learning," she said. "You've certainly learned about false pride and ego. Now you're learning about loneliness and humility. You knew what it was like to be popular. Now you learn how to be unpopular. You had it all, and you'll lose it all.

"These are wonderful lessons to learn," Birdie said. "And remember, it's not the problem—it's how you handle it. If you handle it with fear and doubt, you'll have to learn it again. If you handle it with love and acceptance, you'll move on." She got very serious for a second. "Again Michael, you must make a decision what side to be on—the light or the dark." She smiled. "I'll pray you make the right decision," she said, and that was it. She got up, walked out of the room, and without turning around said, "I love you, honey."

I wasn't sure what to do with what she just said. Then that part about losing it all, what was that? At the time, I figured she meant my whole reputation. But it turned out she meant *it all*.

It started with my dad. He had worked hard for years to prove to people he was somebody, and the only thing he proved was that he could have a heart attack at forty just like everyone else. He bought the exotic cars, fancy clothes, and swinging bachelor pad—but it didn't make him happy. He had done the dad thing and that didn't satisfy him. So he decided it was time to be a hippie. He convinced my mom to not bring him to court for unpaid alimony, filed bankruptcy, and moved to San Francisco. Before he moved, he sold the boat, the cars, cashed in the college fund he had set aside for me, and anything of value was either hidden or taken by the bank.

With the money gone, we had to put the house up for sale, fast. This probably would have been a bigger deal to me, but I didn't think we would sell the house.

I also didn't believe we would move because I knew my dad would come through with the money to pay for the house. The whole time growing up, he assured us we'd be taken care of financially, and the whole time I was growing up, we were. When anyone turned sixteen, they got a car or some big thing, or if one of us was bored he'd give us a stack of dough to spend at the local mall. It was an ego thing for him and we kids knew it—and took advantage of it.

So when I saw him decide to be a free spirit, I saw it as a positive move. He was just becoming hip. Maybe he'd lighten up a bit and then we could really get some green. There was no way he didn't have money. He always had money. It was just too important for him *not* to have it.

However, for my dad there was no *we* in mid-life crisis. If he had money, he wasn't going to share it with the family. Not this time. We had let him down too many times by not going with him on the boat any more, or by getting in trouble with drinking or at school. This *new deal* was hard to take. He told me before he left for California that he had spoiled the rest of the family and he didn't want to spoil me (like he was doing me a favor). I tried to express to him that I was already spoiled, so a lesson this big wouldn't work, but he only laughed.

"It's never too late to learn," he said.

He didn't realize I was dead serious.

It was all getting to be too much. Everywhere I turned a major shift was happening in my life. I had been a rich kid my whole life. My whole identity was around money and who had the most of it. We had the biggest boat, the coolest cars, and all the newest toys. That's who I thought I was, and that's who I thought I would be. There's comfort in that way of thinking, as long as you're doing well. I remember my parents' friends going through hard times financially and how my mom and dad separated themselves from these people like they had smallpox. I felt badly for these people, but even at an early age, I saw the need to shut those people out. Survival of the fittest, you might say. I judged other people according to how much they had and now, with the money gone, I was going to be judged. I guess this was part of karma.

Karma came in all sorts of forms and lessons. It could be a subtle thing, like with me. A year ago I was making fun of people who wouldn't get high, and now they were making fun of me for not getting high.

Or it could be more dramatic, like with my buddy Rich. Rich liked to steal stuff, tacky stuff, for his room. He'd go to the store, steal what he could, and keep it all in his room. He wasn't a popular guy or a strong guy or a even a nerd. He was just a guy, and I think he wanted to be something other than just a guy, so he stole stuff. I liked Rich because at the time I got to know him, I was no longer popular or even cool, and he liked me for the broken-down outcast that I was.

One day Rich came home to fire trucks and police cars. Somehow, while Rich was at school his room caught fire, and everything he stole along with everything else in his room was destroyed. Nobody knows how it started, but the only room affected was Rich's room. That to me was karma—not necessarily a punishment, but a balancing of things or an opportunity to feel both sides of something. Sometimes, karma isn't as obvious. Sometimes it takes awhile for it to make sense. Like the time I went to this party with my buddies, Jim and Phil.

Phil was going out with Sue, the girl who was having this party, so there was a pretty good chance we weren't going to see a lot of Phil when we got there. Those two were inseparable. You'd need the Jaws of Life to get them apart. I wasn't drinking, which in itself was odd, and Jim didn't seem to be having the best of times either. With the party winding down and Jim and I being the only ones left, we decided it was time to leave.

We went upstairs to Sue's bedroom to tell Phil to say his good-byes. We knocked on the door a few times and pleaded with Phil to hurry up. We heard the front door open and an older man said *what the hell's all this beer doing around here*.

Jim and I looked at each other like *oh crap*, and decided we'd better stay.

We opened the door to Sue's room and mouthed the words *your parents are home* to a half-naked Sue. Jim motioned to Phil, who was totally naked and completely flustered, to get under the bed and Jim headed for the closet. That would have been my first choice, the closet. Now my only choice was the under the bed with naked Phil. I waved to Sue and followed Phil under the bed. Now, we're screwed. Unless Sue's parents decided to hit the hay, we were stuck in our positions until they did. Judging by the way they sounded, we weren't going anywhere for a while. Sue's parents were more than just a little pissed off; they were furious. Because Sue and Phil had been fooling around all night, Sue didn't have a chance to clean anything up. There was booze and drugs and all sorts of paraphernalia that one usually finds at parties like that, but the way Sue's parents were acting, they'd never seen the likes of it before. They were crazy, yelling and screaming *what's this, oh my God, what's this*?

Things really got bad when Sue's mom came in to yell at Sue and found a condom wrapper on Sue's bedroom floor. She screamed so loud I thought the lamp was going to burst.

This is where the karma comes in. That wrapper could have been on the other side of the bed where Phil was hiding, or by the closet door where Jim was standing, or anywhere else in the room. Instead that wrapper had to be lying just three feet from where I was hiding under the bed. And since there was such little space underneath her bed and I had my choice of turning my head toward Phil and looking at his nakedness or facing my head toward the feet of Sue's mom, the first thing she saw when she bent down to pick up the wrapper was my smiling face. I said *hi* like most polite people would do and she went off like a roman candle.

"DICK, GET IN HERE! THERE'S A PERVERT UNDER SUE'S BED!"

When her mother left screaming out of the room, armed with the condom wrapper to show her already-angry husband, I realized I was about to get my ass kicked, and for a second I felt it was unfair. After all I wasn't the one deflowering their daughter, Phil was, and just because he made it under the bed before me didn't mean I had to die.

Then it hit me. I had done my share of premarital sex and most if not all of the girls I had been with had parents. Maybe this was for those times. Maybe this was my *karma* and if this was my *karma* I would do the only thing a person can do at those times and take it like a man.

I turned my head to Phil to give him a dirty look, when I felt the hand of a very animated and angry father pull my body from under the bed and out into the room. He was ranting and raving, slapping the back of my head, pushing me against the wall, whirling me around, screaming at me, and all the while I felt nothing—not fear, not anger, nothing. I just went with it.

He demanded I admit to being with his daughter, but I insisted I wasn't. He threatened to call the police, but I knew he wouldn't. At one point he even grabbed a bat and threatened to bash me over the head with it unless I admitted I had done something to her, but he didn't seem the type. I just looked as scared as I could and gave him the impression I would never do this again (which wasn't that hard to do). Eventually he grew tired of hitting me and threatening me and threw me out of the house. I was glad he did. What I was really afraid of was him calling my mom. I was already in so much Dutch with her I could only imagine her reaction to this. I had made it out alive and now all I had to do was relax and wait for the fireworks to happen when he found the other two in the room.

But, the fireworks never came. Instead, Jim and Phil simply walked out the front door, unscathed and unaffected. Apparently they came to the conclusion that since Sue's dad was tired from kicking my ass, they could just walk out without too much trouble and that's exactly what happened. Both of them being six-foot-three also helped.

Neither one of them said much to me about getting thrown around like a super ball, but they did appreciate me not saying anything about them. That was never an option for me because this was my karma, not theirs.

The trick with karma is not to feel like a victim. Somewhere, somehow, everybody has to deal with karma. So if you realize you are not being punished, you're just paying an old debt, it helps take the sting out of it. Of course, with me, when one debt gets paid, I usually go and charge something else on the old karma credit card. I'm not quite ready to be debt free if you know what I mean.

Birdie was funny. She always had an answer for everything and it usually fell under the category of karma or past lives or something.

I'd ask her: *so Birdie, why do innocent people get shot or victimized?*

She'd say *maybe they victimized someone else in a past life.*

I asked *you mean I have to deal with my karma from other lives as well as this life*, and she said: *of course dear, that's why some people choose to come down as a different race, or poor. Because in a past life they may have been bigoted or uncaring and they have to deal with that karma.*

Sometimes a soul will change its mind when it comes down and decide to come down later. *That's why there are SIDS babies, or babies who die shortly after being born.* You could never have a light conversation with Birdie.

This whole past-lives thing was a hard thing for me to get excited about. Not because I couldn't get behind the concept. It fit with my beliefs that we are here to overcome our shortcomings, and to do that you need a few lifetimes. It just looked like all the people who claimed to remember their past lives were usually Cleopatra or Joan of Arc, and rarely just mud dwellers.

For some people, it made sense to find out who they were in their past lives. Echo found out she was burned at the stake and that's why she was so afraid of fire. My other sister, Nikki, thought she was drowned because she has such a huge fear of water. Other people really did have unresolved issues from past lives. Some were drawn to certain countries, almost haunted by them until they went there. Others were fascinated by a particular time in history, making it hard to be here now. Some wear clothes from certain eras, not knowing why it just feels right.

Not me. I have always felt we were here in this time for a reason, to learn whatever lesson this time could teach us. Besides, if I was anything in a past life, it was probably a cave cleaner or a duck slayer, nothing grandiose—which would explain my lack of desire to check it out.

Twelve
Cleaning House

"If you want to overcome fears, you have to face them, if you let fear take you over, it will run your life," our swimming instructor said as he tried to pump us up for the high dive. He continued, "I've been cliff diving, sky diving, I've even gone bungee diving, and every person who went with me and faced their fears was a much better person because of it." We all looked at each other with reassuring smiles. "Well, except Timmy boy, but his chute didn't open, so what could you do? Okay," he continued. "Who wants to be first?"

Life continued to get worse. My dad hadn't paid a mortgage payment in months. The bank was starting to call and the bills were piling up. The flow of money that made life easy for us wasn't there anymore. My mother could no longer afford to house and feed the hordes of people that were staying with us. She decided it was time to clean house. She gave most of the people living with us their walking papers and even limited the kitchen crew meetings to once a week. My little drug problem also had a big effect on her ability to tolerate other people's drugs and drinking habits. She had none. After she said enough is enough to me, she just kept saying it to everybody. She told my cousin and his friends they could no longer get high at our house and threatened to throw anyone who did in jail. People jumped ship like rats off a burning boat. The party was finally over at the funhouse.

Within months of my mother's awakening, the house was nearly empty. Coming home from school was eerie because the house felt so huge with everybody gone. The first couple days it was okay, but then I started to miss the distractions. Even the kitchen was empty and somehow eating a bowl of cereal without the chatter of neurotic psychics seemed wrong. My mother had to work and the only job she could get because of her lack of experience was this odd parttime job counting trucks for a construction company. She sat at a construction site and counted the dump trucks that came in and went out. The guy who owned the construction company saw she was in trouble and invented this job for her so we wouldn't go under. It was strange having her gone. A year earlier it would have been great, but now I missed her and that felt weird.

My cousin decided to move his act west. He moved to California and Nikki soon joined him. Bucky was out of reform school, but trying to make a go of it at home. He didn't want to hang out with me now that I was sober. He was still my friend, but something was missing. That left me in the big house with all the ghosts and goblins that nobody bothered to tell the party was over. And since they scared the crap out of me and finding people to hang out with me was hard, I'd sit in the middle of the cul-de-sac waiting for someone to come home.

All this time, Birdie kept asking me *what are you learning*. Instead of saying *hi* she would say *what are you learning, Michael,* "what are you learning?" She wouldn't wait for my reply. She'd walk away and do something else. But enough times of her asking made me stop and ask myself *what was I learning*.

Everything Birdie said had come true. I had lost it all—my friends, my courage, my belief that everything was going to be okay. Even the house I'd lived in most of my life was on shaky ground. *Karma*, Birdie would say, *was just like being in school. You learn the lesson and you move on.*

I didn't feel that way. I felt like things were going to get worse before they got better, no matter how much I learned. I sat there in the middle of the cul-de-sac, bitter at it all, thinking about Jerry and Bucky and J.J. I thought about Mrs. Olsen and Birdie and all the psychics that hung around our place, the church, the camps, and what happened to my life. Mostly, I thought of that house and how those stinking ghosts had ruined my life.

This continued the rest of the summer, then into early fall. I'd do things with the few friends I had left, but if I got home and nobody was there, I ended up sitting in that stinking circle. That was a long and depressing summer. I wasn't able to find my niche like I had with drinking. Now the parties were going on all around me. People my age were just getting into drugs, and their excitement only made me feel more isolated. I felt like Pete Best, the drummer for the Beatles, who was fired right before they came to America. I once was part of something and now that it was popular, I was an outcast. So there I sat stewing, and getting more and more resentful. September, October, and then finally late November something happened that affected my feelings toward ghosts and how I dealt with them,

I was sitting in my usual spot in the middle of the cul-de-sac, freezing my butt off, watching the house and waiting for someone to come home. It was cold and gray and lonely. I heard a familiar voice behind me; I turned around and there was Jerry.

It had to have been at least a year since I'd seen Jerry. I'd often wondered what became of him, but I'd stopped short of asking him to come back. The last time we had seen each other we were both sick of each other and needed to part ways. But now sitting there lonely and cold, I had to admit I was glad to see him.

My face lit up. "Jerry, why are you here?" I asked.

"To talk to you," he said in a friendly, familiar voice.

We looked at each other and that excitement faded as we both re-membered why it had been so long since we'd talked.

"Oh. About what?" I said in a more subdued tone.

He looked at me impatiently. "Look you asshole, it's dark, you're freezing, and you're talking to yourself. Not that I give a rip, but you're making an ass of yourself, and your neighbors are probably in their house laughing at you as we speak."

He was right. I did look pretty stupid sitting there, rocking back and forth, mumbling all my frustrations to myself, but at the time I didn't care what the neighbors thought. I'd like to see them in my house, alone with all those dead people.

Jerry continued "You are such a wimp. Go in there and kick those creeps out."

I felt a twinge in my stomach. He was telling me stuff I already knew, but I was embarrassed he was telling me. He went on. "Look, the reason they're so big to you is because you make them big. Get pissed," he said. "Take away their power. You wouldn't put up with this kind of crap if the house was filled with jerks. You'd kick them out and watch TV."

He was right.

"Go get rid of them and then let's celebrate," he said, and I saw that evil, nasty side of him.

"Screw you, Jerry," I said. "Go find someone else to bug." I turned my back on him and stared once again at the house.

"Sorry I bothered you, nature boy," he said. "You be sure to wear a scarf, now." I heard him laugh, and then he was gone.

It all came back to me with that laugh. Jerry could be such a jerk, and at the same time, helpful. I did need to do something. It was get-ting cold and I was tired of feeling like a loser.

I stood up and headed for the house. I could see through the hedges the white and off-white figures going back and forth by the windows. It didn't help my anxiety level when the wind started howling. I got to the end of the driveway and started walking toward the front door. I kept repeating to myself *I do have power, I do have power.*

As I got closer, I could see the front door doorknob move and then the door started opening by itself. This scared the hell out of me. I thought for a second that maybe I should try again in the spring, but at that point I was too afraid to turn back, so I kept on going. As a way to break the tension, I said out loud *funny, real funny.*

I got to the front door and walked inside. There, in the front entryway, were about a dozen flying dead people all around me, buzzing me like gnats. My heart was pounding, my legs felt weak, and all I could think about was what a big mistake this was. I wanted to pass out, but I was convinced some demented dead guy would jump inside my body if I did. Suddenly the front door slammed shut and there I was standing in the middle of the walkway looking lost.

A funny thing happened to me at that point. As afraid as I was and as active as they were, I normally would have bolted out of there and not looked back. But I started getting angry. Not just about that time, but about all the times I had been afraid. *What am I so afraid of?* I asked myself. *What could they do to me that I haven't done to myself?* I put myself through all sorts of anxiety because of what *might* happen. I decided right at that point I wasn't going to do that anymore.

I stood there and I realized I did have power. I was in control. And as I was feeling stronger and stronger, the spirits got smaller and smaller. My fear was going away, and that awful feeling that followed me for years was gone. I walked around the house, daring whatever negative spirits might be there to try to scare me, but there was nothing. All that time being afraid and that was all I had to do—face the fear.

I went over to the TV and turned it on. I didn't feel rushed or anxious, I felt liberated—free not only because of getting my power back, but now I didn't have to wait for my mom to come home to come inside. It's more than a little humiliating being a teenager and having to wait for your mommy. From then on, I knew I didn't have to be afraid of ghosts, spirits, or anything else that went bump in the night.

As I was sitting there rediscovering the joys of being home alone, Jerry popped back. "Well, well, it's about time you got some balls," he said. "What do you say we go find some alcohol to ingest, and celebrate?"

The way he put it reminded me of the dark times with Jerry. It was clear why he was so friendly and helpful outside—he just wanted to go get high. And because he helped me, he probably thought I owed him. I didn't and since I didn't want to go there, I proceeded to lay into him for leaving me out in the cul-de-sac for so long.

We went back and forth. His point was I would have never listened to him until I was ready. My point was he was an asshole. For a while it was just like old times. Eventually he figured out I wasn't going to bend on getting high, and he left.

I felt a little better. I was able to come home and be alone, except for the dead guys, of course. And I finally had some control over something that had bothered me for years. It felt like it was something I could build on. The house was still weird. It felt sad and empty. I spent most of the time in my bedroom watching TV. It was the only thing that took my mind off the loneliness and isolation I felt. None of my friends called anymore or asked me to do things with them. If I did do something with someone, it was because I invited myself.

For my birthday, my mother decided to throw a surprise party for me. Three people showed up and two of them were family members. I was so humiliated I wanted to kill myself. The ironic thing was when I was getting high, I couldn't have cared less about people. They were a means of getting high sometimes, but usually they wanted something from me. But since I sobered up, my feelings were coming out all over the place. I wanted people to like me. I wanted to connect with J.J. again, be like we used to be. But now he was just as much of an asshole as I was when I was getting high. I thought a lot about people I knew and spent time with, and I regretted the way I'd behaved. Karma.

I also regretted allowing that door to open between me and Jerry. After that night, he started popping up again, and each time he did, he felt darker and darker. When I'd feel him, I'd feel anxious and depressed. He wouldn't always show himself to me when he was around so it felt a little creepy, like he was watching me and enjoying making me feel uncomfortable.

It got to the point where I asked my mother what to do and she suggested I call Birdie. I wasn't sure I wanted to call in the big guns, but something had to change. And if I'd learned anything from that night on the cul-de-sac, it was *you have to take action or nothing will change.*

I called Birdie and as I was about to explain my reason for doing so, she interrupted me and finished my story. She told me it was time for me to release Jerry. I asked her how I would go about doing this and she told me she would do it.

She also said the key to Jerry leaving was my true desire for him to do so, that in order for him to get the message I would have to tell him out loud I wanted him to go. She asked me if I was willing to do that. I said I was. I asked her if this process would hurt Jerry in any way and she said because he was so self-absorbed and angry the only thing it might do is piss him off. I asked her if it would hurt me and she reassured me it wouldn't. I was glad. I wanted a clean break. We ended our conversation with her planning to come over the next day and I hung up the phone.

I sat for a while contemplating life without Jerry. I had thought of this many times, but this time I believed it would actually happen. Part of me felt guilty setting him up like this. But I had the same guilt when I brought my wiener dog Sassy to be neutered. I knew it was for the best, but still.

The next day was a Saturday. I woke up late, got a bowl of cereal, and plopped in front of the TV. My favorite cartoon, *Jonny Quest*, was just starting, so I settled in. I wasn't thinking about Birdie's visit or Jerry's demise until I heard a voice comment on one of the cartoon character's sexual preference. I turned to my left and there stood Jerry. He had on his usual cocky grin, and was eager to argue about everything. Before we could get started I heard another voice, this time a cackling high-pitched sound, and I knew it was Birdie.

Birdie came through the door like an Avon lady with a bladder infection. She was in a hurry to do something. Her mouth was moving faster than her body, and for a woman who prided herself on being calm, this was unusual. She told me to shut off the TV and come into the kitchen, now. She didn't want to waste any time getting started. She didn't even ask for my mother, who was at the store. I turned to Jerry to excuse myself and he flipped me the finger. I rolled my eyes and went to the kitchen. Birdie gave me a smile as if to reassure me everything was okay and then asked me to bring Jerry into the kitchen.

I trusted Birdie for the most part, but when it came to Jerry I wasn't sure she knew what she was doing. Jerry was a slippery little spook. Even without a physical nose, he could smell a rat. He wasn't the most trusting soul to begin with and for me to ask him to come into the kitchen with Birdie, he had to know it was a setup.

I did what I was told and as I expected, Jerry took off. I turned to Birdie to educate her on the ways of Jerry, but she put her finger up to her mouth to shush me, and a smile came over her face. She closed her eyes and started talking to herself. At this point I figured she blew her bulb. She probably thought she could control this situation like she did everything else, and when it was so easy for ole Jerry to give her the slip, it was just too much.

Birdie opened her eyes and again asked me to tell Jerry to come into the kitchen. I didn't want to upset the lady. She had a look on her face like she just got dealt a royal flush. But I was sure we'd just tried that and Jerry took off. I assumed she had a plan so I asked Jerry if he would please come into the kitchen. To my amazement, he came.

Only when I saw him this time he looked scared, really scared. He didn't even look at me. He turned all his attention to Birdie, who was talking to him about going to the other side.

Whatever Birdie said to him must have been powerful, because Jerry was putty in her hands. I felt sorry for him. He looked like he was about to cry, and that was something I never thought I would see. She asked me if I wanted Jerry to leave me alone and go to the light. I meekly nodded and she repeated the question, this time telling me to tell Jerry I wanted him to go to the light. I looked at Jerry and told him.

As I did, Jerry looked at me for just a second, almost shamefully, and said, "Okay. I'll go."

Birdie continued to talk to Jerry, but I wasn't paying any attention. I just kept staring at him, in shock at how afraid he looked. His presence became weaker and weaker until finally he was gone.

"Birdie, how did you do that?" I said. "One minute he's his normal cocky self, and the next he's about to soil himself."

More than a little proud of herself, Birdie said, "I got his mother."

"You did what?" I said.

"I brought his mother down to help me bring him over," Birdie said.

"I didn't even know he had a mother. How did you know to do that?"

Birdie smiled. "Everybody has a mother, dear. He wasn't hatched."

This was too much. First she gets rid of Jerry, then she says something funny.

"His mother was angry with him for his behavior. She told me on the way here," she continued.

"Wow," I said. "Jerry had a mother."

I asked her why his mother hadn't come down earlier to get him. She said it wasn't up to her then. She said that Jerry chose to stay earthbound, but he had abused his time here and it was time for him to go back. Birdie finished her job by saying a prayer and asking me to *God bless* Jerry's spirit. I did.

There was an immediate difference with him gone, something I hadn't noticed when Jerry left in the past. It was a lighter feeling, a more positive feeling, Birdie explained the reason I felt it now when he left, but hadn't in the past, was that now the cord was broken between us and he was really gone this time. She suggested Jerry might want to come back so I shouldn't bring up his name for a while, in case he heard me.

I agreed.

She gave me a hug and looked in my eyes. "Michael, life is about lessons," she said. "Learn everything you can so you can help others learn."

The way she said it made me nervous because it was as though she was looking at my soul and talking about things to come.

"Remember," she said, "ask yourself what am I learning."

For the moment I was happy. Jerry was gone, the kitchen crew along with all the psychic wannabes was gone. The drug leeches, the phony friends, all took off in search of somebody else to use. Even the ghosts who were so attracted to the place for so long were one by one hitting the road.

In the days and weeks to come, life continued to be difficult. And I asked myself *what am I learning* many times. It didn't always make sense. But if I saw things as lessons it made going through them a little easier.

I learned about fear when I sobered up. I started having anxiety attacks—complete and total fear for no reason. I thought I was going crazy and my self-esteem got much worse. There was no way to predict when one would come and I found myself obsessed with *when*. Would it be while I was at school or out with a girlfriend? The only person I could tell was my mother and I was scared to death to be too far from her in case I had another attack.

The therapist I went to talk to about my anxiety attacks told me I wouldn't go crazy as long as I had someone around to hold on to. *A grounding source,* he said. He didn't tell me I wasn't crazy or that these attacks were just one way my body dealt with stress. He gave me the impression I could go crazy unless I was around someone. So then instead of being afraid of being away from my mom, I became afraid to be alone. He also tried to have sex with me, which completely freaked me out, so I stopped seeing him.

I learned about true love from a brown-eyed, curly-haired beauty at age sixteen. And then I learned what it felt like to have my guts ripped out and served to the neighbors.

I learned about eating disorders when I developed one shortly after my anxiety attacks started. Food scared me and I stopped eating. I was afraid it might be poisoned, which I found out later meant I felt my life was out of control. Before I got better, I was six-foot-two and weighed only 125 pounds. This didn't help my self-worth.

I learned about loss. Another girl I fell in love with had a child. We both watched as the child died from a lung disease. The strain from the loss eventually destroyed our relationship. I developed a thing called shingles, which up to that point I thought were only found on top of houses. It turned out to be a painful nerve disorder that makes you break out with welts on your body, like little explosions from the inside out.

I learned about uncertainty. At age sixteen, I helped my father move everything he owned to San Francisco where he would start his new life. We didn't get along on the trip, so as soon as I arrived in San Fran I caught a plane to San Diego, hoping to hook up with my sister, Nikki. I learned how truly good people can be when you're alone and scared, and I learned to stay away from the people who saw you as merchandise. I went from house to house, sleeping on floors and begging for food. I convinced my father to send me enough money for a bus ticket back home and that's exactly what he sent me—just enough to get me home. People on the bus fed me and I was grateful and I saw the kindness of strangers.

I learned spirituality. On that bus ride home we made a stopover in Las Vegas. As we were set to board again, I couldn't find my ticket anywhere. The bus was about to leave without me. I was going to be stuck in Vegas with no money, no food, and alone. I then had one of the biggest anxiety attacks I had ever had. I was never so afraid. My only thought was to ask God to help me. I believed in God, but mostly in theory. Actual practice was another story. I closed my eyes and with all my might said, *God please help me*. And then I waited. Nothing.

My fear grew to the point where I thought I was going to pass out, when suddenly a feeling of complete calm came over me. I felt as though someone had poured the color baby blue all over me and that tight feeling in my chest and throat went away. Everyone I saw, I saw with complete and total love, and I knew everything was going to be all right. It was an amazing feeling. A man who looked like a transient came up to me.

"Heard you lost a ticket," he said. "Here, take this." He handed me a brand new Las Vegas to Minneapolis bus ticket. I didn't even have time to completely thank him. The bus was just about to pull out. I ran to the ticket agent, gave him the ticket, and off I went. When I turned around the guy was gone. From that day I have never doubted the presence of God.

I learned about being poor. Everything that I knew as a child growing up was gone. My mother and I ended up broke and on welfare. We found a two-bedroom apartment on the main drag of Minneapolis in an area called *Uptown*. There was no yard and the place felt more like a bus terminal than a house. Still, we were grateful to be there because the only alternative was living on the streets. I got a job at a local porno theatre while my mom worked as a receptionist at an eyeglasses store.

Growing up around people with money, I got used to pretentiousness. Shining happy people were the norm. If they wanted to walk around with a smile on their face and pretend everything was wonderful, yipitidoo, I didn't see anything wrong with that approach to life. In most cases, people with money were treated better than other people. They got better tables at restaurants, better rates at the bank. My dad could walk into a car dealership and walk out the door with a new car at the best possible price. If you had money, life *was* easier.

I found out that people who didn't have much money had no problem sharing their emotions, a whole different ballgame from the way I grew up. When someone would direct those emotions at me, I naturally thought it was because I was doing something wrong. One of these people was my boss at the porno theatre.

Max was a struggling business owner and not shy about sharing his feelings. He would yell and scream and bark and bitch, and at first I jumped to attention like a first-year cadet at West Point. I felt so bad for whatever I was doing I would try and make up for it by doing whatever he asked. This went on for a month or so, until one of the other guys who worked with me took me aside and said, *boy, you have got to get some street smarts.*

Roy had been telling me for years I needed street smarts. *You wouldn't last a day on the streets*, he'd say and his gaze suggested he was looking at a complete moron. I assumed being street smart meant finding your way home if you were lost, and having been a boy scout for nearly two months before I was kicked out, I knew I had the basic knowledge to get me home from any spot in the city. Any spot with a phone, that is.

But Isaac (my friend from work) wasn't talking about getting home; he was talking about an entirely different thing. Isaac was an interesting guy. He did half the work, but got most of the credit. He was so likable nobody cared. He was the kind of guy who could smile and make everybody feel better. He was also very street smart. He had the ability to spot trouble before it happened. Not that there was a lot of trouble working at a porno theatre, but you'd get the occasional creepy guy once in a while. Isaac would tell me to keep an eye on a certain person and sure enough, the guy would be playing patty cake with himself in the back row.

This is why when he offered advice—unlike with Roy—I paid attention. Isaac asked me if I ever heard of intuition. Having someone ask me that other than to be sarcastic was refreshing. I told him I had.

"Well, good," he said, "because you need to be intuitive to be street smart."

"Really?" I said. "What else do you need?"

"You need to be jaded," he said. Then he explained how being slightly jaded took away that need to please people all the time and if you took that away, he said you were on your way to being street smart. I told him I wasn't sure what he was talking about. He stopped for a second and then gave me this example.

"Okay, you know how you always come in here and do whatever Max says to do?"

"Yeah, but isn't that what you're supposed to do?" I asked.

"Hell, no. This isn't Russia," he said. "If Max comes in and starts barking, ask yourself what's going on with Max. Now he may be telling you to fill up the Jujubees, but what he's really saying is how am I going to pay for my little sugar momma's new ring. That's where the intuition comes in. You got to feel where he's coming from. You take one Jujubee and put it in the bin, and act like you're busy."

"What if we really do need Jujubees?" I asked.

"Man," he said, "we haven't sold a fricking Jujubee the whole time I've been here. This is a porno theatre. People got more important things to do with their hands than eat Jujubees. The point is, stop being so eager to please. You're making the rest of us look bad, and you're wearing me out just watching you."

I told him I would try.

"That's all I'm asking," he said, and he went back to looking busy and watching the show.

Occasionally he would pull me aside and say, *Okay, it's your turn to pick out the creep.* And he would expect me to point out who I thought was going to go jerk off in the back of the theatre. We would then sneak up behind the person and flash our flashlights on them just as they were getting into it. Thinking about it now, it seems stupid, but back then it made the shifts go much faster. I also started trusting my intuition more.

I transferred schools from a mostly white suburban school to an inner-city, racially mixed school. When I showed up with holes in my jeans I was stunned to find I was looked at with pity and disgust—not the way you want to start your new school life. In my old schools, our jeans were ripped and our shirts were tattered because we wanted to give the appearance of rejecting material things. It was cool to be rich, but it was uncool to look rich. You could wear designer jeans but they had to look like dirt. The people who did dress up were looked at as odd because it looked like their parents dressed them. And anything parent-influenced was bad.

But this new school was like being in the twilight zone—parallel universe kind of thing. The better you dressed, the better you were. People actually prided themselves on looking good. They'd spend hours getting ready for school. At first I couldn't believe this was true, but then one day I decide to test this theory and wear something clean. I dug out an old pair of pants a nerd person had given me for Christmas. I put them on and sure enough, that whole day people noticed me and complimented me. It was just too weird for words. What I was finding out was it was much easier to pretend you were poor when you had money, than it was to pretend you had money when you were poor. Poor people didn't like looking poor.

My cousin and my sisters all had hard lessons to learn about drugs, alcohol, and jail. They went off to do those things, leaving my mother and me to figure it out. During all the fallout, my mother met and fell in love with an old gangster named Tony. Tony was strong, tough, and not too excited about sharing his love with a fresh, still wet-behind-the-ears, teenager. This presented problems for my mother. She was caught between Tony and me. At times I felt betrayed because she would choose Tony. At other times I felt guilty for not giving her more room. This was one of the more lonely times in my life, and I couldn't understand why life wasn't getting better.

The reborn Christians who were still hounding us would have me believe I was being punished for my unconventional ways—that God himself was causing all our troubles because of our belief in spirit and reincarnation and healings and intuition. They would come to our apartment and remind us we were still the Devil and we were still going to Hell. I had grown tired of their opinion, and I was actually starting to see them as evil. The Jesus I felt that night in Las Vegas was completely nonjudgmental and totally loving. It only made me feel more alone when those people would come around. The ironic thing was, the people on the other end of the spectrum—the black magic witches and warlocks—were just as bugged by us because we were *too* spiritual.

People who were into black magic were drawn to our family, probably because some people assumed we were evil. If they would come for a reading or advice from my mom and she would mention our love of God, the reaction was just as bad as when we told a Bible thumper we believed in God. *How could you? How could you?* I'd hear these people go off, and just like with a Bible thumper, there'd be a long and boring discussion on why we believe the way we believe. Most of the times we agreed to disagree, but other times one of them would threaten to put a curse on our family (as if there wasn't one already).

The first time one of them threatened to put a curse on me, I was at a party. I had just arrived when I noticed a serious girl dressed in black with black lipstick and black fingernails. I asked her if this was a costume party, thinking that it really might be. She gave me a look that suggested I was the most ignorant, uncool life form on the face of the planet and answered my question by telling me she knew who I was. Judging by the way that she was looking at me, I wasn't sure that was a good thing.

She went on to say that just because my family had some psychic ability didn't mean I was better than other people. I stopped her and tried telling her I didn't mean anything by what I said. Then the host walked by.

"Watch out for that guy," he said to her. "He can read minds."

She looked at me. "So you can read minds, huh? Well, read this. I have power myself and when you're not expecting it, I will show you." She then gave me this corrupt smile and walked away.

I went up to Keith, the host, and asked him who that strange person was. He told me her name was Laurie, but she preferred *Raven*. She was said to be this black magic witch person who could cast spells on people. I asked him why he would invite someone so odd to his party and he reminded me that he'd also invited me. What could I say?

I ran home, scared to death that my leg was going to fall off or my bowels would lock up. My mother wasn't there, so I called Mrs. Olsen. I told her of my potential calamity. She told me to pray and put the white light around me and I would be fine. I asked her why she was laughing, and she said she didn't mean to laugh, but I was so resistant to following my path that she found it amusing. I suppose I should have asked her what the hell she was talking about, but who had time. I had some serious praying to do.

The next time I spoke with Mrs. Olsen, I asked her what she meant, but the only thing she would say was, "When you're on your path, your heart will know."

Talking to these people was like talking to a fortune cookie, but I was really glad she reminded me of the white light. That white light thing saved my ass from both the black witches and the Bible thumpers. Every time one of them would scare me I would see the white light around me and feel better within minutes.

As far as the Devil people and the Bible thumpers, I often thought it would be interesting to put the two groups in the same room and see what happened. I figured after they beat the crap out of each other with their vibes, they'd find out that despite their haircuts, they were very similar.

This is not to say psychics are any more spiritually evolved. I think psychics can be just as self-righteous and petty as any Christian with Jesus envy. When you tell another psychic that you're a psychic, there's always this tension. Who has the biggest third-eye kind of thing, especially with the crawlers.

A crawler was the term used by some of the old psychics hanging around the house for someone who was naïve. The theory was that first you crawl, then you walk, then you run, then you fly. It wasn't necessarily a put-down, just a tolerance word. It was used to describe people who didn't believe in spirit or psychics, or anything else for that matter. It just meant they hadn't learned enough yet to accept other things.

To me, the Bible thumpers were crawlers. They couldn't see the value to all the lessons we learned in those early years, and we could not have gotten through the things we did without them. For instance, that philosophy that we're here to become more caring, understanding, and God-like. I tried to practice that philosophy all the time (maybe not in school, but everywhere else). I had to, otherwise I'd start thinking we were cursed. When even your dog has a nervous breakdown, you start to wonder if maybe some force has it in for you. But if you realize that maybe it's the dog's karma that he flipped out, it makes it easier getting though life.

I also had to remind myself I was on a different path than other people, that everybody's path was different. This was a big help when I saw the people I grew up with go to fancy colleges while I chased perverts out of the porno theater.

I had to keep reminding myself of the positive aspects of all these negative happenings. I would tell myself that this was a learning process, that this wasn't the way it was going to be my whole life. I was just learning more.

Before all this happened my life was shallow, but it was the only reality I knew. Then the bottom fell out and reality took a different turn. I became a *have not*. If I took the attitude that this was the way it was going to stay, I would have given up.

Instead I looked at it like I was learning something my previous peers would probably not learn, like humility. If they were in college and they ran out of money, they could just click their heels three times and their parents would bail them out. If I ran out of money, I was screwed. There's something very humbling about that.

They wouldn't get the chance to really get to know a hooker, unless on a professional basis, and because of that they would never know just how interesting and caring many of these people really were. And not just hookers, but poor people in general had a different feel to them. Not a worse feeling, just different. There was something to learn from them. I was too ignorant to figure out what that was, but I was trying.

At night, when I would be lying in my bed, trying to sleep over the sounds of the buses, cars, and fighting outside my window (which was literally five feet from the street), I would ask God why I was in the situation I was in. And the only thing I could come up with was that I was paying off some karmic debt from a past life. Obviously I was this terrible person who had done terrible things and needed to pay up—like a Roman on the crucifixion crew.

Despite my mother's occasional lack of loyalty, or all our other troubles, we stayed a family—especially my sisters and mom. One reason my mother and sisters stayed close was those early years. The circumstances forced a bond.

My mother and my sister Echo continued to develop their psychic abilities, while I did what I could to squash mine. My mother had a falling out with Birdie because she felt Birdie was too controlling. (This would fall under the *duh* category.) Since their separation, my mother blossomed psychically. She seemed to trust herself and her abilities more.

This confidence was beginning to show, and more people were asking my mother to teach them about psychic awareness. When these students would come over it wasn't that out-of-control feeling like before; it felt natural for my mother to be leading the classes. The student had become the teacher.

Thirteen
Reborn

"Ya know what I love about this town?" the movie star asked as we sat on his balcony overlooking LA. "What?" I asked. "You can reinvent yourself over and over and people don't judge you." "That is a cool thing," I added. "I like the whole nonjudgmental idea. But why would you want to reinvent yourself over and over?" "You're missing the point," he shot back. "Well, one of us is," I said.

I figured somewhere down the line, life would have to get better. I would tell myself this every day on my way to school, as a rabid squirrel would chase me through the park. It was a lifetime ago I felt too cool to take the bus. Now I'd give anything to be on that bus. I missed my life, I missed my friends, I missed my school, the money, the security. And if one more person told me *what doesn't kill you makes you stronger*, I was going to kill them.

It was starting to dawn on me that maybe my dad wasn't kidding. Maybe he really wasn't going to come back and rescue us. All the signs were there. He loved living in San Fran. He had started a new career as a model and was doing well. He had babes galore, and lived in a beautiful, expensive condo in the upper end of town. And the new Porsche he bought just wasn't a good winter car.

As a little added bonus he would send seventy-five or one-hundred-dollar unsigned checks with the note, *these could be yours if you apply yourself.* I wanted to kill him. Maybe he thought he was doing me a favor, but when we were struggling just to buy food it was insulting. He stopped sending them when I started forging his signature. I'm sure I wasn't the only kid to have his father completely blow him off, but I doubt there was anyone who seemed to enjoy it more.

Fall had come and gone. So had my birthday and now the holidays were upon us. The holidays were always a good time for me growing up. The family tried extra hard to get along and everybody liked being together. After my father left, it was still fun—just less traditional. We tended to throw the food more, and eat less. As we got stranger, so did the holidays. Nobody wanted to do the traditional thing anymore—get together, watch the women spend all day making a huge meal, and then eat it all in ten minutes. We wanted to find the meaning to Thanksgiving. My mother would bring in street people or convicts and let them make the food of their choice. We would talk and talk about living and dying and what was in the middle. In some ways it was better than the old days, because we were helping our fellow man. In other ways it was a drag, because some of these people were creepy.

Christmas, on the other hand, was my favorite. When you have money, Christmas has a whole different feel to it. Anything I asked for, I got. Anything I didn't ask for, I got. My father loved to overspend on Christmas. All those years in that orphanage when he only got an apple paid off big-time for me on Christmas. We'd put the tree up right after Thanksgiving so every day leading up to Christmas the house would smell like fresh pine. The house would be full of lights and presents and wrapping paper and little fake trolls and animals. Nat King Cole played on the stereo. There were cookies and nuts and candy canes and popcorn all over the house. On Christmas, the snow sparkled like diamonds. Everybody built fires so the whole neighborhood smelled like a campfire. My dad would only hang purple lights on the outside of the house (something about royalty), but they were beautiful and warm. No matter what mood I was in, if it was close to Christmas my mood got better.

But Christmas wasn't like that anymore. If anything, it was a shadow of itself—sad, hard, a party that was over a long time ago. If you didn't have money, Christmas was hard. Poor people weren't happy and excited for Christmas; they were sad and afraid because they couldn't afford anything. Whatever sacred feelings I had toward Christmas died when Santa threw up on my shoes when I went to put money in his pot. I didn't like Christmas anymore.

On Christmas Eve, I asked God to tell me what my path was. I told him I knew I had a path, because Birdie and Mrs. Olsen and my mother had been telling me for years I needed to get on it. I was so depressed I didn't care if my path was cleaning toilets; I just didn't want to feel so alone and so lost. I wished him Happy Birthday, but, as usual, God didn't get right back to me. I sat in my room staring out at the street, wondering what I was going to do next.

My mother was going to an AA meeting and asked me to come. I hadn't been to an AA meeting in years because I got tired of being the youngest person in the group by at least ten years. But it was Christmas, and every year all the AA people got together to celebrate and have a place to go for the holidays. It was called the alcathon and it was better than being alone.

We arrived downtown and I told my mother I didn't want to stay long. She told me to shut up and grab some groceries. I dreaded being there and she knew it. If I wasn't so lonely I wouldn't have come, but being in that crappy apartment alone on Christmas Eve was too much to bear. I walked in and I heard someone call a name I hadn't heard for two years.

"Bodine, is that you?"

I looked up and right in front of me was a guy I knew from high school named Keith. This is what Birdie would refer to as *a moment*—a moment in time that altered or affected your life. She said we would have many moments throughout our life, but the trick was to recognize and take advantage of those times. I knew right away my life was going to change, and I was ready to take advantage of it.

Keith and I didn't hang out much in high school. I was on the tail end of getting high and he was on the front end. But he was fun to be around even if we were on different paths. When I saw him we both lit up. I asked him what he was doing there and he asked the same of me. I told him I was sober, and I had to come to help out. He said he was sober too, and that another friend of ours, Mike, was also there. Just then Mike, a good buddy of mine from high school, turned the corner.

"Holy shit, Bodine. What the hell are you doing here?" he asked and came up and gave me a huge hug. "Damn, man, I thought you were dead," he said.

"I feel like it," I said, and we all laughed and got caught up on why we were there. We talked about people I had thought about often. We talked about who was cool and who wasn't. We talked about everything I used to talk about and it felt great, like part of me was home.

I realized how much I missed my old friends and how great it was just be able to talk. I was so grateful to see them again. We stayed together most of the night until they had to leave. They had both just gone through treatment and were staying at a halfway house. Before they left we exchanged numbers and they asked me if I was interested in going to an AA meeting with them the next Thursday. I told them I was, and to let me know where and what time. They said it was a group called *Reborn*, and they would call to fill in the where and what time questions. I had heard about this group a year or two ago from an older guy who asked if I was interested in joining. At the time I wasn't into AA because I got tired of being the youngest member by so many years, but maybe it was different now. Maybe there were more people my age. It didn't matter. I was going to go. I knew enough to know that when these moments come, you go with them. Plus, I was excited about seeing my buddies again.

The guys called and told me the time and place. Ironically it was the same church my friends and I would go to, to crash after being stoned all day. Back when I was getting high, the church people had a *drop in* center in the attic, and we used to drop in often. Now the basement was used as an AA meeting place. It made going there somehow poetic.

When I went back this time, you would have thought you were at an Alice Cooper concert. There was a boom in the adolescent recovery field. Anybody under the age of eighteen who got in trouble or got drunk one too many times was thrown into treatment and had to go to AA.

I didn't miss a meeting for nearly two years. At its height, this group had about 130 crazy, sober, and bored to death adolescents. Being a crazy, sober, and bored-to-death adolescent myself, I felt like I'd found a home. The best part of this was, nobody knew about the family business.

As hard as the last few years were, the next few years were some of the best in my life. I met a whole new group of friends. I trusted them and they trusted me. I could talk to most of them about anything, and most of our goals were the same—to learn about ourselves and try to stay sober. My confidence started coming back. People seemed to like me. Some even looked up to me because I had a few years of sobriety and everyone else had maybe a week.

I kept the psychic world private. Whenever the subject was brought up, like if someone said they were going to a psychic to get a reading, I would take the ignorant approach and say I didn't know much about it. Sometimes I'd even suggest that psychics were a waste of time. I wasn't ashamed of the family business, but this way I could feel out who was okay with psychics and who wasn't. Someday I might need to confide in someone about my family and it would be good to know whom I could talk to about it. Besides, my new friends didn't have to know Tuesday night at my house was séance night. It was fun being on the other side of the fence. I felt like a normal person, most of the time.

Winter in Minnesota is so cold if you go outside naked for more than a minute, you die. It's so cold that the moisture from a car's exhaust freezes before it evaporates and it covers the roads with a thing called *black ice*. You don't usually find out you've hit a black ice patch until you're sliding sideways at sixty miles an hour.

One night, I was coming home from a buddy's house at about three o'clock in the morning. It was cold as hell and nobody was on the road. I was driving down this normally busy street when I saw up ahead of me a car wrapped around the stoplight. As I got closer, I could see the wheels of the car still spinning. I saw steam coming from the hood and I realized that the accident had just happened.

I pulled over and got out of the car. I knew whoever was in that car was either hurt or dead, and I wasn't sure I wanted to see either thing, but with the adrenaline pumping and being the only dipstick out there I had to do something. As I started to approach the car I got that feeling that I get when dead people start showing up. I looked at the car and sure enough I saw this spirit coming out of it. It was a man. He looked confused—intact but confused. We made eye contact for a second, then he shook his head as if to say no and kept going. I knew the person who was in that car was dead.

It was so quiet and the only thing I could do was stand there and stare at the mangled car, five feet in front of me. I started to walk toward the car and I got the feeling not to go any further so I didn't. I just stood there in the middle of the street staring at the car, hearing only the sound of my breath for what felt like an hour. Finally the overwhelming silence was broken by the faint sound of a police siren. I waited as it got louder and louder and as it did, I became calmer.

When the cop finally arrived, he jumped out and asked me what happened. I told him I didn't know because I had just gotten there myself. He ran up to the driver's side and looked in. When he did he said,

Oh God, and started walking back toward the rear of the car. He had a sick look on his face and asked me if I saw the driver. I said no and he said good, and then he told me to go back to my car while he radioed for further help. I did as I was told and went back to my car.

I watched him put flares around the car and as more emergency vehicles showed up, my morbid curiosity got the best of me. I got out of the car and walked up to the officer who was talking to another cop. He didn't realize I was there and I overheard them talking about the cause being black ice. I also overheard them talk about the man's head being almost severed from his body and I realized why I got that feeling not to look.

They noticed me standing there and without me asking, told me I could leave. I gladly went back to my car and left. The eeriness of that night stayed with me for months, but I think if I had peeked inside that car and saw that almost severed head I would have been creeped out for years.

Life continued with ups and downs and I was content with my new friends and lifestyle. I turned eighteen, moved out of my mom's apartment, and started as normal a life as was possible for a psychic alcoholic with an eating disorder.

I got a job in a plastic's factory and continued to go to AA meetings. Living away from my mother's place, I wasn't exposed to psychic activity like I was when I lived there, so it was easier to put it out of my mind. Every once in a while, my mother would call and ask me to *pick up* on someone she was having a hard time reading. It was no big deal. If I got something, I'd tell her. If not, I wouldn't.

I had privately made a decision that if I was gong to do this stuff, and there seemed to be no getting around it, that I would only do it on my terms. Mrs. Olsen told me many years ago that I could do that. Maybe for other psychics it was different, but she said I could make choices. So I did. First thing I decided was no dramatics. I didn't want to spin or levitate or talk with my eyes in the back of my head. I wasn't going to let some stone-age spirit jump inside so I could perform for my clients. I was going to be normal, to the point, and as blunt as I could be.

Second, I wasn't going to be a death and destruction expert—meaning I didn't want to predict earthquakes, floods, assassinations, or car accidents. If you tell someone they're about to have a car accident, does that mean that person shouldn't drive for the rest of her life? The whole idea of telling someone that something bad was about to happen to them was more about control or ego than about helping that person. If it is true and we do control our own destiny, then I could see warning someone about something so they could avoid danger. But if there's nothing they can do about it, then just throwing it out there to impress their friends or get it off your chest is irresponsible. Besides, I'm not sure what good it does. If you announce that a big earthquake is going to hit Los Angeles in such and such year, other than freaking some people out I don't think there's going to be a mass exodus. I also think it gives the psychic way too much power.

When I did readings my way, I felt comfortable. I was only doing one or two a month, so I wasn't full time and since I was just helping out, I usually didn't get paid. But it was okay. Life had a balance to it, and I was happy. I had my normal life living with my girlfriend, working, and going to school and I did my duty from time to time with my *gift*. Everything was Jake.

Then one day, my sister Echo called, and told me she had a problem. She said she needed my help to solve the problem. I could tell by the tone of her voice that she was scared, so I actually paid attention. She said she had been lying out in the sun earlier in the day, when a *voice* told her to pack her stuff and go back up to her third-floor apartment. Having just set up outside, she was in no hurry to go back upstairs, but the *voice* kept telling her to go upstairs.

Finally, after about ten minutes, she relented and packed and dragged her stuff back upstairs. She unlocked the door and there in the middle of her room was her rocking chair going back and forth. She went inside, scared to death, and looked around to see if someone was in her apartment, but there was nothing. That's when she decided to call me.

Echo knew I was resistant to getting involved with anything ghostly, so she laid the urgency on thick. But she also knew I had a hard time saying no to her. When I got to her place, she was waiting for me outside her apartment. I asked her what she was doing and she said she wanted to fill me in on other details, but not in her place, just in case *they* were listening. I told her I was pretty sure *they* could hear us just as well in the dark, stinky hall as *they* could in her nice clean apartment. She agreed, and in we went.

Once in, she said the night before this happened she was awakened by the sound of loud banging on her bedroom wall. She said she saw lights flash on the opposite wall facing the window and assumed that since she was three stories up it wasn't the traffic from the busy street below.

As she was telling me all this I got that sinking feeling she wanted me to help her with this problem. My solution would be for her to move out immediately, but knowing Echo she wouldn't go for it. She had been living there for seven years and she wasn't the type who liked to move around. I asked her what I could do to help and she asked if I could *pick up* on anybody in the room. I didn't want to, but to get her off my back I gave it a shot.

Whatever might have been there earlier had either gone or just wasn't interested in talking to me because we sat there for maybe an hour and nothing happened. I couldn't pick up on anything—not on the chair, or the light show, or the loud thumping noises.

As we sat there for a while longer and talked, it hit us that maybe the lack of information was because *they* didn't have anything to say. We both had other things to do so we agreed that if she had any more problems, she could call me.

Later that night, around ten o'clock, Echo called. My girlfriend Patty, who I was living with, answered the phone. When she handed the phone to me, she had a concerned look on her face. Echo sounded scared again. She said that she got home from a meeting and when she got to the door, she knew there was *something* on the other side. This time it was dark, so the thought of seeing a *rocking* rocking chair in the middle of the room was too creepy for her to do alone. Instead of going inside, she went across the street to the pay phone and called me.

By the way she was talking, I thought she was going to ask if she could stay the night at our place. But she surprised me by asking if I would come over again and try talking to whatever might be there. As much as I may have wanted to say no, I couldn't. Echo was like my second mother. She was always there for me. She was always encouraging and helpful. So if she needed me to go in there and get possessed, it was the least I could do.

I filled Patty in on my plans to go to Echo's. I explained what Echo went though earlier in the day and what she was going through now. I tried to keep it light, but the more I tried, the more uncomfortable Patty was with the whole thing. I changed the subject and told her I thought I'd be home later on and not to wait up in case I was too late. I went to the bedroom to grab my keys and when I came out, Patty was waiting for me at the front door with her coat on. I asked her what she was doing.

"I'm not staying here alone after that story," she said.

I said fine, and off we went to save Echo.

When we got there, poor Echo looked bewildered. She was waiting outside for me and when she saw Patty, she seemed relieved, like one more person might help lighten things up. We proceeded up the stairs to Echo's corner apartment and unlocked the door. I went in first and turned on the lights.

Echo lived in an older apartment and the smell of the old wood and carpet reminded me of my grandmother's place. My grandmother on my father's side was a psycho bitch, so it wasn't a good memory. I looked around and saw nothing. It was a small, one-bedroom apartment so scanning it didn't take long. I told Echo and

Patty the coast was clear, and in they came. We sat down on the couch and tried to get comfortable.

We talked about the day's events and how whatever was there earlier was either shy or screwing with us because, again, there was no sense of any odd spirit. I decided to try and contact whatever *it* was. At first I tried talking to the air, then I tried yelling at the air. We didn't know what we were doing back then. I thought that if I pissed off whatever was floating around, *it* would appear and we could deal with *it*. I didn't know how, but I figured one step at a time. I continued to have a conversation with the wind until I felt like a total jerk. It didn't take that long. Echo was frustrated and Patty looked nervous, although I'm not sure about what—a possible ghost or my ranting and ravings. I finally gave in and told Echo it was no use. She agreed and then asked if we would sleep over because she was afraid whatever it was would come out when we left, and we agreed. Patty insisted. She was certain whatever it was would follow us home and murder us in our sleep for yelling at it.

Just about the time we started to figure out the sleeping arrangements, all three of started getting very tired—almost like someone had drugged us. We decided to all sleep in Echo's double bed because nobody wanted to sleep alone in the living room, on the couch.

We all lay on our backs—Echo on one side of me and Patty on the other. The awkwardness of sleeping in the same bed as my sister was offset by goofy conversation. Even though we were all so tired we were also afraid to fall asleep, so we talked.

It was now late, almost three AM. We just started to close our eyes when, bang, we heard this huge noise coming from the wall separating the bedroom from the living room. The girls both grabbed me and insisted I do something about it. I tried to pretend I didn't hear anything, but when there was another bang—this time so loud it knocked a picture off the wall—I had to agree. We had company.

Echo told me I had to go into the living room and find out what *they* wanted. I asked her *why me* and she told me because I was the

man. I tried to explain that just because I had a penis didn't mean I
was more equipped to do the job. I said I thought women were more
suited to do this sort of thing because they were more sensitive.

"Yes we are," Echo said. Then she proceeded to shove me out into
the living room.

"Wait. Keep the door open," I said.

"Sure, sure," they both said and then slammed the door shut.

I stood in the middle of the pitch-black living room. I could feel
the presence of other people in the room, but I was too afraid to look.
Finally, I took my eyes off the bedroom door and looked around the
room. There, staring at me, were three full-figured ghosts—each one
in different corners of the room. I was stunned at how vivid each
one was and how clear their faces were. The person to my right was
female, about twenty-five to thirty years old. The person directly in
front of me was a male about thirty years old. The person to my left
was male too, only he was about forty. Nobody said a word. We just
looked at each other.

I had the strangest tingling sensation standing there staring at
those three ghosts. I was so scared and excited at the same time that
if someone had shot off a starter pistol, I would have gone through
the wall. I got the nerve to ask why they were here, but the only response I heard was Echo and Patty telling me to ask about what sort
of ghouls I was dealing with. They weren't making things any easier. I
tried asking again with a little false bravado, but still they were mute.

The creepy thing about it was the look on their faces. They looked
angry. About what, they weren't saying, but they were definitely
angry. I figured we could be there all night so something had to give.
With all the power of a flea fart, I told them I would get rid of them
if they didn't start talking to me. They were so scared they started to
come closer to me. Something inside of me said *feets don't fail me now*,
and I bolted for the bedroom door.

I turned the knob and ran into the bedroom in one motion. I shut
the door as fast as I could, and I jumped into bed. I told the girls I

didn't want to talk about it and said *goodnight*. Echo and Patty looked at each other like *screw that* and said, *what do you mean you don't want to talk about it, what just happened*? I could tell by their tone that they weren't going to let me sleep, so I decided to fill them in.

"Look, there are three really angry dead people out there and I don't have the slightest clue as to why," I said. I told the girls that whoever the ghosts were, they weren't talking to me, so if they wanted to give it a try, they could go out to the living room and do so, but I was going to bed. I also said that if they did go out and something happened to them not to expect me to help them. My penis and I were going to stay where we were.

They were both amazed, not only by what I'd just said, but because I left whatever was out there, out there. It was obvious they weren't going to deal with it, so we were stuck. It was also obvious nobody was going to get any sleep. We lay there, on our backs with our eyes shut, trying to pretend it was all okay. We knew it wasn't okay, but what else could we do? We talked about cooking and clothes and what each of us was going to do the next day. Then, a loud bang came from the same wall and our conversation stopped. We continued to be speechless when the lights started flickering on the wall. Patty's way of dealing with it was to pull the blanket over her eyes, which meant we all ended up under the blanket. It was a small bed.

I turned to Echo. "Ya know, I don't think I can sleep like this," I said, and just about that time I had the sense that we weren't alone. I asked Echo if she felt it. Her eyes got wide and she said *yes*. Patty also said she could feel something, but I had my doubts. Patty had somehow sucked her head so deep into her neck the only thing you could see was her hair.

I slowly pulled the covers from over my head and there, floating over us, directly in front of our faces, were the three ghosts—staring at us with that same angry look on their faces. Patty and Echo both screamed. I yelled *Jesus* and jumped up and turned on the light. I was scared and angry and I yelled at whoever they were to get the @*&$#! out now! To my relief, they did.

I walked around the apartment and turned on all the lights. My adrenaline was flowing like the river Jordan and I wasn't in the mood to talk about what just happened, but the girls were, so we talked. Patty couldn't believe what she just saw, and Echo couldn't figure out why it happened. I had no answers for any of it, so to me it was frustrating. After a few hours we did manage to fall asleep, more from exhaustion than anything, and the next day, I told Echo I was sorry I wasn't more help. I told her one possible reason for all the weirdness was maybe the dead guys wanted her gone. She said if they kept doing that crap she would leave, and we left it at that.

Later on that day, Echo's car broke down in front of an apartment complex. She went into the manager's office to use the phone and saw there was a vacancy. Because of all the stuff that was happening at her old apartment, she decided to check into it. She went through the apartment, liked what she saw, and because it just happened to be in her price range, she took it.

A week after she moved from her old apartment, there was a fire in her building and the one spot most affected was right where her old apartment used to be. Because the fire broke out at three in the morning, who knows what could've happened if Echo had stayed. A couple weeks after that, another fire broke out in the same part of the building and a month after that, the pipes blew and what was left on that side of the building was flooded.

The apparent cause of the problems was bad wiring or bad pipes. There was no mention of foul play; the building was just old. Echo never did see those spirits again, so we don't know for sure what their intentions were. I'd like to think they were warning Echo—and knowing Echo, they knew the only way to get her out was to come and literally scare her out. The only thing Echo dreaded more than a wrinkled sock was a ghost.

The thing I came away from that experience with was that I didn't like the feeling of not knowing what to do. There had to be a better way than cowering under the blankets. If I was ever in the same situation, I was going to know what to do.

The next few years I started listening more in my mother's classes. I went on field trips to haunted houses, something I thought I'd never do. I became less and less frightened and more secure in my abilities, which were getting stronger because of my willingness to learn. I could see and hear spirits on a consistent basis and I could also not see or hear them if I chose not to.

Slowly, but surely, I let the people around me in on my family business. My new friends saw me as relatively normal, so when I told them about my psychic connection, they didn't freak. Some of them were relieved. They had experiences of their own and now I was someone they could confide in.

I was comfortable learning more psychically because I felt I had a balance. My psychic abilities were coming in handy. I could get general information on a person without having to ask. I tried to keep the two worlds separate because I didn't want my bosses to think I was a witch, but the psychic impressions were starting to feel natural.

If I was in a group setting and I knew psychically that one of the patients was secretly getting high, I couldn't just blurt it out. I had to learn to take my time and work it out of the person. If I had trouble doing that, I'd try to get information on what might help bring it out. The good news was, my bosses thought I was a genius. The bad news was, I was just doing readings.

During this time I was becoming increasingly closer to Echo. We had always been close, but with both of us emerging psychically, we bonded closer together. We got even closer when Echo had another one of her experiences.

Echo had gone on a trip with a guy she had just met. They went to Canada and were going to drive from one side of the country to the other. A hell of a long time to spend with someone you hardly know, if you ask me. And as it turns out, it was. Echo had some emotional experiences with the guy that left her feeling emotionally crippled.

When she got home, she tried to describe what she was feeling to my mother, but the only thing she could do was to cry. This went on for a few days, and finally my mother asked me if I would talk to her. She thought maybe I could *pick up* on what Echo was feeling.

I called Echo and asked her if she wanted to come over. She was reluctant, because the only thing that made her feel better was sitting around her apartment crying. I told her she could cry at my apartment if she wanted to, but I just wanted to see her and see what I could get psychically. After a while she agreed, but only if I met her in the parking lot.

I waited for her to arrive and when she did, I jumped into her car. We both sat there for a second looking at each other, not knowing exactly what to do. Then I asked her how she was doing. She started to talk, but couldn't get the words out before she started crying again. I didn't know what to do so I silently said *God, please tell me what is going on with Echo.* I didn't hear anything at first and figured it was a wash.

Then, something odd started happening. I felt like someone had jumped inside my body. Having had Jerry do this to me several times when I was using drugs, I knew what it felt like. This time though I didn't feel like I was out of my body. I felt more like someone was joining me, and that someone was Echo. I suddenly felt extremely sad and frightened. The real me felt fine, so I wasn't out of control—I was just possessed.

I started telling Echo what she was feeling. I started describing to her what she went through in Canada—the fear, the loneliness, the panic. As I was doing this, Echo seemed to be coming out of her trance, like whatever she went through was leaving her, going through me—and as it was, she was able to see herself and let go.

The whole process lasted only fifteen minutes, but when someone shares your body, it feels like a week. I started feeling normal again and Echo had a huge look of relief on her face. I asked her what that was about and she was as much in the dark as I was.

We went up to my apartment and called my mother. We told her about what happened and she explained that I was used to relieve Echo's anxiety, and from this point on we would be connected. This would prove itself over and over through the years. Whenever Echo would have a headache or go through something heavy, I would feel it. Unfortunately it was a one-way deal. I only felt Echo's pain—she didn't feel mine. Of all the weird things that had happened to me up to this point, this would be the longest lasting.

Armed with our new bond and knowledge of dead people, Echo and I started doing ghost bustings together. We had been doing them separately, but now it felt natural to team up. Echo was much more diplomatic than I was. She could calm the living inhabitants, while I searched the house for the dead ones. When it came time to get rid of the spirits, one of us would talk to the spirit while the other one let the spirit talk through them.

On every ghost busting, we learned something and we applied whatever we learned to the next one. One of the first things we learned was, we were never going to get rich being ghost busters. Most times we didn't get paid and when we did, it was usually just gas money. It wasn't that people weren't willing to pay. They were. Echo and I just had a hard time charging people when we both felt it was our job to help these people. Sometimes—most times—we drove for miles to get to these places and still we felt happiest if we just got rid of the stinking ghost.

As the years went by and we became more popular, we tried being more professional and charging a regular fee, but if the person was broke or between jobs, we wouldn't push it.

Fourteen
In the Public Third Eye

"After the break, we're going to introduce two people who claim to be real-life ghost busters," the shiny, happy, uninterested host said. He looked at the camera until the stage manager yelled "all clear," and everybody relaxed. "What the hell are we doing here?" I asked Echo. "We're dispelling myths," she replied. "Oh please, it's a dumb show, with a hack host who wouldn't know a ghost if Casper kissed him on the butt," I moaned back. Just then the stage manager came up to us and pointed to our ears and then the tiny microphones attached to our shirts. "We can ALL hear everything you're saying, everybody can," he said, and then pointed to the host, who was also holding his ear. "You are so dead," Echo whispered.

As we became better known, we started to get requests to do interviews. We started showing up in newspaper and magazine articles. We did radio and local television shows. Most of the interest came from the family angle. It was a novelty.

The first few television shows we did, we got much the same questions. Did we actually believe in ghosts, what do ghosts look like, how much did we charge, are we currently on any medication, stuff like that. These questions sounded stupid. Asking a ghost buster if they believed in ghosts was like asking an exterminator if he believed in bugs, but we knew going in that there would be dumb questions so we flowed with it and tried to act as accommodating as possible.

As much as I wanted to suggest they evolve, I couldn't attack their ignorant opinions. Most of the themes in those early interviews were about us being odd, and if we acted odd or combative it would only support that opinion. We did the opposite by showing everybody how normal we were. We didn't twitch, we didn't drool, and we didn't overreact. We laughed at the psychic jokes, no matter how many times we had heard them, and if somebody was a real jerk, we let them talk and make a fool out of themselves.

An odd thing was happening to me as I was doing more television and radio. My psychic ability, which should have been an advantage for me, was becoming a hindrance. Question and answer time was always the hardest, not the psychic questions, but the normal, "how'd you get here" questions. I didn't want to open up psychically because with all the people in the audience it was like opening the flood gates, all sorts of information would come out, but I also didn't want to appear like a fake, in case someone would ask me a psychic question. It became a balancing act, and most times I wished I could just shut it off totally. It was the opposite whenever I did any acting.

In acting, my psychic ability would get in the way. When I would do a play and I'd be on stage, I'd find myself picking up on people in the audience. This could be a little bothersome, because as a performer you want to be totally focused on what's happening on stage and not be affected by what's happening in the audience. Sure you want to have a feel for the audience, but when I had a feel, I really had a feel. This got even worse when I tried stand-up comedy.

A friend of mine was an up-and-coming stand-up comic, and the way he talked about the rush he got when he was on stage made me want to try it. I was freaked at the idea, but I thought if I focused, I'd be all right. After watching a few amateur nights, I finally got the nerve to go on stage. The MC introduced me, I went to the stage, grabbed the mike, turned to face the audience, and bam, I'm a deer in the headlights.

Besides the crickets, the only sound I could hear was the pounding of my heart. Whatever routine I had worked out was gone along with the color in my face. I was grasping for some tiny remembrance of what I thought I was going to do, and the only thing that came to me was what was going on in the audience. I knew the skinny guy who was married to the blonde next to him wanted to sleep with the brunette, sitting next to the gay guy who had yet to come out of the closet. I could feel how uncomfortable the lady behind the alcoholic was at watching me squirm, and I could also feel the hostility coming from the kleptomaniac who paid good money to watch me, watching him.

I said a couple of unfunny things and got offstage as fast as I could. I hid out until the show was over and tried to find whatever pride I'd lost on stage. It was nowhere to be found. If there was something funny about that night, it was the fact that there was a news reporter there doing a story on new comics. I remember talking to him for a second or two, but the night was such a blur I wasn't sure what came out of my mouth. I did my best to forget what happened that night and went to bed, grateful that none of my friends—or anybody I knew—had seen me. When I woke up the next day, the phone was ringing off the hook. I had made the cover of the variety section of the *Minneapolis Tribune*. Under a picture of me looking like I was about to throw up was a critique of how bad I was that night.

Now maybe because of the lessons I learned growing up, I realized things like this happen for a reason. It could have meant I was getting too cocky in my life and I needed to be humbled, or maybe stand-up comedy wasn't my thing and I was a fool to even try. Or maybe I was to use this humiliation to my advantage and work through it. The first two thoughts were probably true but being a high-road-thinking kind of guy, I decided to go with the latter.

The next time I went on stage I billed myself as the comic who sucks. It was a truth-in-advertisement sort of thing, which broke the ice and made me feel more comfortable. I wasn't funny, but I didn't give people the bends, like the first time I went on stage. I also used my psychic abilities to help me instead of hurt me by picking on the people in the audience I knew would be okay with it. Eventually I stopped doing stand-up because I didn't have the passion for it like the people who were successful at it had—but like my buddy said, it was a huge rush.

In some cases, using my psychic instincts wasn't always the best thing to do, like when I was a chef. One day my old girlfriend and I were watching television and I saw this ad for chef school. As far as I was concerned this was a message from God. Here was something I could literally sink my teeth into that didn't have anything to do with psychic phenomena. So I signed up for the two-year course, committed to cooking. But when I graduated and was out in the world using my culinary skills, my psychic instincts crept in. I would pick up information on the person I was making the food for. I could tell whether the person liked something or didn't like it, even before I served it. This would drive my fellow workers nuts because sometimes I would throw the food out and start over when there didn't appear to be anything wrong with it. It also made it difficult to keep a job.

I tried bartending for a while, but watching all the spirits jump in those drunk people took the fun out of getting them drunk. I tried selling cars, but there again if I used my psychic ability on a possible client, I ended up getting way more information than I needed and if I didn't use my ability, I was as useless as a lawyer with a soul.

No matter what occupation I got into, it always pointed back to being psychic—something my mother and sister Echo reminded me of on a daily basis. Their contention was I was avoiding the obvious, which was that I was supposed to be doing readings. And I was avoiding doing readings. I wasn't sure I was ready to take this whole thing seriously. I wasn't sure this was something I wanted to do for the rest of my life. But with every television show or newspaper interview we did, the public became more interested. The doors just opened. And when people would call to make appointments I would have been a fool not book them, so I did.

But I kept some of my individuality. I'd give readings at bars or at restaurants. I was brash and cocky. I came to the point and told them right off the bat what I could and couldn't tell them. I probably came off a little unprofessional, but it made it more fun for me. I was amazed people paid me to begin with, and if someone didn't like the reading, I wouldn't charge them.

The weird thing to me was, people liked it. The more blunt I was, the more calls I got. If I was really insulting, they really liked me. Call someone an asshole and I'd get a tip. I became more daring in my predictions and as they came true, I started to believe the things people were saying about me—that I had this amazing ability and I was a master psychic. As my waiting list got bigger, so did my ego.

Another benefit to being more public was that the ghost busting business was also picking up. Before the publicity, we'd do maybe a couple a year. Now with all the attention, we were doing four or five a month. The majority of the calls were just *bumps in the night* calls, not real scary, just ghosts who got bored and wanted some attention. But on the more serious calls, ones where the floors were bleeding or animals were mysteriously dying, we'd bring people with us who'd never seen ghosts before—usually friends or friends of friends.

Sometimes we'd get carried away and bring too many people but we didn't know any better. We were learning as we were going. The first time we brought too many people was when we were called to a house that had been built over the grounds of an old mental institution. The people living there said they heard weird noises, felt a creepy feeling, and things were disappearing and then reappearing for no reason. They said it got to where they were thinking of just moving out, but then seeing us on television, they thought maybe we could help.

At first, this was just a typical call. Echo and I had been on dozens of these kind of jobs and it didn't warrant bringing anybody along. But then the homeowners called back and said things had gotten worse. A bad smell developed in certain rooms, stuffed animals started levitating in the kids' rooms, and a general sense of fear filled their house.

With the new developments, we thought this might be a good time to bring some friends along. We had been promising to bring people with us for so long our list had gotten pretty big, but as long as they didn't make fools of themselves we thought it would be okay. We packed up the van and headed out.

On the way out there we talked about the possibilities of things to come. I talked about the experiences we already had and this turned out to be our first mistake. When you start telling ghost stories to a group of people who have never seen a ghost before, and you're on your way to a ghost busting on a dark and stormy night, tensions will rise. I thought some levity might ease things, so I started joking with Echo that maybe tonight we would see Elvis Presley, something Echo had wanted to do since the big E kicked the bucket.

When we arrived with our throng of anxious friends, about seven more people greeted us at the door. When we were setting this deal up, neither side mentioned that we were inviting other people, so instead of four or five, we had a group of about fifteen. This would be our second mistake. The only thing missing was the circus clowns and they showed up later, floating in the basement.

Echo and I decided to break up the group and put them in separate rooms. If someone saw something odd or unusual, they could yell out to either one of us and we could come and help. By doing this we could go about our business and not have the gallery following us around. But it was also our third mistake. Some of the rooms we were putting these people in were haunted.

One thing ghosts do love is an audience, especially a giddy one. If you have an already giddy group of people and you put those people in a dark, maybe haunted room, giddiness can lead to nervousness. Nervousness and imagination can lead to fear, which can lead to panic, and the only thing a ghost has to do to set the whole group off is whisper *boo* and everybody will start screaming and claim to see floating dolls and hands coming at them.

Such was the case at this house. The people in the haunted rooms started seeing things and screaming. This, in turn, set off the people in the non-haunted rooms. Everybody started screaming. People then started yelling for me to come to wherever they were, but I couldn't be in all the places at one time. I'd run to the nearest room, calm the person down then run to the next room, kinda like Abbott and Costello. Meanwhile, Echo, who was checking out the laundry room and *not* the calmest person on the planet, was having her own little episode. I heard her scream *it's Elvis, it's Elvis,* and caught her as she ran out of the laundry room with her eyes wide open, panting like a race dog. She looked me in the face and swore she'd just seen Elvis in the laundry room.

I rolled my eyes as hard as I could and asked her if it was the skinny Elvis or the one from Vegas. She told me to shut up and go see for my-self. I knew at this point Echo probably didn't see the King in some rural basement laundry room, but I also knew even a broken clock is right twice a day so why not check for myself. I went in. I looked around and sure enough there he was, the King himself. Behind a rack of clothes, on the wall, a four-foot poster of Elvis on stage, in Vegas. I finally got to meet the King.

I went out to the hall and told Echo about the poster. We both had a laugh until our employer came down and asked me if we were really professionals. With all of the screaming and joking going on, I couldn't blame her. We assured her we were professionals and decided to put everyone in the living room with the lights on while we got rid of the spirits.

The job itself didn't take that long, although the spirits turned out to be pretty nasty. They were people who had been in a mental institu-tion for certain crimes they had done and didn't want to go to heaven, fearing they would be punished. We eventually talked them into going to the light and cleaned out the rooms with sage.

From that point on, we only brought two people at the most on a job, and we checked them out beforehand to make sure if they did see anything, they wouldn't freak out. Every ghost busting job we did, we learned another little trick or way of dealing with a ghost. After a few years, we could go into any situation and feel comfortable. It was starting to become routine and as the world was embracing psychics more, it was no longer a novelty in some parts to have your house cleaned by a ghost buster. It was becoming chic.

Meanwhile, my psychic ego was growing to grotesque proportions, so much so that my spirit buddies decided to bring me down a notch. I was doing a local radio show and one of the personalities asked me to do a reading for him. He told me he had gotten other readings, but wanted to see if I was as good as everyone said I was. I figured I would show him what a real psychic could do, and agreed to read him right there on the spot.

A normal reading goes like this. I sit down with people. I concentrate on their first name and like a door opening, I start getting information on them. I see pictures, images, and if they're not shy, I also tap into their spirit guides. Sometimes when a person asks me to do a reading for them, I might do a pre-reading for the person the day before, just to make sure I can pick up on them. But since I became super psychic, I stopped doing any pre-reading jazz and just jumped into it.

When I went to do the reading, everything was as usual. I concentrated on the host's first name, started to get information, and as always, it felt right. I rambled on for a while, telling him about his likes and dislikes, where he'd been and where he was right now. I told him about his wife, her good and bad points. I described his business and how he felt about it, and I told him about his last job and why he had to change.

Normally I don't look at the person when I do the reading because I don't want to get thrown off by their reaction, but I was so sure I was nailing this guy that I had to look up and see the look of awe and amazement as I dazzled him with my gifts. But he didn't look dazzled. In fact he looked anything but. I stopped the reading and asked him if everything was okay, sometimes a reading can be so overwhelming it leaves you speechless, I assumed this was the case. He paused for a second, and then said, "I'm not sure you got the right person, everything you've said so far has been pretty wrong."

"Strange," I thought. Everything I said felt so right. I thought that maybe I was explaining it wrong, so I asked what specifically was *off*.

He looked at me sheepishly and said *"Everything."*

"You mean you don't understand anything I've said?" I asked.

"Oh, no. I understood it," he said. "It just didn't have anything to do with me."

I thought he was kidding. I had never been that wrong before in my life, but judging by the look on his face, he thought I was the joke. I told him I would try again and when I did, I got absolutely nothing.

I started digging for anything I could get. I did what you're never supposed to do in a reading, I asked *him* the questions instead of him asking me. I asked him about his wife, his work, his kids, I interviewed the guy hoping something, anything would come, but nothing came.

Finally, he put his hand up to mercifully stop me from rambling on and reached into his pocket. He had a look on his face I will never forget—embarrassed, uncomfortable, disgusted, and concerned. He pulled out two twenties and handed them to me. "No" I said, shaking my head, mortified he would even think to give me money. He put the bills in my sweaty hand and motioned me not to bother putting up a fight. "You're going to need this," he said. He got up, half smiled and left. I held the twenties in my hand and tried to figure out what the hell had just happened.

The next few months I did readings, I came up with the same results. I either got totally wrong information or none at all. The more

I pushed it, the worse it got. Even people I had done in the past I couldn't do; it was like looking at a blank screen.

As a last resort, I called my mom to see if she knew what I could do. I really didn't want to call her, but things had gotten so bad I had too. When she answered the phone she was upbeat and happy. I told her I was having trouble with my readings, making sure not to mention how bad I was. I asked her if she knew what I could do to get on track.

"Yeah," she said. "You can bake cookies."

I paused, thinking my minimizing had caused her to underreact. "No, Mom, it's a little worse than that," I told her. "I can't get anything on anybody, and nothing I do seems to make a difference."

"Do you have any vanilla?" she answered back.

"Mom!" I said, ready to beg and plead for something from her "I'm serious. I think something's broken."

She laughed. "Honey," she said, "I know you're serious, but somewhere on your way to becoming the Second Coming, you forgot the basic rule of doing readings. It's the information you get, not the person delivering it. I don't know how long it will be before you get it back, hopefully you will, but until then, bake cookies. Clean your room, come over here and shampoo my rug. When it comes back you will know." With that she hung up.

Almost three years later it still hadn't come back, and being normal was becoming a challenge. I took a job at a giant retail chain, selling washers and dryers, stereos and TVs. At first it was simple and I welcomed it. Go to work, do a good job, get a little raise, punch out on time, live for the weekend. When a customer came in, I didn't *feel* their energy, I just sold them stuff. And the more I sold, the better I felt. Nobody knew that I was a psychic, and that, for me, was the best part of the job.

Socially it was school all over again. Nerd types, jock types, overachievers, under-achievers, kiss asses, prima donnas, all worked at various positions, and all bonded by the oppression of the man, or whoever was in charge. MY psychic days seemed another lifetime ago and I wondered if I would ever get them back.

Like school I slipped into the role of class clown. As the boredom and routine became mind numbing, I became less interested in sales and more interested in pranks. Boundaries became the new challenge, stretching, pushing, testing—try as I could, I just couldn't embrace the notion of living a normal life.

But help was on the way. One day as a manager in training was lecturing me on the many reasons why *not* to sell dishwashers using only mime techniques, a wonderful thing happened—my dead guys finally showed up again.

A customer had gone to the manager in training to support his hiring of a mime. He felt that although it took longer to understand what I was saying, in the long run my physical demonstrations were very helpful. The manager in training thanked the customer and then ran to where I was stationed. "Okay, who's the frickin mime," he said, looking around to the three people standing at the work area of appliances. As my two co-workers spread apart like the red sea and snickered to themselves under their breath, I did what every self-respecting mime would do, I treated manager in training to "the box." Instead of laughing, manager in training became angry with each unanswered question by me. His face got red, his veins protruded, and when I tried the invisible "tug of war," he got so upset he pushed my hands down and pointed his finger within an inch of my face. "Don't pull that mime crap on me," he said, spit coming from his mouth.

Normally I would have stopped by then and made the attempt to listen, but I was having too much fun pissing this guy off. Which was odd because he was a manager in training. He could actually write me up, get me in trouble, but somehow I knew he wouldn't. I remember thinking, "Okay, Michael, start pretending like you care," but when I did, out of the blue I heard the words "divorce."

By this time, a small group had gathered to find out why the manager in training was yelling. He was on a roll, I was his chance to make a name for himself and now, with an audience, he was going to assert his authority over me with the flare of Mussolini. But my attention was elsewhere; I was searching my memory banks for that voice. It was a familiar voice, a forgiving voice, a voice from the past. In my need to hear the voice again, I didn't notice the shock in everybody's face when I told manager in training to shut up. I also didn't notice how stupid I looked, straining to listen to a voice only I could hear. But in the five seconds when he and everybody else were stunned, and unsure of what to do next, I heard the voice again and this time it said, "He's in the middle of a divorce, his wife found another man."

It was so good to hear that voice, to know it was talking to me. It was like hearing my mother say, "You're not grounded anymore." I felt forgiven. A smile came over my face and I looked at manager in training with an almost grateful look on my face. He, on the other hand, had turned a slight shade of purple and my newfound nirvana wasn't the look he was hoping for. Nevertheless, I couldn't help myself. It didn't matter what he said, it didn't matter what he did, I felt like I was back.

The voice again said, "He found his wife with another man" and I suddenly realized I needed to be nice. "They" wanted me know this for a reason, and I was pretty sure it wasn't to mock or embarrass him.

Manager in training was beside himself, steam was building up in his little manager head and I knew an apology wouldn't be enough. I leaned into him, so only he could hear. "I know about the divorce thing and I'm sorry, I can only imagine what it felt like to find your wife," and then I motioned up and down with my eyes. "You know," I said. He looked at me like I was Satan, his eyes got huge and his mouth went wide. "And about that whole mime thing. I'm sorry. I won't do that again, I promise," I said as sincerely as I could. He looked around at the silent little group that had gathered and then looked back at me. He put his eyes down and walked away as fast as he came, without saying a word. Maybe he thought everybody else knew and wanted to get the hell out of there, or maybe I just freaked him out. Who knew? The next day I put in my two-week notice and I never saw him again.

The moral of that little experience was to never take myself too seriously. I can be good, bad, somewhere in the middle, but I'm not that great a psychic. Whatever I get, it's because "they" want to give it to me and I will be grateful for whatever "it" is. If not, I can always sell dishwashers.

A few years earlier, I was doing a reading for a girl downtown and she asked a friend to join us. Her friend came down and we all went to a club to go dancing. Her friend said she also wanted a reading and we set it up for a week later. I met the girl at a restaurant to do the reading. Right before I started, I heard the front desk page tell me there was a phone call for me. I went to the phone and it was my mother. How she knew I was there was a mystery, but she asked me to please be nice to the girl I was giving a reading to. I asked her why the interest, and she told me the woman was going to be a major influence in my life. I thought it odd, but I promised her I would.

My mother was right. Four years later we got married. We also bought a fixer-upper house and had two of the greatest kids a person could pray for. When my daughter was born, we got cards and gifts from the old psychics congratulating me on her birth. They all talked about how special she was, and that she was going to be a powerful psychic and healer. Not exactly music to my ears, but one look in her eyes and I knew they were right. She had the look of an old soul and when I held her for the first time, I fell instantly in love with her. I also knew she would teach me more than I could possibly teach her. I decided to wait and see if her psychic ability surfaced and not push it. Hopefully it wouldn't start coming out until she was fifty.

I didn't think I could love a human more than my daughter until we had our son. He is equally special, but for different reasons. He's normal, sensitive, and yet wild like his father. Because I didn't bond with my father, I made it a point to bond with my kids. I stayed home and took care of them while my wife went to work at a beauty salon she bought from her old boss.

After a few years, I slowly and surely came back on line psychically. I don't think I ever lost it; I think it got all gunged up by my ego and insensitivity. I decided that if I was going to do readings again, I was just going to do business readings and stay away from the personal ones for a while.

A few years before my psychic bulb went screwy, I started doing readings for a big-dog businessman named Bob. Bob would have me sneak up the back stairway to his office because his big-dog-in-training son, Bob Jr. (the reborn Christian), thought psychics were evil.

Bob Sr. wanted his son to feel like he was running the business, give him confidence as he passed the torch. In reality, Bob Sr. was running the business and in the process using whatever tool he could to make it more profitable.

He would give me a list of people he was interested in hiring and ask who I thought he should hire. He also wanted to know about in-house promotions. He said he was spending a lot of money promoting people through the company and when they didn't work out, he was out that money. So he would tell me the person's first name and the division they were thinking about promoting him or her to. If it felt like a good fit, I'd tell him. If not, I'd tell him where I thought the person might fit better. We talked about stocks and what to invest in and what not to.

He would tell me the name of a stock and what it was at. I would tell him if I thought it was going to get higher or lower. If it was going to go higher, I'd tell him to buy. If it was going to go lower, I'd tell him to wait and then buy. As long as I didn't do it for money, I did pretty well—about 75 to 85 percent accuracy. But if I started doing it to get a percentage of the profits, or the profits were my only concern, then my accuracy average dropped to about 35 percent and sometimes lower.

It was easy for me to do business readings because, unlike doing personal readings, it was black and white. I didn't have to pick up on any odd relationship or weird psychosis, or try to reassure the person that they weren't going to die within the next week. All I had to do was say buy or sell, hire or fire, and life was good.

After working with Bob for a while, I was slowly introduced to his inner circle, the big financial hitters of our community. Bob would sneak me into his buddies' boardrooms and soon I was knee deep in suits. But for me, this was the best time I had doing readings and it felt like a perfect fit. The first time I walked into a boardroom full of Bob's friends I recognized most of them from either the newspaper or television. I liked that. These were powerful guys and, as a psychic, if you're around powerful people, you feel powerful. Bob walked on in, in front of me, and pointed to a chair at the head of a large oval-shaped desk. I wasn't sure whether he wanted me to stand or sit, so I stood. In front of me sat eight or nine men, all looking to be in their sixties, except one gentlemen who appeared to be in his forties.

Bob said to the group, "This is the kid I've been telling you about, you know the psychic kid." He sat down and looked at the confused faces. "Go ahead, ask him something, he ain't going to bite," and with that Bob gave me a smile. I smiled back and looked at the rest of the group. Nobody knew what to say.

The room stayed quiet until the fortyish-looking man finally spoke up. "Okay, I don't how this works, do you need a birth date or something?"

"No," I said. "Just give me a rough idea of what you want to know."

Again the room went quiet. He looked to the rest of group for a question. It started to feel awkward. Just as I was about to say never mind and give him a general read, Bob jumped in.

"Okay, look, Michael, this is John." Bob looked over at the younger-looking male. "Talk to John like you talk to me, just give him something he would know so he knows how you work." I looked back at

John who was now looking like an expectant mother. As I looked, all his spirit guides showed up and began to talk.

I looked back at Bob, who gave me a reassuring nod, and I went back to John. "John," I said. "You need to wear a blood pressure cuff and a smoke detector wherever you go, because you are one tense mother," I smiled. "You're ambitious, you're creative, and you're bored, that's why you're having the fling with the waitress. If you keep having the fling, your wife will find out, but for now she doesn't know.

Bob started laughing, and the man next to John said, "Damn, I like this kid."

The man next to him said, "He's got you pegged, Johnnie boy."

Bob said, "See, I told you this kid was good."

John, who was stone-faced, looked around to the rest of the group and said, "You ask him something."

The man to Bob's right jumped in. "Okay, I've got a question."

"What's your name, Phil," Bob barked.

"Hey, if he's any kind of psychic he should know my name."

"I'm going to go with Phil," I replied, and the rest of the group laughed.

Phil smiled and continued. "Okay. I'm thinking about merging with a group called Omitech, what do you think?"

I looked at Phil, and again all his "people" showed up. "Dumb idea," I said. "This group has more holes than Swiss cheese, and if you do get in bed with them it will be years before you see any value." Phil looked perplexed. "Your right-hand man has a personal interest in this group and you're being lazy by blindly trusting him."

Again Bob laughed. "I have to agree with the kid on this, Phil, you have gotten soft since you met Julie."

"Phil," I said. "Just look at the books yourself—this is something you would have never done a year ago, because you know there's something screwy going on."

Phil smiled. "Interesting kid," he said, and so it went.

For every question I was asked, it was like I had the answers before they were asked. It was clean, sharp, to the point, and for the first time I didn't feel like a freak show. By the time I was finished I was being offered five thousand bucks to check on people's wives, which I didn't do.

During those few years when I didn't do any readings and I got my humility back in place, Bob Sr. died. The last time I saw Bob, he looked happy. He was in a fun relationship and looked forward to retirement. I thought with his death I wouldn't be seeing any of his friends anymore, but if anything my services became more desired.

Because I thought my psychic ability was off, I didn't even take business calls. But the more I said no, the more they wanted me. When my third eye started getting clearer and I thought I might be ready, the business boys were anxious to go.

With my contacts in business and the people in the acting business, it was only a matter of time before I started reading actors. When Shirley MacClain came out of the closet, a lot of actors started wanting readings, and with my new sense of humility, I came off as grounded.

My life had developed into a manageable psychic lifestyle. I took care of the kids, did mostly phone readings, and was finally phasing out the lifeless ghost busting that we had been doing for way too long.

Fifteen
Full Circle

"I'll tell you one thing," she said, as she ate her soup. "This is the last time I'm coming back." "What?" I replied. "You don't like the food?" "Not the restaurant, you dipstick, here, Earth!" "Oh," I retorted, "and how do you figure that?" She gave me a stern look and then calmly explained her thinking. "I figure we keep coming back until we get it all straight. Then once we do, we don't have to come back." "Well, that's good news for me," I said, rather proudly. "I don't have to come back either." "You!" she shrieked, nearly choking on her soup. "You'll have to come back more times than a Roman."

It was around eight o'clock. The darker side of dusk was coming up, and wanting to wait until it was completely dark before we arrived, we took a stroll around the neighborhood. I was glad for the extra time. I wasn't upset at doing the job, but I wasn't excited either. As we finally drove up the long driveway, I got a glimpse of the house and had a feeling that this one was going to be different. Not because it looked bad. On the contrary, the house looked normal, even comfortable. The lawn was mowed. The bushes were pruned, and a hanging basket of flowers and a night light greeted us as we parked in the driveway.

It wasn't the outside of the house that was bugging me. It was the feeling around the house. When I first looked at the house, it felt cold and empty, like a mausoleum. I looked over at my sister Echo to see her reaction. Usually when we'd pull up to a bad one she'd shiver like a cold Chihuahua, but she seemed fine, so I let it go.

The only reason we even took this job was because we hoped that it was going to be our last job. For years we had been trying to retire, but everyone that we trained to replace us didn't work out. They either let the experience go to their heads, charged way too much, or ended up making things worse. We would end up going back to the jobs that they had started and mopping up their mess—usually for free.

One of the ways they would make it worse would be the way they would go about doing it. Some people feel safer using religion or the Bible to address the ghost. They automatically assume whatever is haunting them is demonic, and rant and rave, using whatever religious symbols they feel will ward off what they see as a demon. Unfortunately by doing this, they give whatever is haunting them more power than most of them deserve.

Ghosts may act like jerks. They may do stupid things and they might even smell bad, but they're not demons. I'm not saying that there are not demons out there. I've met living people who would qualify as demonic. I'm saying the majority of calls we receive are about ghosts, and ghosts are simply dead people. As with some people, alive or dead, you throw a Bible in their face and they might not get the point. They could be Atheist or Hindu or whatever, and not care what it says in the Bible.

The typical ghost busting job should go like this: you go to the house and talk to the people living in the house about what's been happening, then you identify any ghosts. You reassure the living people that they're not crazy. You come up with a plan to get rid of the ghosts. You get rid of the ghosts, and boom, you're done. It's that simple.

Our two new trainees, Jamie and Bruce, had a basic instinct on how to deal with ghosts. They weren't too flaky (you'd have to be a little flaky to do the job). They weren't into the money. They weren't interested in becoming famous. And on the two previous jobs when Jamie and Bruce had come along, they handled themselves well. Also and probably more importantly, they loved doing it. And not just because they might see blood coming through the walls, but they loved the whole process—a feeling Echo and I had lost a long time ago.

So there I was, staring at what I hoped would be the last ghost busting job I would ever need to do. Our trainees were pumped, Echo was ready, and if we hurried, we could get home in time for *E.R.*

When we got to the door and rang the bell, Echo checked my look to make sure I had that professional glow that you need when you tangle one-on-one with the undead. The smile on her face suggested I did.

As soon as the host Vicki answered the door and told us to come in, the smile on Echo's face disappeared. She grabbed my hand as if to stop me from going in. I looked at my hand, then at her. She had a look of fear and anger in her eyes. She asked me to wait. I said okay. I told our trainees to go ahead and we'd be in shortly.

I pulled her aside and told her that the least she could do was wait to freak out until after we saw something. I went on to explain how unprofessional I thought it was to freak out at the door, but Echo wasn't in the mood for my sarcasm. She put her fingers to her lips and gave me the shhh sign.

"We can't do this one," she said.

Any other time, this would have been music to my ears. I was usually the one trying to figure out angles as to why not to do a job. I asked her if she could give me a clue as to why we couldn't do this one. Then she said she knew this woman. She had been calling Echo for months complaining about the black magic spells her ex-husband had put on her and the house. She said she didn't take the job because it felt wrong.

I reminded her that she was the one who booked this deal and asked what changed her mind.

"I didn't change my mind," she said. "I told Mary, the lady who's been calling, we weren't interested in doing the job. I told her to find someone else because we were retiring. But when this Vicki person called and said she just had a few ghosts in her house, would we come and get rid of them, I thought it would be a perfect chance to have Jamie and Bruce see us in action one more time before we retired."

I told Echo that I followed her so far, but didn't get the punch line. She told me to shut up so she could finish. She said Vicki's name wasn't Vicki—it was Mary, the woman who had been calling. I asked her how she knew it was the same woman on the phone and she said she recognized her voice when she answered the door. I asked her why she didn't recognize her voice when she called as Vicki. She said her mother made the call.

Because Echo was so nervous about this one, I wanted to be as light as possible. The truth was, I was a little nervous about this one myself. It did feel wrong somehow, like whatever was going on in that house was none of our business. The feeling in the air had a familiar negativity to it. I couldn't place where I last felt it, but I knew I had felt it somewhere and it wasn't a good experience. I also knew if I acted anxious it would only make things worse for Echo, so I just kept my mouth shut and we went back to the house.

We got to the door and as we went in, I felt that negative feeling getting stronger. Normally this would be a red flag, a warning for me to put extra protection around myself, but for some reason I didn't. I just wanted to get the job done.

When we walked in, Jaime and Bruce were sitting on the couch. Other than looking out of place (like cheerleaders at a biker bar), they were intact. Sitting with them was Vicki and another woman who had come to watch. We apologized for keeping them waiting and sat down to discuss what was going on.

For me this was the worst part of any job—the story. Every job had a story and unfortunately it was just as important to listen to the story as it was to get rid of the ghost. Echo could listen until the cows came home. She actually hated the story just as much as I did, but she came across as more understanding.

Usually while Echo was listening and being understanding, I would try and get a feel for what was going on in the house. When people get into the stories, there tends to be more tension in the air, like when you tell a spooky story around the campfire. What I try and do is separate myself from that drama. I try and picture the house as a salesperson would see it, or a cleaning person. What's my first, second, third impression. Then I do a little psychic sweep of the place and see if any blips come up on the screen. Most of the time I have to excuse myself and walk around alone to do that, and most of the time the people in the house don't mind.

I stood up and asked if I could walk around and see what I could pick up. When I did, Jamie and Bruce wanted to come along but I told them I needed to do this myself and that I'd be right back.

While they stayed in the living room chatting, I went to where the feeling was strongest—the bedroom. For me, the closer I come to a bad spot, the tighter my gut gets. It's like being in line for a roller coaster—the anticipations builds as you get closer. In most cases it's more excitement than fear—but not this one. As I said it felt scarier than most. When I got to the bedroom, I turned the lights off and stood in the middle of the floor. I shut the lights off because it's easier to see spirits in the dark and I stand in the middle of the room so I feel as much of the room as possible, Normally, if a spirit is around I will see or feel it within the first couple of minutes. If a spirit leaves before I come, I can still feel the presence of that spirit much like you would feel the presence of someone who just left your house.

Judging by the way I felt before I got to the room I fully expected to see something as I stood in the middle of the room. But after five minutes went by and I didn't feel or see even the slightest entity, I assumed my radar was off.

I sat on the bed and tried to figure out what was going on. The room was still dark, but my eyes were adjusting to the lack of light and I could see the room clearer. It looked like a party room. One wall was covered with pro-drug, anti-establishment posters, and the other walls were covered by hand-painted notes and scenes painted by friends or people who had spent a lot of time there. Besides the frameless bed, the other main bit of furniture was a stereo and on it, an overfilled ashtray along with a bong. In a lot of ways it reminded me of my cousin's room in the basement of our old house, only smaller. It had that crash-pad feel to it and it hit me that maybe that was where that familiar feeling was coming from. It also hit me that I was starting to feel dizzy, real dizzy. I thought I might be picking up on whoever had last slept on the bed, which can happen from time to time. But as I stood up to get my bearings, a rush of anxiety and fear overtook me, and I knew this was different. I could still hear the people talking in the other room, but it sounded like I was underwater.

I walked out to the hall and then the bathroom. I wanted to put water on my face and try and snap out of whatever was happening to me. I could feel my heart pounding and for a second I thought I might pass out. I got to the sink and turned on the faucet. I put my face down close to the water and splashed my face while I talked myself down. I knew whatever was happening to me didn't have to do with me—it had to do with the house—but I also knew I needed to be careful because whatever it was, was strong. I lifted my head and looked in the mirror and there in the reflection was Jerry.

I turned around and faced him. He looked weathered and old. But the familiar dark and scary aura that always seemed to be around him was still as strong as ever. They say that if an alcoholic goes back to drinking, even if he's been sober for thirty years, his body and mind reverts back to who he was when he last drank. Seeing Jerry for the first time in twenty-five years had the same effect on me. I was back in the early seventies, and I felt small and uncertain. I didn't feel like I knew what I was doing, and Jerry, although technically just another spirit, felt huge to me.

But something *was* different, and not just because I was taller, or my stomach was bigger. I was different, I wasn't the same kid who got a tight gut every time I saw Jerry, I'd learned a few things since those days and my adult side seemed to want to kick in. I reminded myself of some of the experiences I'd been through, since the last time I saw Jerry. Like the time I saw slap marks appear on a man six-foot-two and two hundred pounds after he was hit by a female spirit who was jealous of his girlfriend, or the welt marks I saw on Echo's face after she was struck by a spirit on a ghost busting job. I saw a spirit put their hands around my wife's throat, and I've had my hair pulled back and my hands grabbed by blacked-gloved female spirits. I've been engulfed by blackness so dense I couldn't see my hand in front of my face. I've had things thrown at me and things knocked out of my hands. I've been pinched, poked, and prodded. I've been whispered to, yelled at, and screamed at by ghosts who hated my presence. I've seen countless floating heads, hands, arms, and bodies.

And even though these experiences were unnerving and some downright scary, I knew I could handle it. I knew the spirits that were doing this stuff wanted to see how I would react. If I freaked out, it was to their advantage, but if I didn't, it was to mine, because once you take their power away, they become small.

I decided to start from scratch and protect myself as much as I could. I started with the basics: I surrounded myself with white light, I prayed to replace my fear with love, and I grounded myself the best I could. I thought of the people I love and I felt my heart become lighter. I must've done that same ritual a thousand times and each time I did, it amazed me how quickly it worked. The calmness came and I stopped being afraid, mostly.

No matter how calm I felt, Jerry still looked scary. I asked him why he was there, but he didn't answer, he just stared, a cold, detached stare. I asked him again, but this time I didn't wait for an answer, I kept talking. I decided if he didn't want to talk, I would talk for him, which in the past always pissed him off. Sometimes in situations like this, it turns into a standoff—if you underestimate a spirit, tell the spirit to leave and it doesn't, you end up looking stupid, or worse, ineffective. You have to find a middle ground, an angle in which to connect to the spirit. It's up to the living person to find the angles to get them to talk. The reason you want them to talk is so you can better help them go to the other side, which is really your job. Sometimes you have to bring in a relative who has also passed, to help bring the spirit to the other side. But what you don't want to do is give the spirit a sense they have the control. Be kind, but not weak. If you come off weak you could be there all night.

When I went to that camp, and the Yoda dude drew me a picture of Jerry and told me he was my spirit guide, I believed him. As I grew up and Jerry and I became close, I still thought of him as my spirit guide. But spirit guides don't scare you and they don't jump inside your body and they don't feel better when you feel bad. Jerry did all those things and more.

When Birdie and I sent Jerry on his way, I remembered his fear of going to the other side as the main reason for his staying earthbound. Spirit guides don't do that either.

What I started to realize was that Jerry was an unevolved spirit, or soul, who, for whatever reason, stayed earthbound, I reminded myself that psychics are often wrong, as was the case with Yoda, and I reminded myself that Jerry wasn't different, he was just better at staying earthbound.

"Jerry," I said. "I gotta go. You want to be in this house with all the drama and depression, I'm not going to stop you." I turned my back and started out the door.

"I've always been here, I never left," he said. "I'll always find a place to be—you were right not to try."

When I heard him speak, it was like going back in time. I turned around and looked at him, and he smiled. "I like it here," he said. "I like depression, I like drama, what's your excuse?" And then he smirked, just like the old Jerry. "I tell ya who needs to not be here," he continued, "that's you, pal." He paused and then with bone-chilling detachment said, "Remember?"

If you've ever thought of someone or something and it comes to you with such detail and clarity that you can almost taste or smell the place you're thinking about, then you know how it felt, when Jerry said that to me. Just like that, I was back in the kitchen listening to the old psychics.

We were talking about choices and how life was all about what we decided. It was a topic we discussed a lot, and actually one of my favorites. The old psychics believed we could have anything we wanted, good or bad. It was as simple as believing you were going to have it. The problem, they said, was most people talked or acted like bad things were expected, mostly so they wouldn't get disappointed if good things didn't work out. But by thinking bad things were going to happen, most of the time they would. It all boiled down to self-worth—if you didn't feel like you deserved good things, then you didn't get them. This conversation would almost always loop around to self-love and God issues, but the first part was my favorite.

The kitchen crew would talk for hours about this "wand" we all had and how we could use it any time we wanted. The theory was, first you decide what you want. It could be a car or a new job or more money, or whatever. Then the next step, you visualized it, seeing it in your mind's eye. The third thing, and probably the most important step, was expecting it to come. That was the key, *the knowing* you were going to get it. The old psychics likened it to sending mail. You write the letter, you put it in an envelope, and then you put the envelope in the mailbox. You don't stand there with the letter in hand praying it will be delivered, you trust it will, and let it go. But each week a new person would say something stupid like "Hey where's my car?" or "I didn't get that job I ordered," and the old psychics would just roll their eyes, because they knew that person didn't get it. "You'll see it when you believe it," they would say, and put their energy into people they thought took it seriously.

And the "wand" did work. Story after story, people who believed would tell us about things they wanted and got, and then comment about how easy it was.

I loved those stories, I believed those stories, I saw it working and I wanted to know exactly how it was done. Jerry, on the other hand, liked the people who didn't get it, and did nothing but complain. Their stories were about how hard life was and how so-and-so never got a break. And for them, they never did get a break.

The part that got me was the realization that however my life ended up was basically because of choices I made. All these years I had felt cursed because I was a psychic. I felt like I had no choice but to talk to dead people and tell fortunes. And now with this little trip down memory lane I was reminded that all along it was my choice. I was the one who chose to be the psychic, I was the one who always went back to being a psychic when the other jobs didn't work out. It was one of those "Oh shit" moments that come along ever once in a while, and in this case the timing couldn't have been worse.

He looked at me with a cocky smile and asked me again, "So what *are* you doing here?"

This was a good question, probably the only good question Jerry ever asked. It could be applied either philosophically or literally—I wouldn't have a good answer for either one. And he knew it was a question I often asked myself, including the forty-five times I'd asked myself since walking in the door. But I don't think either of us was expecting the answer that came to me so clear and simple.

His point, at least from what I felt psychically, was I hated my job, hated my job choices. And if that was the case, how could I effectively sway anybody to make changes in their life if I couldn't do the same for myself?

"So what?" So what if I didn't like what I do, *lots* of people don't like what they do, but they do it, because they know how to do it or they do it for the money or they do it because they have to, but they do it. And these aren't bad people; they're just doing their jobs. And that was what I was doing: my job. For some reason that simple notion took all the weird psychic responsibility off of my shoulders, and I stopped feeling guilty for not liking my job.

Jerry's cocky smirk was gone when I looked at him.

"I'm here to get rid of the rotten ghost," I said. "But I have the feeling you're not ready to go to the other side." I felt clear as I was talking to him, like this was just my job and not some world event that could change life as I knew it if I didn't get rid of him. If he didn't go, he didn't go. I didn't care either way.

And Jerry knew it. "What, are you crazy?" he said. "You think you have the power to send me to the other side?" He looked at me with both fear and anger. "See ya," he said, and just like that he was gone.

I gathered my thoughts and walked out to the room where everybody was sitting. I motioned to Echo to come to me and when she did I told her this wasn't going to work. I told her the spirit in the house wasn't going to leave, no matter what we did, and since we weren't going to make a difference we should pack our things and go. A half a second later she agreed. We all went out to eat afterward, as usual after a job, but instead of talking, I sat and listened. They all talked about how strange the place was, and how they felt this bad thing or that bad thing. They wanted to know more about what went on in the room, but I told them I really couldn't get any real vibe so I left it alone. As I watched and listened, I felt a peace I hadn't felt in years. Whatever was lifted in that room felt permanent, and it changed the way I look at doing my job.

With all the things I still have yet to learn, I think back to the last time I talked to Birdie and what she taught me. With Birdie, it was an unwritten law that when she called and gave you psychic information, it was your obligation and duty to then give her something back. This would usually make me nervous, because she was *The Master*. But it was also a chance to show her I could pick up stuff on her. I didn't want her to think all her teachings were falling on deaf ears. I also wanted to show her I wasn't afraid to trust what I was getting. Birdie hated it if you didn't trust what you were getting. To her it was an insult if you didn't trust spirit, no matter how stupid or odd it felt to say. I did learn to say whatever it was I was getting for her.

But on this day, I was finding it difficult to come up with anything other than that she was going to die soon. This information wasn't all that shocking considering she was three hundred years old, but it wasn't something I wanted to talk to her about either. Not because I was worried about her reaction, I just didn't want to go there.

I decided to do what I was taught you never did with Birdie and that was, to lie to her. I'm not sure why I thought that was a good idea. It had never been up to that point, but bringing up death to someone I loved was too hard for me to do. I hemmed and hawed and tried to make up something that wouldn't sound too bizarre. But I was shooting blanks. It bothered me I was picking up on her death, and it bothered me she knew I was picking up on her death. I couldn't figure out why she was torturing me like that.

"Birdie, I said, "I'm sorry, but the only thing I can get is you're going to pass on soon."

She didn't say a thing. Maybe she was in shock—I didn't know. But when she broke the silence by laughing and saying, *I know that dear, but what else do you have,* it was me who was shocked.

Not the response I was expecting. If someone were to tell me I was going to die soon, you might see me running out of the room with my hands over my head screaming, but I doubt I'd ask *what else.* I sat for a second and thought maybe she wanted me to tell her something that would wrap up her life in a sentence—something deep, yet simple. But if that was the case, she was barking up the wrong tree. It's not like I work for Hallmark. I'm not that deep of a guy.

I struggled again, trying to come up with just the right words to say. *Keep in touch* seemed too casual; *Say hi to Elvis* wasn't any better. But anything meaningful seemed trite; how do you sum up what she had meant to me, what she'd meant to everybody, in a word or two? There just wasn't enough time. Finally, I told her I couldn't get anything else, and said I was sorry. I didn't want to let her down. I loved Birdie, but she overestimated my ability to come up with what she needed. I was embarrassed. She paused for a second, maybe waiting for some last-minute inspiration on my part, and when none came, in a quiet voice she said, "You have to say goodbye."

This obvious statement made us both laugh and made me feel sad. I told her she was right—I needed to learn to keep it simple. I kept my goodbyes short, figuring I'd see her again before she died, but a month later, she was gone.

I've often thought about all the things that she and other people taught me—Mrs. Olsen, Nonette, all the old psychics. They're all gone now and sometimes life seems colorless without them. I miss not being able to chat with them from time to time. You'd think given what I do, that I'd see them more now that they've gone, but so far I haven't.

Not long after Birdie died, my three-year-old daughter Bianca came up to me. "The lady upstairs told me grandma has to see a doctor," Bianca said. "She's sick."

"Oh really, honey? Where's she sick," I said. Bianca pointed to her stomach and said *her tummy*. Now I thought she was just being adorable, but since you never know in this family, I called my mother and asked her if she was okay. She said she was fine, but instead of letting it go, I asked again.

"Mom, are you sure you're okay," I said. "Bianca seems to think you're sick."

"Well my stomach hurts a little, but my stomach always hurts," my mom said. That was true. She's had the same stomach ache since 1957. I asked her to please have it checked so my daughter could sleep, and that was that.

A few days later my mother called and said she did go to the doctor. They found some tumors on her ovaries that, because of her age, might be cancerous. The doctors felt an operation was needed as soon as possible. She then asked me if Bianca had said anything else about being sick. What she was really asking was, did Bianca mention seeing my mother playing Barbies in heaven in the near future.

I told her Bianca didn't say anything else, but that I thought she was going to be okay. Even though my mother was convinced, I wasn't sure I wanted to believe my daughter was being psychic.

My mother had the operation and had both ovaries removed. The tumors turned out to be benign, but the doctors agreed had they stayed in, they might have turned cancerous. While my mother was recovering, she asked Bianca to tell her about the nice lady who talked to her about my mother. Bianca was more than willing to do so. It turns out they had played together a few times, and Bianca had grown to like her.

My mother grabbed her purse and rummaged around in it until she produced a picture. She handed it to Bianca and asked her if she could recognize the woman in the picture. Bianca looked at it and immediately said, *that's Lala*. My mom told Bianca thank you, and Bianca said you're welcome, and then she went back to playing Barbies. My mother got quiet and her eyes got sad. I asked her what was going on and she handed me the picture. She looked out the window.

"It's your grandma Laura," she said. I looked at the picture and then over at Bianca. *And so it starts*, I thought.

I can't escape the fact that my family is psychic. Whether I wanted it or not, that's just the way it is. And I'm not doing cartwheels knowing my kids are showing signs of psychic abilities—especially with all those right-wing conservatives out there just ready to poison their heads. But the truth is, I wouldn't want them growing up with anyone else. Not just because I love them with every cell in my body, but because I know as their psychic abilities develop, they're going to need to understand what's happening to them, and who better to be there for that, than me.

There are still things I haven't come to terms with as far as all the psychic happenings that I've experienced. I'm skeptical of people who claim that they let three-hundred-year-old spirits enter their body so they can rant and rave and charge whoever's stupid enough to believe them a fortune to watch.

And it would be nice if the psychic community were more evolved, but it's not any different than a business atmosphere. It's all about who's got the biggest third eye or who's the most famous. And the people who are successful tend to endure the back stabbing and jealous behavior you'd find in any business situation. Echo is always hearing about other psychics putting her down or accusing her of not giving enough back to the community.

But as much as I've felt uncomfortable with the psychic world and my abilities, I have to say that there are days I love being psychic. In the movie *Star Wars* they talked about *the Force*. They described it as the power in everything alive—trees, animals, plants, even rocks and soil. That's what it feels like to be psychic sometimes. There are days I feel so connected and so alive it truly does feel like a sixth sense. It feels powerful and calming at the same time. There are times too when I can feel a break in the force.

Because I know that force does exist I also have to believe we can all tap into it. I doubt it's all for me. And at the risk of sounding like a tree-hugging hippie, its power is unlimited. When an athlete competes they say it's ninety percent mental. When a person hires you for a job, it's not always your qualifications that make the difference. It's that something extra the interviewer sees in you. And they say one of the most appealing qualities in both men and women is confidence—not cockiness, but real belief in themselves. I believe all these things come from that force and if we want, we can tap into it.

Knowing this has been a problem. Before all this psychic stuff happened, my life was mapped out for me. I'd go to school, get married, have kids, work at some cool job, and play and travel my whole life. I wasn't going to be a deep guy; I'd be rich. Rich people get a free pass when it comes to a lot of things and that's one of them. But then my eyes were opened and my life changed and everything started to have meaning except what I thought was important. I miss the ignorance of seeing life one-dimensionally.

I'm not an expert at all of this and if you run across someone who claims to be a master psychic, do me a favor and whack them in the groin. Remind them as they're lying on the ground holding themselves that there is no such thing as a *master psychic*—then maybe help them up. There are too many *experts* in this field. But the more someone says they know, the less they actually do.

I don't think my life experience makes me a more advanced person spiritually than someone who hasn't gone through the same things. If you know me, you know I've done some dumb things and I still amaze myself at some of the decisions I make. But I do think once you know the power that's at our disposal, you have to use it.

So if you want to get a reading, get one. I would suggest getting a referral first and then go. But do yourself a favor and ask yourself the same questions you'd ask the psychic. *Does it feel like you're going to get that job? Do you really think a biker named Tiny is your soul mate?* Ask yourself honestly. Trust your intuition. Psychics are wrong a lot of the time. We know some stuff, but nobody has the power to show you all the decisions you need to make. We can help support you or encourage you or warn you, but even then our timing can be screwy. Trust yourself.

If you've got a ghost, tell it to leave. Ghosts have no right bugging the living. Don't be taken by a moving lamp or floating poodle—it's all about getting your attention. I say kick 'em out—and yes, it can be that easy. But if you do need help, make sure you get someone who knows what they're doing. Heat sensors, Geiger counters, things that go *Whoop* are fun to watch but not all that helpful. Also if they charge too much don't be scared to say no thanks. The ghost won't get stronger if you kick the ghost busters out.

Ghosts and spirits and things that go bump in the night do exist. If you want to shut yourself off from it, more power to you. So what if thirty-five million people claim to have had some sort of psychic event happen to them or someone they know. And forget all those pictures and videos and sworn affidavits or even your own eyes, just keep your head in the sand as long as you can and find out for yourself when you die.

But if you've had an experience, seen a ghost, or picked up on someone or something and you're not sure what to do about it, be calm. Don't just assume you're crazy—the more you learn the less you become afraid, and the better you become at handling it.

Professionally, psychics are more respected now but listing psychic as your occupation on a house or car loan application still doesn't cry out stability. It usually goes like this. You go to the bank, show them your application, they ask if you're really a psychic, you say yes, and they respond, *then you must know you're not getting the loan.*

I can't speak for all psychics, but I'm sure there are some people who can do amazing things with their abilities. We all have different takes on things, and that includes the way we do readings. Some of us are blunt, some cryptic. Some like to perform while others tend to be more real. I've seen psychics twitch or hum and I've been to psychics who sit and talk to the air. There are mean psychics, indifferent psychics, sweet and understanding psychics, good, bad, and even *master* psychics. (How you become one of those, you tell me.) There are psychics who charge a lot for a little information and others who ask for nothing and give you more information than you'd care to know.

As different as we are in the way we do readings, we're equally varied in the gifts we've received. And like with most things, each gift has its good and bad points. Some psychics' specialty is finding keys, jewelry, or even people. (I've lost five pairs of glasses in the last three years, so I can tell you this is definitely not my area.) Others specialize in predicting global events or world disasters. Nostradamus was one of those guys who had the ability to predict global events. From what I've read about him, he wasn't comfortable with it. I got the impression that he just wanted to develop smells—like musk or patchouli—rather than get involved with predicting the future. But like it or not, there he was getting pictures of WWI, WWII, the H-bomb, the Kennedy assassination, and the possible end of mankind. On and on he would see images of these things and his only release was writing the stuff down. Fortunately I'm not that affected.

I do know that my generation is getting older, many people are dealing with the reality of death, and many are looking deeper into the possibility of life after death. I think that as long as people keep digging and looking for answers, psychics are going to pop up all over the place, hoping to help, but I do have hope for the generations to come.

When my son was eleven, we had just pulled into the driveway from the store when we noticed a man waiting for us at the front door of our house. It was around five o'clock in the afternoon and still light outside. He looked pretty serious—he was wearing a suit and tie and carrying a brief case. The thought occurred to me I might have forgotten I had an appointment. I wasn't expecting one, but I have been known to forget them from time to time.

Blake, who was eleven at the time, was sitting in the front seat. He turned to me, put his hand on my knee, and said, "Dad, you really have to do something about these people." His look suggested he was frustrated at my irresponsibility.

I looked back at him with surprise. "Sorry buddy," I said. "I must have forgotten I had somebody coming. Tell you what, I'll talk to him and have him come back after dinner," thinking that would make him feel better. But he looked at me again and rolled his eyes. "No, Dad, *these* people," and he looked back at the man who was now coming toward us.

I took a closer look at the man. "What are you talking about?" I asked.

"His feet, Dad, look at his feet," he said and opened the door to get out. I looked at the man's feet, and sure enough he didn't have any, he was just floating down the sidewalk, looking like he was on his way to a meeting. I looked back at Blake and then back at the man, who was now gone.

I sat in the car amazed. I didn't know who that guy was, where he came from, or why he was there. And I really didn't know why he was so clear. Usually if a dead guy that obvious shows up at your door, he must be there for a reason.

My son, on the other hand, could not have cared less. "Coming?" Blakey asked smiling.

I shook my head and smiled back. "Weird," I said and started to get out of the car.

As I stepped out, my son, who was ten feet in front of me, turned and smiled. "No offense, Dad, but you kinda suck at this ghost busting thing."

I thought for a moment. "First off," I reminded him. "I'm not ghost busting, I'm coming home from the store. Secondly, the creepy guy probably showed up to make sure you cleaned the bathroom. And thirdly, even exterminators get bugs sometimes."

He turned his back and kept walking "Whatever, Dad," he said. "But if he shows up in my room tonight, I'm sending him down to you."

I loved that, to be so unaffected by what would freak out anybody else gave me hope that someday everybody will just trust their intuition, or not think twice about seeing a ghost.

Shortly before I finished my book, my father passed away. He had been sick for some time with diabetes, and by all accounts had given up on taking care of himself. On one of the days just before he died I was on my way to the hospital, listening to our local sports talk radio show. The topic that day was psychics. The host's contention was that anybody who believed in psychics or ghosts was a nut job. His wife was a big believer, but she was a woman and women are strange.

His callers seemed to agree. Call after call, they supported his beliefs. Some suggested psychics were merely confused or want-to-be actors. Others went so far as to call psychics con artists and gypsies, just looking for an easy mark. The host even questioned how a person in "that" profession could look themselves in the mirror. I had to check the paper to make sure we weren't back in the 1600s.

As I listened, I thought back to the days before all this stuff happened and I found myself missing the simplicity of not knowing. I couldn't really blame these guys (all the callers were guys) for their attitudes because there was a time when I felt the same way. Psychics *were* whack jobs. Family, sports, school, friends—those were the things that mattered. Ghost stories were things you told around campfires or at sleepovers. And when you woke up, there was comfort in knowing they didn't exist. Girls believed in psychics because girls were from a different planet. And if you believed in ghosts and you were a guy, you were from that planet and therefore a girl.

It was clear as black and white.

I missed that.

But as I pulled into the hospital parking lot and made my way to my father's room, my thoughts turned to him. It had been very hard for me, those last few days, to see my father. It was surprisingly sad. Not because of the relationship we had, but the one we didn't. We never did get close. The knowing we would never be close hit me harder and harder as I watched him go.

I was also worried about him being alone. Not physically, my siblings had been very attentive, but on the other side. The last several years my father had chosen to be alone. People seemed to annoy him and he had little issue with sharing his contempt with the general public. Even before his exile from society, I knew him as having few, if any, friends. And on the last day before he slipped into a semi-coma, when I told him I loved him for the last time, I saw fear in his eyes, like a child would look on their first overnight away from home. It was because of this I worried he would be alone on the other side.

As I turned the corner and entered his room, my fears were lifted. I saw "people" waiting for him by his bed. A man in a Navy uniform was watching him by the foot of the bed. Two other women, both looking to be in their forties, were standing by his head, and an old man with white hair, his chin resting slightly in his chest, was standing near his shoulder. All four had a look of unconditional love to them, and all four could not have cared less if I was there or not. The feeling in the room felt light and peaceful. All of those thoughts of wishing I was never introduced to the psychic world went away. I knew my father would not be alone.

I'm glad my cousin saw what he saw forty years ago, and I'm grateful for what our family has gone through. I believe everyone has psychic abilities in different degrees and different ways, and we use them every day. Hunches, feelings, intuition—we experience them all the time.

Sometimes when I'm being psychic, I'm not psychic. That is, "they" will give me some of the information, but not all of it.

Such was the case with my friend Harold.

Harold was someone I knew for only a short period of time, but who made a major impact on my life. I never met Harold face to face, but we talked on the phone, sometimes three to four times a day. Harold was a thirty-four-year-old struggling producer who wanted desperately to break into the film industry. He lived alone in Boston. He was single. He was broke. And he was hopelessly gay.

Normally being gay isn't an issue psychically, unless the person who is gay has a problem with being gay. And Harold did. He accepted that he was gay, but up to this point had not allowed himself to be in a relationship with another man. He felt maybe someday, when he achieved some form of success, he would do so.

But, success seemed to elude Harold. No matter how hard he tried, no matter how long he worked, he could never seem to get anywhere.

Another friend, to whom I had given a reading, introduced us one day. At the time of that meeting, Harold was a true skeptic. Psychics for him were right up there with the Easter Bunny and the Tooth Fairy. His lack of faith was so bad he had lost his belief in God. Faith was for suckers. And trust? Forget it.

But months after our initial meeting, he finally got so desperate that he sought me out for a reading.

During his reading, I was shown all of the things *they* wanted me to see. His loneliness. His desperation. His doubt. They also showed me the opportunities and the breaks that were coming his way. *They* seemed excited for him and when I shared their excitement, he became excited. I liked Harold, and I couldn't help but think that all his hard work was about to pay off.

During the reading I was lucky enough to hit on several things that helped "legitimize" me. A few actually seemed to scare him. The next day he called me back and asked me how I knew these things. I responded with "I eat a lot of fiber" and when he actually thought I was serious I found myself liking him more. Harold was an innocent, sweet, kind person regardless of his bitterness toward the hand life had dealt him. I felt really happy for him that things were going to look up.

The next day he called me again, but this time to offer me a business proposition. He said the next *big thing* on the East Coast was for people like me to have representation, like a psychic agent. He offered to hook me up with readings and appearances in exchange for hooking him with all my film industry buddies.

I told him I would be happy to connect him with my contacts in LA, but I'd pass on the agent idea. "No offense, pal," I explained, "but when it starts to be about money, the dead guys give me a busy signal."

He told me he would send a contract for me to read "just in case." Knowing it wouldn't change my mind, we resumed chatting about his reading.

Over the next several months I connected Harold with the people I knew in LA. Everyone who met him liked him, even though they had no idea what to do with him. Every conversation seemed to end in "but I really liked him." He seemed a little happier making connections, but he was still struggling financially. His money situation or lack thereof became the main topic of conversation. I felt the top was about to pop off, he felt the bottom was about to fall off, but still he remained upbeat.

The last time I talked to Harold he was getting ready to go to LA. This time, to look for a place to live. He still seemed happy. Hopeful. And hanging on.

A week later I got a call from his sister.

Harold had killed himself.

His sister had the unimaginable job of calling all the people in his Rolodex to tell them not only what had happened, but to look for information on Harold's last days.   Since my last name began with a B, the tragedy and her brokenness was still pretty raw.

"So Michael, how did you know my brother?" she questioned with a restrained underscore of anger.

My first instinct was to admit I was his psychic. But my guilt at not knowing how bad off he was stopped me.

"Just friends…" I fibbed.

"Did you know he was worried about money?" she asked.

"Yes," I answered. "Well, I uh, I knew he was worried about it but not to this point…" was my clumsy offer.

Then she started to sob. I didn't know what to say next. I was sad, also stunned that I had had absolutely no clue. I was also feeling paranoid she might really know I was his psychic and want to blame me for not saving him.

Before I knew it I choked out "I'm so sorry" and I could feel myself getting ready to confess who I was and come clean.

"No ..." she sobbed. "You don't understand. A fifty-thousand-dollar check came in the mail today, along with a one-year contract for another two hundred thousand dollars. If he just would have waited one more day he'd still be alive."

Now she was sobbing so hard it was difficult to understand her words. I was stunned to the point of being speechless.

"This is such a mess." she moaned. "I have to go." And with that, she hung up.

I sat, rocking back and forth, and stared at the phone for an hour.

I have struggled for years about Harold's decision that day.

———

The reason that I chose to end the book with this story is that it sums up everything I've learned and believe about being psychic.

The truth is this. A psychic can pass on information. But I've never known one that can perform a miracle.

And miracles happen every day. They don't just happen to holy people or blind men, they happen to average, everyday people. Every day.

The universe opens up its loving arms, presents us with opportunity, and then disappears.

And we are left with a choice. To seize the opportunity presented to us, or to hide in the false comfort of the status quo. To choose to dismiss it as a random moment or recognize it for the potentially life-altering event it may prove to be.

Although we think of them as extraordinary, miracles are presented to us sometimes when we least expect them.

When I think of Harold, I wonder what might have happened to him if he had hung on just one more day. He had mapped out his future as one of enormous failure, not knowing or believing that something could happen to shape his destiny in a way he could not even imagine.

The most important lesson he might have learned was that the universe has much bigger plans for us than we have ever dreamed of for ourselves. And to not trust in that is to let pass the greatest miracle of all.

Everything in this book is true, as much as the people I've talked to and I can remember it. Trust me, I even had a hard time believing some of the things that happened and I was there.

Family Photo Album

Life on the St. Croix River, in Dad's boat

*Echo with a beehive,
at seventeen*

*My first fish, a Northern—I was
worried it would attack me*

Dad and me

Mom and me, around the time things were heating up at our house

When we opened this cupboard door, whatever we wanted
would slide off the shelf into our hands

Echo, in uniform, headed to work at Uncle John's Pancake House

Echo and me

My dad called this Mom's Mary O. look

Mae (Mom), Michael, and Echo Bodine

To Write to the Author

If you wish to contact the author or would like more information about this book, please write to the author in care of Llewellyn Worldwide and we will forward your request. Both the author and publisher appreciate hearing from you and learning of your enjoyment of this book and how it has helped you. Llewellyn Worldwide cannot guarantee that every letter written to the author can be answered, but all will be forwarded. Please write to:

Michael Bodine
℅ Llewellyn Worldwide
2143 Wooddale Drive
Woodbury, MN 55125-2989

Please enclose a self-addressed stamped envelope for reply,
or $1.00 to cover costs. If outside U.S.A., enclose
international postal reply coupon.

Many of Llewellyn's authors have websites with additional information and resources. For more information, please visit our website at http://www.llewellyn.com.